Critical Essays on H. L. Mencken

Critical Essays on
H. L. Mencken

Douglas C. Stenerson

G.K. Hall & Co. • Boston, Massachusetts

Library of Congress Cataloging in Publication Data

Critical essays on H.L. Mencken.
    (Critical essays on American literature)
    Includes index.
    1. Mencken, H. L. (Henry Louis), 1880–1956—Criticism and
interpretation. I. Stenerson, Douglas C.
II. Series.
PS3525.E43Z547   1987   818'.5209   86-22752
ISBN 0-8161-8694-4

CRITICAL ESSAYS ON AMERICAN LITERATURE

This series seeks to anthologize the most important criticism on a wide variety of topics and writers in American literature. Our readers will find in various volumes not only a generous selection of reprinted articles and reviews but original essays, bibliographies, manuscript sections, and other materials brought to public attention for the first time. This volume on H. L. Mencken contains a selection of reprinted reviews and comments by many of the leading figures in modern letters, including George Jean Nathan, James Weldon Johnson, Percy H. Boynton, Edmund Wilson, Walter Lippmann, Irving Babbitt, Reinhold Niebuhr, Van Wyck Brooks, and Joseph Wood Krutch. In addition to an extensive introduction by Douglas Stenerson, there are a revision of a previously published article by Vincent Fitzpatrick and original essays by Fred Hobson and Charles Scruggs. We are confident that this volume will make a permanent and significant contribution to American literary study.

JAMES NAGEL, GENERAL EDITOR

Northeastern University

To my wife
Marjorie Barrows Stenerson

CONTENTS

INTRODUCTION

H. L. Mencken is so closely identified with the 1920s we sometimes forget he was of the older generation of leaders of the moral and literary revolt that climaxed in that decade. His highly productive career stretched from 1899, when he started as a cub reporter on the *Baltimore Morning Herald,* to 1948, when a cerebral thrombosis incapacitated him for any further reading and writing. He always regarded himself as primarily a newspaperman, but he was equally successful in such separable but often overlapping roles as magazine editor, popularizer of European artists and thinkers, literary critic, social and political commentator, and self-taught pioneer analyst of the American vernacular. He was, in addition, a demanding critic of the American press. For a layman, he was unusually well informed in the biological sciences and in medicine. As a music lover and enthusiastic amateur performer on the piano, he ventured occasionally into music criticism and, in his later years, devoted himself to studies of religion and ethics, three volumes of nostalgic memoirs, and a new edition and two huge supplements to his *The American Language*. He was also one of the most prolific, incisive, and entertaining letter writers of this century. Unlike many lesser mortals whose versatility prompts them to spread themselves too thin, he had remarkable energy and the self-discipline to direct it to whatever ends he chose. During his lifetime he produced an estimated 8,000,000 words of copy and 200,000 or more letters, yet, even with this prodigious output, he was a conscious artist who perfected a style so distinctive that it frequently won the admiration of those he ridiculed or denounced. Many young writers in the twenties imitated him, but no one could duplicate his tragic vision of life united with joy in living, his imaginative and rhetorical resourcefulness, his contentiousness redeemed by common sense and robust humor, and his absorption in all things American and his concern for the quality of life and literature in "these states."

As Mencken himself suggested and modern scholarship has confirmed, the "prejudices" he flaunted in six volumes during the twenties originated within the context of thought and feeling in which he grew up in Baltimore and the border state of Maryland. The oldest of four children, Henry Louis Mencken was born in 1880 into a German-American middle-class family

1

sustained by a comfortable income from the cigar factory of which his father was co-owner. In the three-story row house at 1524 Hollins Street in West Baltimore he experienced the loving, secure, and stable home life he recalls fondly in *Happy Days* (1940). At Knapp's Institute, a private school, and at the Baltimore Polytechnic, a public high school from which he graduated as class valedictorian, he found that he could always win out in fair competition with students from the dominant Anglo-Saxon culture. He shared with his father and paternal grandfather a homebred agnosticism for which he discovered a fuller rationale in Darwinism and contemporary science as interpreted by Herbert Spencer and Thomas Henry Huxley. He took over from his father a faith in capitalism and its economic virtues and a preference for the managerial class that were reinforced by his reading of William Graham Sumner. Among the other attitudes Mencken absorbed were a sense of belonging to a hereditary elite and a sympathetic response to an idealized version of eighteenth-century plantation society.

For Mencken, as for most German-Americans, civilized living meant sharing heartily in the social pleasures summed up in the concept of *gemütlichkeit*, which, as he once explained, signified "politeness, urbanity, hospitality, friendliness, sociability, toleration, general good humor."[1] This suggests the positive norms of honor, decency, and common sense, to which he often referred, and also his positive social ideal, with its emphasis on the innocent enjoyment of sensuous pleasures. In their negative aspects, these same standards compelled opposition to anything threatening the way of life that upheld them. Mencken was like most German-Americans, whether or not they were professing Christians, in his violent reaction against the puritanism, blue laws, and temperance crusades sponsored by the Anglo-Saxons and their churches. His early newspaper writings reveal the strong iconoclastic impulse that persisted throughout his career: the desire to lash out at the individuals, groups, or practices that violated his sense of what is decent and right.[2]

Had Mencken been content to express his rebellion in journalistic clichés or the florid rhetoric of political oratory, he might have ended up like such nineteenth-century iconoclasts as William H. Brann or Robert Ingersoll, renowned in their own day but almost forgotten a generation or two later. Mencken attracts new readers in each new generation because he had the talent, the literary ambition, and the will to achieve a fresh and individual style. A strong urge for self-expression accompanied his intellectual and artistic awakening. In the workshop of daily urban journalism from 1899 to 1908 he cultivated the ability to see the life about him and interpret it vividly. As a play reviewer he took to heart the advice of an older colleague to trust his own impressions and communicate them with appropriate humor, ridicule, or ferocity. As a fledgling satirist he worked consciously in the tradition of Mark Twain. Inspired, in addition, by the vogue of muckraking, his favorite paper the *New York Sun*, and writers as diverse as Thomas Huxley, Thackeray, Kipling, Shaw, O. Henry, Ambrose Bierce, James Huneker, and George Ade, he sought to combine lucidity with a verve and color matching his own individuality. He knew that, in the end, his success would depend upon his winning over a large group of readers within the majority audience whose puritanism and credulity he often attacked. To capture their attention, he wanted to startle, stimulate, and entertain as well as to convey a point of view. What gave this style much of its shock value was that his readers, like himself, were in varying degrees moving beyond the genteel tradition while still committed to many of its values.

Part 1 of this volume samples the writings of those who knew well the private Mencken behind the public image projected in his writing. The selections in parts 2 through 5 illustrate the changing fortunes of Mencken's critical reputation between 1905 and 1984. Because Mencken wrote, edited, or contributed to more than fifty books, some of which appeared in more than one edition, reviews of his works in American newspapers and magazines run into the hundreds. These reviews consist typically of summary, illustrative quotations, and some more or less discerning judgments. Although a few such reviews are reproduced here, the main emphasis is on review essays and critical essays which move beyond one specific work to a broader interpretation of Mencken's ideas or significance. Since each major book receives some attention in these more comprehensive essays, no effort has been made to print a review or review essay on every volume. Decisions as to what to include have been made on the basis of literary interest and merit as well as of the typicality and importance of the ideas and attitudes expressed.

Chronological order is followed in presenting the selections, all of which come from American publications, with more from magazines than from newspapers. Excerpts from books have been kept to a minimum. Taken together, the reviews and essays examine the full range of Mencken's work and represent the chief points of view in the controversies surrounding him. The selections are complete except for cases in which some editing is clearly justified. In these instances omissions are indicated by ellipses. Obvious typographical errors or proofreader's oversights have been silently corrected.

Throughout the introduction an asterisk (*) following an author's name—or the title or similar reference if the piece is anonymous—designates a selection included in this collection.

Each of the essays in part 1: "Intimate Impressions and Insights," finds some contrast between the public and the private Mencken. George Jean Nathan,* in 1920, saw his fellow *Smart Set* editor when hard at work as hopelessly at odds with his pleasure-loving "corporeal self." In 1927 Elizabeth Shepley Sergeant* discovered that "our most terrible and earth-shaking critic" was at the same time "a solid, Germanic sentimentalist." In a retrospective article written after Mencken's death in 1956, Gerald W. Johnson* distinguished between the often hated H. L. Mencken and the Henry Mencken whose zest for life, wit, and incandescent conversation helped transform the lives of his intimates.

Among other articles in which friends have portrayed Mencken with understanding and insight are Alfred A. Knopf, "For Henry with Love" (1959); Hamilton Owens, "A Personal Note" (1961); Philip M. Wagner, "Mencken Remembered" (1963); and Louis Cheslock, "Some Personal Memories of H. L. M." (1974).[3]

Essays that movingly depict Mencken in his later years include Alistair Cooke, "The Last Happy Days of H. L. Mencken" (1956); Robert Allen Durr, "The Last Days of H. L. Mencken" (1958); and William Manchester, "Last Years of H. L. Mencken" (1975).[4]

In her *The Constant Circle* (1968) Sara Mayfield re-created with an insider's knowledge the social worlds in which Mencken moved in both Baltimore and New York.[5]

The selections in part 2 illustrate Mencken's rise from local prominence to national fame between 1905 and 1918.[6] While still in his teens Mencken had started writing verses, some in the French forms then popular and some modeled on Kipling. His first book, entitled with appropriate modesty *Ventures into Verse* (1903), was issued in 100 copies by three friends setting up a printing business who needed a sample to attract customers. One reviewer, noting that a number of the rhymes had appeared in popular magazines, liked their "froth, sizz, sparkle and tang" but adjudged them "salable rather than sincere."[7]

Mencken had already turned away from versifying to writing short fiction. In the artistically flatulent first decade of the century, the fascination both the realistic and the aesthetic phases of the literary movement of the nineties had for him anticipated much more than his verse or short stories the course he would take in future. His reading of Zola, Dreiser's *Sister Carrie,* and Conrad confirmed his preference for literary realism and naturalism. In his concept of the critic as artist and in his partisanship for the new drama he resembled cosmopolitan critics like James Huneker and Percival Pollard, but he differed from these forerunners in his Darwinian orientation and his enthusiasm for mimetic fiction. Through his play reviewing on the *Herald* he found his métier as a critic of ideas. As the result of his having outlined a proposal which John W. Luce & Co. accepted, *George Bernard Shaw: His Plays,* which he always considered his first real book, was put on the market in the fall of 1905.

A common reaction among critics was that Mencken grossly overstated Shaw's importance.[8] The reviewer in the *Nation,* observing that Mencken "rather describes than interprets," felt that he lacked the equipment "to go all the way with" his subject as Shaw had done years before in his *The Quintessence of Ibsenism.*[9] Newspaper reviewers, on the whole, were more appreciative. The *Chicago Tribune* reviewer,* for example, recognized Mencken's ability to bring "a satirist's comprehension to a greater satirist's work."[10]

At the suggestion of his editor at John W. Luce & Co., Mencken next wrote *The Philosophy of Friedrich Nietzsche* (1908), in which he interpreted the German thinker as "a thorough Darwinian."[11] The more uniformly positive tone of the reviews showed that Mencken's approach and style had matured considerably. A perceptive critic in the *New York Times Book Review** aptly summed up the qualities the book revealed: a "clear, forceful, even ardent style, a keen and thoroughgoing intellect, knowledge of men, and a sense of humor." Reviewers in the *Catholic World* and the *Dial* dissented from Mencken's appreciation of Nietzsche, but praised the organization and style.[12] An academic accolade came from a critic in the *Educational Review*.[13] A reviewer in the *Nation* was exceptional in faulting Mencken for not having the breadth of learning to relate Nietzsche accurately to the intellectual background.[14]

Mencken's *Nietzsche* had to be reprinted that same year, and a new edition was published in 1913.[15] Meanwhile, in *Men versus the Man* (1910), an exchange of letters with the wealthy socialist Robert Rives La Monte, Mencken was able to express his social and political views more fully than had been possible in his *Nietzsche*.

Men versus the Man, issued by Henry Holt, did not catch on with the public and was soon remaindered. Perhaps a reviewer in the *Living Age* was right in thinking that most readers would be familiar with the arguments. Some critics were quick to notice that Mencken built his case against socialism on the premises of conservative social Darwinism. Sidney A. Reeve, for instance, pointed out that Mencken, by seeing man only in the context of natural selection, ignored the fact that human institutions and "collective interaction" also help shape society.[16]

World War I caused a crisis for Mencken and other German-Americans by transforming their friendly rivalry with the Anglo-Saxon majority into sharp conflict. "The Free Lance" column Mencken had started in the *Baltimore Evening Sun* in 1911 was quoted so frequently in other papers it enhanced his national reputation, but he terminated it in 1915 because his opposition to the growing anti-German hysteria and the Wilson administration's violations of neutrality was at odds with the *Sunpapers'* editorial policy. When he returned in March, 1917, from service as a war correspondent in Germany, superpatriotism and intolerance were at their height. He was abused, vilified, and forced into silence on war issues. Newspapers and magazines other than the *New York Evening Mail,* the *Seven Arts,* and the *Smart Set,* for which he had become the book reviewer in 1908, were closed to him.

In 1916 John Lane Co. printed two books by Mencken: *A Little Book in C Major,* a gathering of humorous epigrams from the *Smart Set,* and *A Book of Burlesques,* a collection of satiric sketches and parodies that later went through several different reprintings and editions under the Alfred A. Knopf imprint. During some of the leisure the war forced upon him, Mencken carefully revised the material that went into his essays on Conrad, Huneker, Dreiser, and "Puritanism as a Literary Force" in *A Book of Prefaces* (Knopf, 1917), a major work of literary criticism. The volume at first reached only a small audience, but it helped establish his leadership in the new movement marked by Joel Spingarn's "The New Criticism" (1911), John Macy's *The Spirit of American Literature* (1913), and Van Wyck Brooks's *America's Coming-of-Age* (1915).

The reviews of *A Book of Prefaces* made it easy to sort out Mencken's allies from his enemies. In Chicago, Burton Rascoe,* in the most thoughtful and sustained estimate anyone had yet done, emphasized themes to which later critics recurred again and again: Mencken's "imagistic, colorful, dynamic" style; his intimate knowledge of "the whole process of daily life in this republic"; his importance as "a satirist and humorist of a high order"; his personal brand of puritanism that propelled him to fight the moralists; even "his share of intellectual fourflush." In the *Liberator,* successor to the *Masses* recently suppressed by the government, Louis Untermeyer rejoiced at "the author's vitality, vivacity, variety, and . . . vulgarity."[17] Randolph Bourne,* in the *New Republic,* took the middle ground, admiring the treatment of Conrad, Huneker, and Dreiser but decrying the way Mencken had allowed himself to become "the victim of that paralyzing Demos against which he so justly rages." Mencken's lustiest opponent was Stuart Sherman,* a professor at the University of Illinois who championed the New Humanism of Irving Babbitt and Paul Elmer More. Quick to exploit wartime prejudice, Sherman ironically praised Mencken's "purely aesthetic ministry to the American people" before intimating that his real loyalty was to Germany.

Mencken was also being heeded by black writers. In an article in the *New York Evening Mail* (13 November 1917) he called the entire South "The Sahara of the Bozart." When Mencken returned to this theme in "Mr. Cabell of Virginia" (3 July 1918), James Weldon Johnson,* a black poet and novelist, commended Mencken for the "electric shock" of his style and his ability to cut through "sentimental and mawkish morality."

In 1918 Mencken compiled two more books, both issued by Philip Goodman, a convivial Jewish friend who had decided to venture into publishing. *Damn! A Book of Calumny* brought together some short, pithy essays. *In Defense of Women,* swiftly but artistically edited, combined irony, comedy, and common sense in dealing with such topics as "The Masculine Bag of Tricks," "Woman's Equipment," "The Emancipated Housewife," and "Equal Suffrage." Goodman did little to publicize either volume. Knopf reissued both that same year, but, of the two, *In Defense* proved much more durable, with new printings and editions extending well into the twenties.

The documents in part 3 show how and why Mencken reached his heyday in the 1920s. The lifting of restrictions on free speech and the disillusioned and questioning mood after the war enabled him, together with the increasing number of recruits rallying to his cause, to bring his campaign to a successful conclusion. In the next few years he was accepted as a mentor by many young intellectuals in the process of self-discovery and in search of fresh values. On topics ranging from the Ku Klux Klan to the Red Scare, from fraudulent advertising to sexual morality, from James Branch Cabell to Sinclair Lewis, he voiced with gusto and humor, burlesque and invective, the kinds of attitudes toward which young people were reaching. Since becoming co-editor of the *Smart Set* in 1914, he had been strategically placed to encourage aspiring writers and in many instances publish their work.

Vincent O'Sullivan was probably the first to recognize the exasperated affection intermingled with the rage and scorn Mencken directed at the "mob."[18] This sense of kinship with the common people and their vernacular provided much of the motive force behind *The American Language* (1919), a work of major literary as well as linguistic importance. Most reviewers, while taking exception to some examples or conclusions, recognized the book's trail-blazing value. Francis Hackett* (the *New Republic*, 31 May 1919) remarked that Mencken combined in one person "the benign pedant" who organized the huge mass of material and "the anarchist that has breathed fire into it." As a result "we . . . form a new view of our own spoken and written language." Critics in the *Boston Transcript* and the *North American Review* were similarly enthusiastic.[19] The academic critics Mencken had often denounced could not help but be impressed by his scholarship and his orderly and graphic exposition.[20]

Prejudices: First Series (1919) also attracted extensive critical comment. Aldous Huxley described how Mencken contemplates "with a civilized man's astonishment and horror" "the solemn mammoths of stupidity," then deflates them with his sharp and unerring pen. George F. Whicher asked, "Is this that 'barbaric yawp' which Whitman hailed as the language of the future?" Philip Littell was sure that Mencken would never be able to distinguish between his "extraordinarily able things" and his "howlers." Stuart Sherman derided both Mencken and the pretty but only superficially educated *jeune fille* of immigrant stock who presumably looked to him for guidance.[21]

Early in 1920 Ernest Boyd,* the Irish critic, broached in the *Freeman* a controversy Mencken had helped precipitate: the clash between writers who vigorously asserted their national identity and "the professorial guardians of colonial precedents" who, during the war, "were enabled to lynch their opponents in the name of patriotism." In reply, Percy H. Boynton* of the University of Chicago satirized Mencken as the cheerleader of "the tart set": "young Americans . . . whose acquaintance with the country has seldom taken them west of Tenth Avenue" but who vociferously belittle Puritanism and demand a literature "independent of old-world standards." Fred Lewis Pattee of Pennsylvania State College made the diagnosis more specific. Mencken suffered from the journalist's disease—"obsession by contemporaneousness."[22]

When "The Sahara of the Bozart" was reprinted in revised form in *Prejudices: Second Series* (1920), damning Mencken was more than ever a favorite southern pastime, but through its shock treatment the essay helped stimulate the southern literary renaissance. Among the articulate southerners who accepted it as an appropriate challenge was Hunter Stagg,* who, in the first issue of the *Reviewer*, commented appreciatively on the strategy of contrasting the culturally deprived New South with the high civilization which, according to Mencken, had prevailed in the Old South.

A seminal essay by Edmund Wilson* that may mark the floodtide of Mencken's influence on the young intellectuals appeared in the *New Republic* in mid-1921. The"intelligentsia," said Wilson, are greatly indebted to Mencken for discrediting "optimism, Puritanism, and democratic ineptitude" and championing "the kind of literary activity of which we have now become proudest." Mencken's gloomy prose listings of such types as " 'Farmers plowing sterile fields behind sad meditative horses' " are a suitable modern equivalent of Whitman's exuberant catalogs. "For Mencken," Wilson summed up, "is the civilized consciousness of modern America," "a great satirist to arouse us against the tragic spectacle we have become."

At this same time some young writers felt they had absorbed Mencken's message and moved beyond him. F. Scott Fitzgerald implied as much in a review of *Prejudices: Second Series*. Burton Rascoe, now a literary editor in New York, was saddened by Mencken's newly acquired respectability which has deprived "the literary youth of America of an agitator." With its growing sophistication, "the literary generation now gaining recognition has progressed beyond the reaches of Mencken's aesthetic equipment." Newton Arvin, citing defects in Mencken's theory of criticism and in his view of poetry, argued that Mencken was not a literary critic at all, but "a social critic, and besides that, a humorist of a very high order."[23]

Even before the young writers started to question his qualifications as a literary arbiter, Mencken was turning away from literary to broadly cultural concerns. The *American Mercury*, a monthly edited at first jointly with Nathan and then by Mencken alone, and backed by Knopf, had a literary dimension but was designed to comment extensively on the whole gaudy, gorgeous American scene. First issued in January 1924, and reaching its peak circulation of 77,000 in 1927, the *Mercury*, covering a wide range of approaches and opinions, appealed to a "civilized minority" that embraced every segment of the middle class from business leaders to college students.

Expanding in the *Mercury* on a practice started on the *Smart Set*, Mencken sought out black writers, most of them active in the Harlem Renaissance, and published many of their articles. The black writers acknowledged his courage and fairness and welcomed his advice. Walter White, for example, approvingly described how Mencken risked going to jail by openly defying the Boston Watch and Ward Society when it proceeded against the *Mercury* for April 1926, containing Herbert Asbury's "Hatrack," a story about a small-town prostitute.[24] When Mencken published an article on the prospects for black intellectuals and artists (*New York World*, 17

July 1927), George S. Schuyler,* a frequent contributor to the *Mercury,* replied with an appreciation and critique. Kelly Miller complimented Mencken on "his perennial freshness and novelty" and on his opening up the magazine to "the Negro theme."[25]

By 1925 Mencken had the distinction, rare for a writer in his mid-forties, of having two books devoted to him. Isaac Goldberg's full-length biography *The Man Mencken* was valuable chiefly for the information Mencken furnished in a thick sheaf of autobiographical notes. Goldberg's own commentary is often diffuse and badly organized. In the much briefer *H. L. Mencken,* the estimate Ernest Boyd gave of his friend as American, philosopher, and critic is concise, witty, and judicious.[26]

Mencken's *Notes on Democracy* (1926) prodded critics into a wide variety of interpretations. Viewing the book in the perspective of English political thought, Rebecca West deplored the ignorance, misconceptions, and lack of definition that marred Mencken's polemic. The English experience, she maintained, shows that there are just as many "boobs" capable of arrogance and evil in the aristocracy Mencken prefers as in the mass he condemns.[27] Both Simeon Strunsky and Bluce Bliven sensed that Mencken's fulminations concealed a real love for democracy.[28] Walter Lippmann,* in the *Saturday Review of Literature,* began by calling Mencken "the most powerful personal influence on this whole generation of educated people." By appealing "not from mind to mind but from viscera to viscera," he is dispelling the mystique surrounding "the divine right of demos" much as earlier agitators like Tom Paine assailed "the kings, the nobles, and the priests." Edmund Wilson saw in the "boob" Mencken had created "an ideal monster, exactly like the Yahoo of Swift," that "has impressed himself on the imagination of the general public."[29]

A few critics in the late twenties analyzed Mencken's much touted style. In *The Outlook for American Prose* (1926), Joseph Warren Beach found that Mencken's writing conveys "the excitement of an accelerated heartbeat." V. E. Simrell, in 1927, demonstrated through the use of examples that Mencken brilliantly practiced the arts of persuasion recommended by Aristotle.[30] In "H. L. Mencken: Doctor Rhetoricus" (1920), I. J. Semper,* with a liveliness that belied his title, examined the "eight-cylinder vocabulary" as well as the other resources that made Mencken "a brilliant and provocative rhetorician of the bellicose type."

From socialists on the left to the New Humanists on the right Mencken was in no danger of running out of antagonists. Somewhere between these extremes was Ernest Hemingway, who, in *The Sun Also Rises* (1926), has Harvey Stone say of Mencken, " 'He's through now. . . . He's written about all the things he knows, and now he's on all the things he doesn't know.' " Among the radicals, V. F. Calverton (whose real name was George Goetz) characterized Mencken in 1925 as "The Vaudeville Critic,"—an "anti-bourgeois in morals, . . . a thorough bourgeois in economics." In 1927 Upon Sinclair, who could not fathom the humor of his long-time correspondent, predicted that as "the masses of labor" become more discontented, Mencken would "have to . . . choose between the bloody reaction of Fascism and the dawn of industrial brotherhood."[31]

As for the New Humanists, Stuart Sherman charged that Mencken stooped to the methods of the "literary proletariat" in his onslaught against "The American Tradition" in *Prejudices: Fourth Series* (1924). Paul Elmer More, in one of his few inspections of contemporary literature, pushed restraint aside in complaining that "the critical ideas of the immature and ignorant are formed by brawling vulgarians like H. L. Mencken, who in stentorian tones champion any crude product of modernism which appeals to their own half-educated taste."[32] On the other hand, Irving Babbitt,* in "The Critic and American Life" (1928), admitted that Mencken, despite his reducing "criticism . . . to the uttering of one's gustos and disgustos," had "certain genuine critical virtues—for example, a power of shrewd observation." What he lacked, in Babbitt's opinion, was discrimination: the ability to mediate wisely between past and present by adapting traditional values to current needs.

Between 1930 and Mencken's death in 1956, the period with which part 4 is concerned, his reputation at first declined, not to revive until after World War II. Late in the twenties, there were already signs that Mencken had waged his various campaigns so effectively that his influence was on the wane. In 1927 Frederick Lewis Allen admitted that the debunking by Mencken, Sinclair Lewis, and "the disillusioned young highbrows" had been salutary, but contended that "the pendulum has swung too far. It is almost time that the debunkers were themselves debunked."[33] This was only one of a number of articles on the same theme.[34] Other evidence also pointed to a decline in Mencken's prestige. The circulation of the *Mercury* peaked in 1927, then gradually fell off. The first series of *Prejudices* (1919) had sold 16,500 copies; the sixth and last (1927) only 4,100.[35] As a harbinger of the Great Depression, the stock-market crash in October, 1929, ended the Age of Mencken.

While the audience for his social commentary was diminishing, Mencken was already becoming engrossed in other concerns. Early in 1930, as James Branch Cabell said, he "graduated *cum laude* from the 'twenties' " with the publication of *Treatise on the Gods*.[36] The book was well received, although Mencken's self-styled "amiable skepticism"[37] in the tradition of Thomas Huxley did not please orthodox Christians. Granville Hicks liked the *Treatise's* "urbane, orderly, and discriminating progress," and Henry Hazlitt regarded it as "a work of genuine scholarship." Michael Williams, a Catholic spokesman, dubbed the book "a new Bible for boobs" by "an unshaken apostle" of strict Darwinism.[38] Reinhold Niebuhr,* in the *Atlantic Monthly* for June 1930, emphasized that Mencken's thesis that religion is magic cannot account for the insights of the prophets and mystics concerned "not with bending physical circumstances to the human will, but with . . . the appropriation of all the inner and outer beneficences of life as the grace of God." As long as Mencken denied the validity of mystical experience, he was merely showing "how one fanatic feels about other fanatics of a different stripe." The volume sold so well that it went through numerous reprintings prior to the issuing of a second edition in 1946.

Mencken the journalist dominated *Making of a President: A Footnote to the Saga of Democracy* (1932), a timely compilation of a *Mercury* editorial and his *Evening Sun* dispatches on the Republican and Democratic national conventions. Mencken voted for Franklin Roosevelt in 1932, but by early 1933 he was worried about the New Deal "visionaries whooping up gaudy schemes to succor the depressed and lay on new taxes."[39] The times had changed, but Mencken had no desire to change with them. His staunch economic conservatism, which had rarely attracted attention in the prosperous twenties, now stood out prominently. In the midst of widespread unemployment and suffering his advice to wait for the economy to right itself and his protests against the assertion of federal power had little appeal. An editorial in the *Christian Century** (18 October 1933) sensitively commented on the "change in the American mood" that prompted Mencken to retire from the *Mercury*.

Mencken's *Treatise on Right and Wrong* (1934) was organized on the same plan as *Treatise on the Gods,* but fared less well with reviewers. James M. Gillis and Idris W. Phillips complained that the book was weak in definition, inconsistent, and often inaccurate, Irwin Edman that it was "capricious" in its learning and condescending in attitude, and C. E. M. Joad that it was "facetious without humour . . . and serious without scholarship."[40] This second "treatise" also sold much less well than its predecessor.

Mencken's greatest accomplishment in the thirties was the fourth edition of *The American Language* (1936), embodying an enormous amount of information accumulated since the third edition of 1923. Abandoning his previous view "that the differences between American and English would go on increasing," Mencken now argued that "since 1923 the pull of American has become so powerful that it has begun to drag English with it."[41] The review by J. B. Dudek,* in its enthusiasm for "a phenomenal achievement" of scholarship and for the "diverting" writing, its summary of the approach and contents, and its notice of a few "sins of omission" typified the responses of many critics.[42] Edmund Wilson incorporated into his review an assessment of the historical and cultural significance of the first edition.[43]

Within a dozen years Mencken crowned his fourth edition with two additional thick volumes: *Supplement I* (1945) and *Supplement II* (1948), both of which elicited thoughtfully appreciative reviews. A good example is Harold Whitehall's evaluation of *Supplement I** as "superb compilative and organizational scholarship" animated by a "still pungent, still vigorous" style.[44]

Beginning in 1936, Mencken tapped a rich vein of reminiscence in a series of articles for the *New Yorker* which, with some other material, formed the substance of his *Days* books: *Happy Days, 1880–1892* (1940), *Newspaper Days, 1899–1906* (1941), and *Heathen Days, 1890–1936* (1943).

In his comments on the first two of these volumes, Hamilton Owens,* like many reviewers, invoked the powerful mood of nostalgia pervading them. *Happy Days*, Owens emphasized, reveals "a sensitive individual with a highly developed power of selection (i.e. an artist) from the very beginning." In regard to *Newspaper Days*, Owens speculated that the fact that Mencken was entertained rather than shocked by the seamy side of urban life may help account for his ability later on "to evoke and direct the literature describing it."

A *Mencken Chrestomathy* (1949), a collection of out-of-print writings edited and annotated by Mencken, was timely because it coincided with an upturn in public interest generated, at least in part, by *The Days* books. Shortly before his death he managed, with help from others, to choose from his memoranda the miscellaneous items for *Minority Report: H. L. Mencken's Notebooks* (1956).[45]

Much of the criticism of Mencken well into the forties followed patterns laid down in the twenties. Benjamin de Casseres's *Mencken and Shaw* (1930) was a scattergun variation on the more orderly approach of Goldberg and Boyd. Cabell, in *Some of Us* (1930), resembled Wilson and Lippmann in classifying Mencken as "that force which has reshaped all the present world of American letters." Nathan, in his *Intimate Notebooks* (1932), chatted in lighthearted mood about his relations with Mencken.[46] Edmund Wilson, despite his journey to the political left, devoted a sizeable section of his anthology *The Shock of Recognition* (1943) to Mencken.[47]

Older academic critics like Pattee and Boynton continued to express ambivalent attitudes about Mencken in their literary histories and essay collections,[48] but now they were joined by a younger generation of literary historians. Russell Blankenship, Granville Hicks, and Walter Fulton Taylor mentioned Mencken only briefly.[49] Ludwig Lewisohn, on the other hand, gave a full account of "The Great Critical Debate," with Mencken the satirist pitted against More the critic. Fred B. Millett, in 1940, viewed Mencken as "almost a forgotten man" who had made his great contribution as a critic of "the bourgeois way of life and of the enfeebled gentility of academic criticism." Alfred Kazin balanced Mencken's faults, such as "a fatal want of generosity," against the "uproarious gift for high comedy" shown in his role as "Civilization Incarnate."[50]

As more intellectuals moved close to or into the Communist party, the assault on Mencken by radicals became more vehement. In 1934 Malcolm Cowley, incensed by Mencken's ridicule of proletarian writers, dubbed Mencken "the former fugleman" and accused him of an anti-Semitism worthy of Joseph Goebbels.[51] According to Louis Kronenberger,* writing in 1936, Mencken had moved farther to the right, indulging in "cheap word-juggling on Roosevelt and the New Deal" and on "the proletarian school of novelists." V. F. Calverton, who rejected Communist totalitarianism, realized that Mencken, instead of "retrogressing" as Kronenberger assumed, had stood still all the while. The fault lay with the young men who, in the twenties, had failed to detect Mencken's "shallowness and shoddiness" and "hopped on the anti-Puritan bandwagon, just as a decade later they were to leap on the Red Bandwagon." In one of the most temperate essays by a Marxist, Bernard Smith, in 1939, argued that Mencken's "aristocratic attitude based on laissez-faire sentiments" had been "a revolutionary force" in "the fat years" of his forays against "comstockery, philistinism, and gentility," but in "capitalism's desperate hour" it was useless.[52]

A new development was Mencken's appearance in autobiographies by contemporaries, biographies of Dreiser, and intellectual and social histories. Among the autobiographies were those by Emily Clark, who recalled Mencken's help to her and the *Reviewer;* Harold Stearns, who acknowledged Mencken's assistance in finding contributors for the anthology *Civilization in the United States* (1922); Louis Untermeyer, who analyzed Mencken's style as essentially dionysian; and Richard Wright, who revealed how Mencken's writings stimulated him to read widely and to dream that he, too, might use words as weapons.[53] In their biographies of Dreiser, Dorothy Dudley, Robert Elias, and F. O. Matthiessen traced in some detail his relations with Mencken. Mencken also earned a place in a number of histories, including those by Frederick Lewis Allen, Mark Sullivan, Curtis D. MacDougall, and Eric Goldman.[54]

As measured by the amount of attention Mencken received in newspapers, magazines, and books, his reputation was at its lowest from 1944 through 1945. As soon as World War II ended, a revival of interest started which climaxed with his seventy-fifth birthday in 1955 and his death the following year. As part of this upswing, Jacques Barzun explored the implications of *The American Language* for the national psyche, Roger Butterfield interviewed Mencken about his political views, and Maxwell Geismar interpreted Mencken's inconsistencies and exaggerations as uncontrollable tensions that made him "the captive of his own aesthetic, . . . led to the void by his own antics."[55] In the prestigious *Literary History of the United States* (1948), Robert E. Spiller minimized other influences on Mencken in finding that "Nietzsche's dominant concepts . . . remained his substitute for the decalogue."[56]

By 1950 the time was ripe for two new biographies, the first since Goldberg's. Edgar Kemler's *The Irreverent Mr. Mencken* is a well organized and readable account handicapped by coldness toward its subject, oversimplification, and snap judgments. William Manchester, in *Disturber of the Peace* conveys much more vividly Mencken's personality and outlook, but his youthful partisanship makes him deflate others in order to magnify his hero.[57]

At this same juncture Alfred A. Knopf and Carl Van Vechten saluted Mencken in two reminiscent essays.[58] In "Bouquets for Mencken" (1953) a dozen writers paid their respects to the editor who had helped and encouraged them.[59] In a major essay surveying Mencken's whole career, Van Wyck Brooks* held that Mencken had a mind too "coarse" for literary criticism, but exactly suited to breaking down the colonial tradition and creating a "new interracial point of view." Reaching a different conclusion in another important reassessment, James T. Farrell was convinced that, in addition to being "a voice for civilized values, . . . for honesty of insight and expression," Mencken was "a sound critic of fiction" who "stated his likes frankly, clearly, forcefully, and with intelligence and feeling."[60] Among the younger academic critics, Oscar Cargill, in "Mencken and the South" (1952) turned to a neglected topic, and Frederick T. Hoffman, in his comprehensive *The Twenties* (1955), focused on Mencken's "paradoxical" portrayal of the middle class.[61]

Two anthologies of Mencken's writings, each with a useful introduction, appeared: *The Vintage Mencken,* gathered by Alistair Cooke (1955), and *A Carnival of Buncombe* (1956), in which Malcolm Moos assembled sixty-nine political articles from the *Evening Sun.*[62]

As if to offset any encomiums, Charles Angoff, once assistant editor of the *Mercury,* etched in acid his *A Portrait from Memory* (1956), from which Mencken emerges as a talented journalist inhabiting the same body as a callous, boorish—and anti-Semitic—buffoon.[63]

Out of many commemorative articles following Mencken's death two may be taken as representative. From an English perspective, D. W. Brogan recognized that the memoirs centering on Baltimore had helped save Mencken from oblivion, for "Antaeus-like, he drew strength from the soil that bore him."[64] Joseph Wood Krutch,* in an eloquent tribute, concluded that Mencken will live on not because of the causes he embraced or abhorred, but because his was "the best prose written in America during the twentieth century.[65]

Mencken left his personal library and the bulk of his meticulously kept archives, including typescripts, his *American Language* notes, clippings, and other memorabilia, to the Enoch Pratt Free Library in Baltimore. By so doing, he provided much of the data for the extensive body of scholarly and journalistic writing sampled in part 6, "Recent Perspectives and Interpretations, 1957–1984." It was largely through the efforts of Miss Betty Adler, who was in charge of the Mencken Room at the Pratt from 1956 until her death in 1973, that Mencken became one of the best bibliographed of American authors. First, she compiled with the assistance of Jane Wilhelm, *H. L. M.: The Mencken Bibliography* (1961), with an extensive coverage of Mencken's writings followed by an annotated list of secondary sources exclusive of reviews. In 1962 Miss Adler became the founding editor of *Menckeniana,* a quarterly journal that features short articles and bibliographical check lists. She also compiled the following, all published by the Pratt Library: *A Descriptive List of H. L. Mencken Collections in the U.S.* (1967); *Man of Letters, A Census of the Correspondence of H. L. Mencken* (1969); and *H. L. M.: The Mencken Bibliography, A Ten-Year Supplement, 1962–1971* (1971). Another *Supplement, 1972–1981,* prepared by Vincent Fitzpatrick, is scheduled to appear soon. Those concerned with the Mencken-Dreiser relationship should also consult *Theodore Dreiser: A Primary and Secondary Bibliography,* comp. Donald Pizer, et al. (1975).[66]

All this bibliographical activity is only one of the signs indicating that since 1957 Menckenian studies have come of age. In strong contrast to the situation in the twenties, when most academic critics either ignored or looked askance at Mencken, college professors have in recent years been among his main proponents and interpreters. A number of the foremost Mencken scholars converted their Ph. D. dissertations on him into books. Journalists, many of whom revere Mencken as the newspaperman's newspaperman, frequently quote and otherwise publicize him. Although the Mencken revival has not caught on with the general public, there has been an audience large enough to justify publishers in keeping many of his books in print and issuing new anthologies of his writings as well as scholarly studies.

The collections of Mencken letters published or planned illustrate the general trend. The trove of correspondence in the Princeton University Library, the New York Public Library, and the Dreiser Collection at the University of Pennsylvania, with many smaller holdings in other libraries, was too tempting to be disregarded. Robert H. Elias included some Mencken letters in his *Letters of Theodore Dreiser* (1959). *Letters of H. L. Mencken,* ed. Guy J. Forgue (1961), highlighted literary correspondence. Carl Bode, in *The New Mencken Letters* (1977), ranged more broadly, having at his disposal much material not available to Forgue. P. E. Cleator, an English writer, edited *Letters from Baltimore: The Mencken-Cleator Correspondence* (1982).[67] Thomas P. Riggio has completed a scholarly edition of the Dreiser-Mencken correspondence, to be issued by the University of Pennsylvania Press. The exchange of letters between Mencken and Sara Haardt, whom he married in 1930, is being edited by Marion Rodgers for a book to be issued by McGraw-Hill.

Books reprinting Mencken's writings continued apace. The broadest selection is in *The American Scene,* ed. Huntington Cairns (1965). Also of general interest are *Prejudices: A Selection,* ed. James T. Farrell (1958), and *The Young Mencken: The Best of His Work,* ed. Carl Bode (1973). *H. L. Mencken's Smart Set Criticism,* ed. William H. Nolte (1968), generously samples reviews otherwise inaccessible to most readers.[68] Newspaper pieces are on center stage in *A Bathtub Hoax and Other Blasts and Bravos from the Chicago Tribune,* ed. Robert McHugh (1958), and *Mencken's Last Campaign,* ed. Joseph C. Goulden (1976), which assembles *Sun* articles on the national political conventions and the presidential campaign of 1948. Mencken as watchdog of the press is featured in *A Gang of Pecksniffs,* ed. Theo Lippmann, Jr. (1975).[69] *H. L. Mencken on Music,* ed. Louis Cheslock (1961), is sympathetically judicious in both its selections and in its introduction and headnotes.[70]

On Mencken, ed. John Dorsey (1980), contains selections grouped by topic, with each set preceded by an appropriate commentary by a Mencken specialist.[71]

Because of the proliferation of criticism on Mencken since 1957, this introduction must concentrate on book-length studies and a sampling of significant essays. The autobiographies and collections of letters by contemporaries who knew Mencken, as well as the biographies and critical studies about them, are too numerous to be considered here. These and other more specialized sources can easily be located in the appropriate bibliographical references.

As this introduction and the selections for the period starting in 1957 illustrate, Menckenian scholarship ripened quickly, producing in the 1960s an efflorescence that has not since been equaled. This decade was distinguished by a large number of illuminating individual essays as well as of important books. Among the books were two substantial biographies. Guy J. Forgue's *H. L. Mencken: l'Homme, l'Oeuvre, l'Influence* (1967) is comprehensive and thoroughly researched, with much close analysis of the cultural background and of Mencken's ideas and style. One may balk at some of its judgments—for example, that *In Defense of Women* hides beneath the surface both a misanthrope and a misogynist—but Forgue always argues cogently. In his *Mencken* (1969), Carl Bode, following a more traditional concept of biography, is less concerned with analysis than with constructing a well documented, smoothly written narrative. Particularly valuable is the new information he presents about Mencken's relationships with friends of both sexes. In his pamphlet *H. L. Mencken* (1966), Philip Wagner packs a sensitive characterization into forty pages.[72]

In the 1970s articles on Mencken in journals and magazines declined in both quantity and quality, with relatively few using new material or attaining fresh insights, but collections of his writings and books about him continued to be published at the same pace as in the sixties. Several intellectual histories appearing in the seventies had a forerunner in *The End of American Innocence* (1959), in which Henry F. May charts Mencken's relationships to major cultural trends. In *H. L. Mencken: Iconoclast from Baltimore* (1971), Douglas C. Stenerson discusses how Mencken's ideas and values and the style in which he expressed them originated and developed and why his peculiar blend of iconoclasm and artistry fitted many of the needs and moods of the twenties. W. H. A. Williams's *H. L. Mencken* (1977), concerned with similar issues but extending its analysis beyond the twenties, is especially astute in discerning the strengths and weaknesses of Mencken's social and political commentary. The detailed, topically arranged presentation of ideas in Charles A. Fecher, *Mencken: A Study of His Thought* (1978) is strongly colored by the author's "thesis . . . that Mencken's influence was all to the good."[73]

An essay by Gerald W. Johnson in the *New Republic* for 30 September 1957, stimulated a debate in the "Correspondence" section that stretched into early 1958, with Charles Angoff affirming, and Arthur Schlesinger, Jr., Alfred A. Knopf, and Guy J. Forgue denying, that Mencken was pro-Nazi and anti-Semitic. In 1961, Forgue, in an article in the *Nation*, cited evidence from Mencken's actions and letters to refute four "myths": that Mencken was disloyal to his country during World War I; that he was pro-Nazi; that he was anti-Semitic; and that he was anti-Negro.[74] When the pro-Nazi and anti-Semitic charges were revived shortly before the Mencken Centennial in 1980, Gwinn Owens, in a thoughtful essay, conceded that "German chauvinism" made Mencken slow to see the evil in Hitler, but by 1936, as one of his letters shows, he was denouncing the Führer's "gross brutality to harmless individuals." Mencken's unfavorable criticism of Jews, Owens pointed out, was not all-inclusive, but followed the same selective pattern as his criticism of other groups.[75]

Also discussed was Mencken's social and political commentary. In his introduction to *A Carnival of Buncombe* (1956), Malcolm Moos had observed that Mencken was rarely right in predicting political trends or the outcome of elections, but was often unerring in his capsule estimates of individual politicians. In *Writers on the Left* (1961), Daniel Aaron, portraying Mencken as the leader of "the Journalistic Shockers," traced the ambivalent attitudes of radical critics toward him.[76] Douglas C. Stenerson,* in the *American Quarterly* (Winter 1966), used the "Forgotten Man" image as a focal point of the many conflicting elements in Mencken's social and political thought. John W. Aldridge's far-ranging "In the Country of the Young" (1969) contrasted the "strongly individualistic and aesthetic premises" of Mencken and other like-minded critics in the twenties with the herd mentality of many intellectuals and young people in the sixties. While Mencken and his colleagues "wanted tolerance for enlightened opinions and for an emancipated and more rigorously humane existence," their counterparts forty years later sought the good life "not . . . in the development of the self in spite of or in opposition to society, but rather in the transformation of the structures of society. . . ." George H. Douglas started out promisingly in his *H. L. Mencken: Critic of American Life* (1978), but in maintaining that in "any of Mencken's essays . . . you will invariably be rewarded by a solid and coherent piece of thinking" he did not sufficiently recognize the emotional appeals and the shifting and ambivalent values in the commentary he summarized.[77]

Another subject to be re-examined was Mencken's role as a literary critic. Louis D. Rubin, Jr., in 1966, felt that Mencken was at his peak in the 1910s when, in his *Smart Set* reviews, he dismantled "venerated nineteenth-century literary attitudes which . . . had to be destroyed if future American writers were to do their best work." In his *H. L. Mencken: Literary Critic* (1966) William H. Nolte gave an enthusiastically pro-Mencken version of the *Smart Set* reviewer's achievements.[78] Nolte exercised more restraint in his succinct introduction to *H. L. Mencken's Smart Set Criticism* (1968). Richard Ruland's *The Rediscovery of American Literature* pute with the New Humanists that has not been surpassed. Arthur Frank Wertheim, in his *The New York Little Renaissance* (1976), devoted a chapter to "Mencken, Dreiser, and *The Smart Set*" and related Mencken to contemporary cultural trends and to other critics.[79]

A number of critics were intrigued by Mencken's style and his modes of humor and satire. In "H. L. Mencken's Poetry" (1964) Edward A. Martin* argued persuasively that the "poetic, Whitmanesque sensibility" evident in *Ventures into Verse* helps account for "the startling imagery, the emphatic cadences, and the sharply defined dramatic voice" in Mencken's best writing. C. Merton Babcock compared the satirical aims and methods of Mencken and Mark Twain. Norris W. Yates, in *The American Humorist* (1964), demonstrated that the masks of the aristocrat and the solid citizen formed a "Janus-faced image" Mencken could change in mid-essay when that suited his purpose. Douglas C. Stenerson based his "Mencken's Newspaper Experience: The Genesis of a Style" (1965) on the apprentice journalist's news reports and humor columns.[80] M. K. Singleton,* in "Rhetoric and Vison in Mencken's Satire: The 'Medieval' Mob" (1966), concentrated on the effective marshaling in the *Prejudices* of metaphors and epithets from words like *peasantry, knave, demonology,* and *moutebankery.* Joseph Epstein, in 1979, theorized that what makes Mencken "an artist, perhaps the greatest of the American essayists," is his point of view combining a tragic sense of life, joy in living, skepticism tempered by "a certain humility," a grasp of reality, a humane code of behavior, and a passion for knowledge.[81]

Mencken as magazine editor was scrutinized in M. K. Singleton's *H. L. Mencken and the American Mercury Adventure* (1962) and in Carl Dolmetsch's handsomely produced and illustrated *The Smart Set: A History and Anthology* (1966).[82] Singleton carefully documented his study of the *Mercury* from the planning stages in 1923 until 1933, but he seemed unable to decide whether Mencken *qua* editor was a humane libertarian or a cynical opportunist. Dolmetsch considered the Mencken-Nathan teamwork, their relations with contributors, and the problem posed by the *Smart Set's* shaky finances. In "Mencken as a Magazine Editor" (1967) Dolmetsch* emphasized how Mencken, through his precise suggestions, became "an unexampled schoolmaster of the literary arts to a great many (perhaps fifteen hundred) of the younger generation of writers."[83] Frank Luther Mott surveyed both the *Smart Set* and the *Mercury* in volume five of his *A History of American Magazines* (1968).[84]

The task of assessing in detail how Mencken and the various editions of *The American Language* transformed philological study in the United States awaits some historically minded linguist. In 1963 Knopf issued still another version consisting of the Fourth Edition and the two Supplements abridged, with annotations and new material, by Raven I. McDavid, Jr., with the assistance of David Maurer. The introduction to this volume is only one of several essays by McDavid in which he helped lay the groundwork for further investigation. In "The Impact of Mencken on American Linguistics" (1966), for example, McDavid* gave his explanation of what qualities of mind and heart account for the far-reaching influence of *The American Language*.[85]

There is a sizeable literature on the Mencken-Dreiser friendship, the most enduring and culturally significant literary relationship in which either writer was involved. Two recent examples of research in this area are Vincent Fitzpatrick,* "Private Voices of Public Men: The Mencken-Dreiser Inscriptions," based on a previously published article revised by the author for this collection, and Thomas P. Riggio, "Dreiser and Mencken: In the Literary Trenches" (1985).[86]

Within the last ten years some scholars have surveyed stretches of Mencken terrain formerly mapped only in part. Considerable reconnoitering was done, for example, to estimate the effect "The Sahara of the Bozart" and related writings by Mencken had on southern culture and letters, but it remained for Fred Hobson to consolidate and expand on such earlier efforts in his *Serpent in Eden: H. L. Mencken and the South* (1974).[87] In " 'This Hellawful South': Mencken and the Late Confederacy," written especially for this volume, Hobson* places the same topic in fresh perspective. Except for a few suggestions here and there, the importance of Mencken's friendly relations with and encouragement of black writers was overlooked until Charles Scruggs started the research informing his *The Sage in Harlem: H. L. Mencken and the Black Writers of the 1920s* (1984).[88] In "H. L. Mencken and James Weldon Johnson: Two Men Who Helped Shape a Renaissance," here published for the first time, Scruggs* shows how the interactions of the two writers on the eve of the Harlem Renaissance anticipated many of its major themes. Edward A. Martin followed up a series of distinguished essays with his *H. L. Mencken and the Debunkers* (1984).[89] The first half of the book covers familiar ground but is notable for its emphasis on the muckraking and progressive aspects of Mencken's career, including his consistent advocacy of women's rights. The more venturesome second half relates Mencken's satire to the work of fellow debunkers ranging from William E. Woodward and Stuart Chase through Sinclair Lewis and Don Marquis to Ring Lardner, Frank Sullivan, E. B. White, and Nathanael West.

Even the brief survey in this introduction attests that Menckenian studies are healthy and hardy. They are likely to stay that way because a writer as versatile, vigorous, prolific, entertaining, and controversial as Mencken constantly invites re-evaluation. In 1974 Louis D. Rubin, Jr., challenged biographers and critics to probe more deeply into Mencken's psyche—to examine, for instance, the troubled teens neglected in his *The Days*, the effect upon Mencken of "the searing experience of the First World War," the connection between his view of life as a meaningless tragedy and his humor and comedy.[90] Even though Rubin may have exaggerated the degree to which such issues had been ignored, he raised a valid

(1967) contained a thorough and even-handed analysis of Mencken's disquestion: To what extent have we discovered the quintessential Mencken?

In addition to testing the findings from past research, we need fresh starts on such topics as Mencken's relationship to the American traditions of humor and satire and of opposition to literary censorship. As mentioned earlier, no one has gauged the effect of Mencken and *The American Language* on linguistic study in the United States. A good beginning might be an anthology of reviews of the various editions and supplements together with a comprehensive introduction. Little critical analysis has been made of either Mencken's letters or of *The Days*. Mary Miller Vass and James L. W. West III, in their "The Composition and Revision of Mencken's *Treatise on the Gods*" (1983), called upon others to join in studying his methods of composing and revising.[91] Mencken's services as a literary scout for Alfred A. Knopf have not received much attention. A study of the estimates of Mencken in the letters and autobiographies of his friends and other correspondents would be revealing. So, too, would a consideration of his relationships with young writers as reflected in their correspondence and in what he accepted for publication in the *Smart Set* and the *Mercury*. His critical reputation in England and on the Continent, especially in Germany and France, still awaits its chroniclers. And this list is by no means exhaustive. Future investigators will, however, profit from being able to build upon the work of a long line of worthy predecessors.

The most challenging task in preparing this volume has been deciding what to select out of the rich stores of criticism accumulated over more than eighty years. My sincere thanks go to Fred Hobson and Charles Scruggs for contributing original essays written especially for this collection. I am pleased to acknowledge helpful suggestions from Neda Westlake, Guy J. Forgue, Thomas P. Riggio, Louis D. Rubin, Jr., and the late Raven I. McDavid, Jr. James Nagel, the general editor of this series, always stood ready to offer sound advice.

The dedication expresses my appreciation to my wife Marjorie for her constant support and able assistance.

DOUGLAS C. STENERSON

Roosevelt University

Notes

1. Review of I. A. R. Wylie, *The Germans*, in "The Prophet of the Superman," *Smart Set* 36 (March 1912): 157.

2. Mencken gives his own account of his formative years in *Happy Days, 1880–1892* (New York: Knopf, 1940). For a more complete analysis of the ideas and attitudes he derived from the Baltimore context, see Carl Bode, *Mencken* (Carbondale and Edwardsville: Southern Illinois University Press, 1969), 9–26, and the following by Douglas C. Stenerson: *H. L. Mencken: Iconoclast from Baltimore* (Chicago: University of Chicago Press, 1971), 34–81, and

"Baltimore: Source and Sustainer of Mencken's Values," *Menckeniana*, no. 41 (Spring 1972): 1–9.

3. Alfred A. Knopf, "For Henry with Love," *Atlantic Monthly* 203 (May 1959): 50–54; Hamilton Owens, "A Personal Note," in *Letters of H. L. Mencken*, ed. Guy J. Forgue (New York: Knopf, 1961), v–xiv; Philip M. Wagner, "Mencken Remembered," *American Scholar* 32 (Spring 1963): 256–74; and Louis Cheslock, "Some Personal Memories of H. L. M.," *Menckeniana*, no. 49 (Spring 1974): 3–11. See also Theodore Dreiser, "Henry L. Mencken and Myself," in Isaac Goldberg, *The Man Mencken* (New York: Simon and Schuster, 1925), 378–81; and Joseph Hergesheimer, "Mr. Henry L. Mencken," in *The Borzoi, 1925* (New York: Knopf, 1925), 102–6.

4. Alistair Cooke, "The Last Happy Days of H. L. Mencken," *Atlantic Monthly* 197 (May 1956): 33–38; Robert Allen Durr, "The Last Days of H. L. Mencken," *Yale Review* 68 (Autumn 1958): 58–77; and William Manchester, "Last Years of H. L. Mencken," *Atlantic Monthly* 236 (October 1975): 82–84, 86, 88, 90.

5. Sara Mayfield, *The Constant Circle: H. L. Mencken and His Friends* (New York: Delacorte, 1968).

6. On Mencken's critical reputation, see G[uy] [J.] Forgue, "La Carriére de H. L. Mencken et les Critiques," *Études Anglaises* 12 (April–June 1959): 112–23; Huntington Cairns, "Mencken, Baltimore, and the Critics," *Menckeniana*, no. 45 (Spring 1973): 1–9; and George H. Douglas, "Mencken's Critics in the Twenties," *Menckeniana*, no. 53 (Spring 1975): 1–5. Excerpts from selected reviews and critical essays may be found in "H(enry) L(ouis) Mencken," *Twentieth-Century Literary Criticism*, vol. 13 (Detroit: Gale Research Co., 1984), 355–98. A useful, although incomplete and sometimes inaccurate, list of reviews appears in *Literary Writings in America: A Bibliography* (Millwood, N. Y.: KTO Press, 1977), vol. 5, 6888–903.

7. Review of *Ventures into Verse*, *Chicago Record-Herald*, 17 August 1903.

8. See, for example, "Comment on Current Books," *Outlook* 82 (10 February 1906); 323–24; "The Book-Buyer's Guide," *Critic* 48 (May 1906): 471.

9. Review of *George Bernard Shaw* in the *Nation* 82 (1 February 1906): 103–4.

10. See also "The Searchlight on G. B. S.," *Philadelphia Record*, 17 December 1905; "Topics of the Week," *New York Times Saturday Review of Books*, 23 December 1905, 914.

11. *The Philosophy of Friedrich Nietzsche* (Boston: John W. Luce & Co., 1908), note 3, 141–42; see also 35–36.

12. Reviews of *Nietzsche* in the *Catholic World* 87 (June 1908): 398–400; and in the *Dial* 45 (1 July 1908): 19.

13. The evaluation of *Nietzsche* in the *Educational Review* 35 (May 1908): 508–9, was the first in the "Reviews" section and may well have been by Nicholas Murray Butler, editor of the *Review* and president of Columbia University.

14. Review of *Nietzsche* in the *Nation* 86 (2 April 1908): 312–13.

15. A British edition was published by T. Fisher Unwin (1908). Between 1909 and 1918 Mencken edited or contributed to six other volumes in which he popularized European figures including—in addition to Nietzsche—Ibsen, Eugène Brieux, and Oscar Wilde. In the twenties this role was a less conspicuous, but still important one, as witnessed, for example, by Mencken's translation of Nietzsche's *The Antichrist* (1920). For complete listings, see *H. L. M.: The Mencken Bibliography*, comp. Betty Adler with the assistance of Jane Wilhelm (Baltimore: Johns Hopkins Press, 1961), 21–28. Hereafter this work is referred to as *H. L. M.: The Mencken Bibliography*.

16. Review of *Men versus the Man* in *Living Age* 265 (23 April 1910): 254; review by Sidney A. Reeve in the *Yale Review* 19 (August 1910): 203–5. See also Marcus Hitch, "Marxian vs. Nietzschean," *International Socialist Review* 10 (May 1910): 1021–27, and the review in the *Independent* 69 (18 August 1910): 367.

17. Louis Untermeyer, "A Preface To—," the *Liberator* 1 (May 1918): 43–45.

18. Vincent O'Sullivan, "The American Critic," in *H. L. Mencken* (New York: Knopf, 1920), 16–20, reprinted from the *New Witness* (London), 28 November 1919.

19. Review of *The American Language* in the *Boston Transcript*, 2 April 1919; Lawrence Gilman, "The Book of the Month," *North American Review* 209 (May 1919): 697–703.

20. For grudging praise from a philologian who concentrated on Mencken's technical errors, see James Root Hulbert's review in *Modern Philology* 17 (September 1919): 118–19. For favorable appraisals by academics, see Brander Mathews, "Developing the American from the English Language," *New York Times Book Review*, 30 March 1919, 157, 164, 170, and the reviews by J. M. O'Neill in the *Quarterly Journal of Speech Education* 5 (May 1919): 313–14, and by George O. Curme in *Journal of English and Germanic Philology* 18 (July 1919): 480–83.

21. A[ldous] L. H[uxley], "American Criticism," *Athenaeum* (London), no. 4679 (2 January 1920): 10; George F. Whicher, "Cross-Sections," *Nation* 110 (24 January 1920): 111–12; P[hillip] L[ittell], "Books and Things," *New Republic* 21 (21 January 1920): 239; Stuart P. Sherman, "Mr. Mencken, the *Jeune Fille*, and the New Spirit in Letters," *New York Times Book Review*, 7 December 1919, 218.

22. Fred Lewis Pattee, "A Critic in C Major," *Side-Lights on American Literature* (New York: Century Co., 1922), 56–97.

23. F. Scott Fitzgerald, "The Baltimore Anti-Christ," *Bookman* 53 (March 1921): 79–81; Burton Rascoe, "Notes for an Epitaph," *New York Evening Post Literary Review*, 4 March 1922, 459–61; Newton Arvin, "The Role of Mr. Mencken," *Freeman* 6 (27 December 1922): 381–82. Two other essays emphasizing Mencken's importance as a social critic are Carl Van Doren, "Smartness and Light: H. L. Mencken, A Gadfly for Democracy," *Century Magazine* 105 (March 1923): 791–96, and Frank Harris, "H. L. Mencken, Critic," *Contemporary Portraits: Fourth Series* (New York: Brentano's, 1923), 143–54.

24. Walter White, "The Spotlight," *Pittsburgh Courier*, 17 April 1926.

25. Kelly Miller, "Kelly Miller Says," *Baltimore Afro-American*, 8 October 1927.

26. Isaac Goldberg, *The Man Mencken* (New York: Simon and Schuster, 1925); Ernest Boyd, *H. L. Mencken* (New York: McBride, 1925). Two bibliographies had also been published, the first of which, done by Mencken under the pseudonym F. C. Henderson, appeared in the publicity pamphlet *H. L. Mencken*, 21–32 (full citation in note 18). To the second, Carroll Frey, comp., *A Bibliography of the Writings of H. L. Mencken* (Philadelphia: Centaur Bookshop, 1924), Mencken contributed a foreword.

27. Rebecca West, "In Defense of the Democratic Idea," *New York Herald Tribune Books*, 14 November 1926, 4. Like Miss West, two anonymous British reviewers objected to Mencken's shaky logic. See "The Innocence of Father Mencken," *Saturday Review* (London) 143 (19 February 1927): 276, and the review of *Notes on Democracy* in the *New Statesman* 29 (16 July 1927): 458.

28. Simeon Strunsky, "About Books, More or Less: A Distinguished Recruit," *New York Times Book Review*, 28 November 1926, 4; Bruce Bliven, "Mencken, Coolidge, and Democracy," *Forum* 77 (March 1927): 471–73.

29. Edmund Wilson, "Mencken's Democratic Man," *New Republic* 49 (15 December 1926): 110–11.

30. Joseph Warren Beach, *The Outlook for American Prose* (Chicago: University of Chicago Press, 1926), 81–105, and passim; V. E. Simrell, "H. L. Mencken the Rhetorician," *Quarterly Journal of Speech Education* 13 (November 1927): 399–412.

31. Ernest Hemingway, *The Sun Also Rises* (New York: Scribner's, 1954), 43; V. F. Calverton, *The Newer Spirit: A Sociological Criticism of Literature* (New York: Boni & Liveright, 1925), 165–79; Upton Sinclair, "Mr. Mencken Calls on Me," *Bookman* 66 (November 1927): 254–56.

32. Stuart P. Sherman, "Mr. Brownell and Mr. Mencken," *Bookman* 60 (January 1925): 632–34; Paul Elmer More, "The Modern Currents in American Literature," *Forum* 79 (January 1928): 127–36.

33. Frederick Lewis Allen, "These Disillusioned Highbrows," *Independent* 118 (9 April 1927): 378–79.

34. See, for example, Henry Sydnor Harrison, "Last Days of the Devastators," *Yale Review* 18 (September 1928): 88–103; William Saroyan, "The American Clowns of Criticism," *Overland Monthly and Out West Magazine* 87 (March 1929): 77–78, 92–3.

35. These sales figures are from Philip M. Wagner, "The Wages of Literature—II," *Philadelphia Evening Bulletin*, 3 March 1969, quoted in *Menckeniana*, no. 31 (Fall 1969): 14.

36. James Branch Cabell, *Some of Us: An Essay in Epitaphs* (New York: McBride, 1930), 113.

37. *Treatise on the Gods* (New York: Knopf, 1930), vii.

38. Granville Hicks, "Primer to Religion," *Forum* 83 (April 1930): vi; Henry Hazlitt, "The Gods Damned," *Nation* 130 (19 March 1930): 328–29; Michael Williams, "Mr. Mencken's Bible for Boobs," *Commonweal* 11 (2 April 1930): 607–10.

39. "The Tune Changes," *Baltimore Evening Sun*, 27 March 1933, reprinted in *H. L. Mencken on Politics: A Carnival of Buncombe*, ed. Malcolm Moos (New York: Vintage Books-Random, 1960), 285.

40. [James M. Gillis], "Mencken, Moralist!," *Catholic World* 139 (June 1934): 257–66; Idris W. Phillips, review of *Treatise on Right and Wrong* in *Philosophy* (British Institute of Philosophy) 10 (January 1935): 121–22; Irwin Edman, "Treatise on Mencken," *Saturday Review of Literature* 10 (7 April 1934): 603, 607; C. E. M. Joad, "Ethical Fireworks," *Spectator* 153 (12 October 1934): 530, 532. Among the favorable reviews were those by H. M. Parshley in *New York Herald Tribune Books*, 8 April 1934, 7, and by Max C. Otto in the *American Journal of Sociology* 40 (January 1935): 555.

41. *The American Language*, 4th ed. (New York: Knopf, 1936), vi.

42. Reviews of *The American Language*, 4th ed., roughly similar to Dudek's in tone and format include those by Charles Earl Funk in the *New York Times Book Review*, 10 May 1936, 2, 13; H. W. Seaman in the *American Mercury* 38 (August 1936): 501–5; John T. Flanagan in *Minnesota History* 17 (September 1936): 319–20; and William Carlos Williams in the *North American Review* 242 (Autumn 1936): 181–84.

43. Edmund Wilson, "Talking United States," *New Republic* 87 (15 July 1936): 299–300.

44. For comparable reviews, see, for *Supplement I*, the evaluation by William Cabell Greet in *American Literature* 18 (May 1946): 177–79, and Robert J. Menner, "A Patriotic Linguist," *Yale Review* 35 (Winter 1946): 354–56. For *Supplement II*, see George Genzmer, "Mr. Mencken's Life Work," *Nation* 166 (1 May 1948): 472, 474, and M[ax] J. H[erzberg], "Mencken Concludes," *Word Study* 23 (May 1948): 1–2. Raven I. McDavid, Jr., analyzed both volumes closely and, on the whole, favorably in *Language* 23 (1947): 68–73, and 25 (1949): 69–77.

45. For a listing of other books Mencken wrote, edited, or contributed to between 1930 and 1956 see *H. L. M.: The Mencken Bibliography*, 14–18, 30–34.

46. Benjamin de Casseres, *Mencken and Shaw* (New York: Silas Newton, 1930), 3–103; Cabell, *Some of Us*, 108; *The Intimate Notebooks of George Jean Nathan* (New York: Knopf, 1932), 94–121.

47. *The Shock of Recognition* (New York: Doubleday, 1943), 1155–1245. Wilson reprinted some of his own pieces on Mencken in *The Shores of Light: A Literary Chronicle of the Twenties and Thirties* (New York: Farrar, 1952).

48. Fred Lewis Pattee, *The New American Literature, 1890–1930* (New York and Lon-

don: Century Co., 1930), 415–32; Percy Holmes Boynton, *The Challenge of Modern Criticism* (Chicago: Rockwell Co., 1931), 29–46, 52–69, and *Literature and American Life* (Boston: Ginn and Co., 1936), 774–76, 778–79, and passim.

49. Russell Blankenship, *American Literature as an Expression of the National Mind* (New York: Holt, 1931); Granville Hicks, *The Great Tradition* (New York: Macmillan, 1933); Walter Fulton Taylor, *A History of American Letters* (Boston: American Book Co., 1936).

50. Ludwig Lewisohn, *Expression in America* (1932; rpt. New York: Modern Library-Random, 1939), 415–61; Fred B. Millett, *Contemporary American Authors* (1940; rpt. New York: AMS Press, 1970), 191–92, 480–86; Alfred Kazin, *On Native Grounds* (New York: Reynal, 1942), 189–204, and passim.

51. Malcolm Cowley, "Mencken: The Former Fugleman," *New Republic* 81 (21 November 1934): 50–51; Mencken's article was "Illuminators of the Abyss," *Saturday Review of Literature* 11 (6 October 1934): 155–56.

52. V. F. Calverton, "Henry L. Mencken: A Devaluation," *Modern Monthly* 10 (December 1936): 7–11; Bernard Smith, *Forces in American Criticism* (New York: Harcourt, 1939), 302–13. See also Mike Gold, "At King Mencken's Court," *The Hollow Men* (New York: International Publishers, 1941), 11–25.

53. Emily Clark, *Innocence Abroad* (New York: Knopf, 1931), 109–26; Harold Stearns, *The Street I Know* (New York: Furman, 1935), 193–206; Louis Untermeyer, *From Another World* (New York: Harcourt, 1939), 184–205, and passim; Richard Wright, *Black Boy: A Record of Childhood and Youth* (New York and London: Harper, 1945), 214–18.

54. Dorothy Dudley, *Forgotten Frontiers: Dreiser and the Land of the Free* (New York: Harrison Smith and Robert Haas, 1932), 259–66, 327–71, 395–404, and passim; Robert Elias, *Theodore Dreiser: Apostle of Nature* (New York: Knopf, 1949), passim; F. O. Matthiessen, *Theodore Dreiser* (New York: William Sloane Associates, 1951), 105–7, 177–80, and passim; Frederick Lewis Allen, *Only Yesterday: An Informal History of the Nineteen-Twenties* (New York and London: Harper, 1931), 230–44; Mark Sullivan, *The Twenties* (New York and London: Scribner, 1935), 413–21 (*The United States, 1900–1925*, vol. 6); Curtis D. MacDougall, *Hoaxes* (New York: Macmillan, 1940), 302–9 (Mencken's bathtub hoax); Eric Goldman, *Rendezvous with Destiny* (New York: Knopf, 1953), 315–17, 343.

55. Jacques Barzun, "Mencken's America Speaking," *Atlantic Monthly* 177 (January 1946): 62–65; Roger Butterfield, "Mr. Mencken Sounds Off," *Life* 21 (5 August 1946): 45–46, 48, 51–52; Maxwell Geismar, *The Last of the Provincials: The American Novel, 1915–1925* (Boston: Houghton Mifflin, 1947), 3–66, 355–77.

56. Robert E. Spiller, et al., eds., *Literary History of the United States*, 3 vols. (New York: Macmillan, 1948), 2:1141–45; bibliography, 3:654–56.

57. Edgar Kemler, *The Irreverent Mr. Mencken* (Boston: Little, Brown, 1950); William Manchester, *Disturber of the Peace: The Life of H. L. Mencken* (New York: Harper, 1950).

58. Alfred A. Knopf, "Reminiscences of Hergesheimer, Van Vechten, and Mencken," *Yale University Library Gazette* 24 (April 1950): 145–65; Carl Van Vechten, "Random Notes on Mr. Mencken of Baltimore," ibid., 165–71.

59. William Manchester et al., "Bouquets for Mencken," *Nation* 177 (12 September 1953): 210–14.

60. James T. Farrell, "H. L. Mencken: Criticus Americanus," *Reflections at Fifty and Other Essays* (New York: Vanguard Press, 1954); 42–57.

61. Oscar Cargill, "Mencken and the South," *Georgia Review* 6 (Winter 1952): 369–76; Frederick T. Hoffman, *The Twenties: Writing in the Postwar Decade* (New York: Viking, 1955), 304–14, and passim.

62. *The Vintage Mencken*, ed. Alistair Cooke (New York: Vintage Books-Random, 1955); *A Carnival of Buncombe*, ed. Malcolm Moos (Baltimore: Johns Hopkins Press, 1956).

63. Charles Angoff, *H. L. Mencken: A Portrait from Memory* (New York: Thomas Yoseloff, 1956).

64. D. W. Brogan, "H. L. Mencken," *Spectator* 196 (17 February 1956): 212.

65. See also Gerald W. Johnson, "Henry L. Mencken [1880–1956]," reprinted in Part 1 of this volume.

66. *Theodore Dreiser: A Primary and Secondary Bibliography,* comp. Donald Pizer, Richard W. Dowell, and Frederick E. Rusch (Boston: G. K. Hall, 1975).

67. *Letters of Theodore Dreiser,* 3 vols., ed. Robert H. Elias (Philadelphia: University of Pennsylvania Press, 1959); *Letters of H. L. Mencken,* ed. Guy J. Forgue (New York: Knopf, 1961); *The New Mencken Letters,* ed. Carl Bode (New York: Dial Press, 1977); *Letters from Baltimore: The Mencken-Cleator Correspondence,* ed. P. E. Cleator (Brunswick, N. J.: Associated University Presses, 1982).

68. *The American Scene: A Reader,* ed. Huntington Cairns (New York: Knopf, 1965); *Prejudices: A Selection,* ed. James T. Farrell (New York: Vintage Books-Random, 1958); *The Young Mencken: The Best of His Work,* ed. Carl Bode (New York: Dial Press, 1973); *H. L. Mencken's Smart Set Criticism,* ed. William H. Nolte (Ithaca, N. Y.: Cornell University Press, 1968).

69. *A Bathtub Hoax and Other Blasts and Bravos from the Chicago Tribune,* ed. Robert McHugh (New York: Knopf, 1958); *Mencken's Last Campaign,* ed. Joseph C. Goulden (Washington, D.C.: New Republic Book Co., 1976); *A Gang of Pecksniffs and Other Comments on Newspaper Publishers, Editors and Reporters,* ed. Theo Lippmann, Jr. (New Rochelle, N. Y.: Arlington House, 1975). For further interpretation of Mencken's newspaper criticism, see the following two review essays on *A Gang of Pecksniffs:* Thomas Stritch, "Mencken on American Journalism" *Review of Politics* 38 (April 1976): 266–72; Louis D. Rubin, Jr., "That Wayward Pressman Mencken," *Sewanee Review* 86 (Summer 1978): 474–80.

70. *H. L. Mencken on Music,* ed. Louis Cheslock (New York: Knopf, 1961).

71. *On Mencken,* ed. John Dorsey (New York: Knopf, 1980).

72. Guy J. Forgue, *H. L. Mencken: l'Homme, l'Oeuvre, l'Influence* (Paris: Minard, 1967); Carl Bode, *Mencken* (Carbondale and Edwardsville: Southern Illinois University Press, 1969); Philip Wagner, *H. L. Mencken* (Minneapolis: University of Minnesota Press, 1966).

73. Henry F. May, *The End of American Innocence: A Study of the First Years of Our Own Time, 1912–1917* (New York: Knopf, 1959); Douglas C. Stenerson, *H. L. Mencken: Iconoclast from Baltimore* (Chicago: University of Chicago Press, 1971); W. H. A. Williams, *H. L. Mencken* (Boston: Twayne, 1977); Charles A Fecher, *Mencken: A Study of His Thought* (New York: Knopf, 1978).

74. Guy Jean Forgue, "Myths about Mencken," *Nation* 193 (16 September 1961): 163–65.

75. Gwinn Owens, "Mencken and the Jews Revisited," *Menckeniana,* no. 74 (Summer 1980): 6–10. Owens was replying to Robert Kanigel, "Did H. L. Mencken Hate the Jews?," ibid., no. 73 (Spring 1980): 1–7. Both articles originally appeared in the *Baltimore Jewish Times.*

76. Daniel Aaron, *Writers on the Left* (New York: Avon Books, 1961), 45–46, 125–31, and passim.

77. John W. Aldridge, "In the Country of the Young," *Harper's* 239 (October 1969): 49–64; George H. Douglas, *H. L. Mencken: Critic of American Life* (Hamden, Conn.: Archon Books, 1978).

78. Louis D. Rubin, Jr., "H. L. Mencken and the National Letters," *Sewanee Review* 74 (July–September 1966): 723–38; William H. Nolte, *H. L. Mencken: Literary Critic* (Middletown, Conn.: Wesleyan University Press, 1966).

79. Richard Ruland, *The Rediscovery of American Literature: Premises of Critical*

Taste, 1900–1940 (Cambridge: Harvard University Press, 1967) 97–165; Arthur Frank Wertheim, *The New York Little Renaissance: Iconoclasm, Modernism, and Nationalism in American Culture, 1908–1917* (New York: New York University Press, 1976), 187–98, and passim.

80. C. Merton Babcock, "Mark Twain, Mencken, and 'the Higher Goofyism,'" *American Quarterly* 16 (Winter 1964): 587–94; Norris W. Yates, *The American Humorist: Conscience of the Twentieth Century* (Ames, Iowa; Iowa State University Press, 1964) 142–64; Douglas C. Stenerson, "Mencken's Early Newspaper Experience: The Genesis of a Style," *American Literature* 37 (May 1965): 153–66.

81. Joseph Epstein, "H. L. Mencken: The Art of Point of View," *Menckeniana*, no. 71 (Fall 1979): 2–11. See also James J. Kilpatrick, "The Writer Mencken," ibid., no. 79 (Fall 1981): 2–10.

82. M. K. Singleton, *H. L. Mencken and the American Mercury Adventure* (Durham, N. C.: Duke University Press, 1962); Carl Dolmetsch, *The Smart Set: A History and Anthology* (New York: Dial Press, 1966).

83. See also Carl Dolmetsch, "'HLM' and 'GJN': The Editorial Partnership Re-examined," *Menckeniana*, no. 75 (Fall 1980): 29–39, and Alfred A. Knopf, "H. L. Mencken, George Jean Nathan, and the *American Mercury* Venture," ibid., no. 78 (Summer 1981): 1–10.

84. Frank Luther Mott, *A History of American Magazines*, vol. 5 (Cambridge: Harvard University Press, 1968). For articles on specific aspects of the two magazines, see the listings in the Mencken bibliographies.

85. See also Raven I. McDavid, Jr., "Mencken Revisited," in *Language and Learning*, ed. Janet A. Emig, James T. Fleming, and Helen M. Popp (New York: Harcourt, 1966), 112–29; "H. L. Mencken: *The American Language*," in *Landmarks of American Writing*, ed. Hennig Cohen (New York: Basic Books, 1969), 261–69; and "H. L. Mencken and the Linguistic Atlas Project," *Menckeniana*, no. 73 (Spring 1980): 7–9.

86. Thomas P. Riggio, "Dreiser and Mencken: In the Literary Trenches," *American Scholar* 54 (Spring 1985): 227–38.

87. Fred Hobson, *Serpent in Eden: H. L. Mencken and the South* (Chapel Hill: University of North Carolina Press, 1974).

88. Charles Scruggs, *The Sage in Harlem: H. L. Mencken and the Black Writers of the 1920s* (Baltimore: Johns Hopkins Press, 1984).

89. Edward A. Martin, *H. L. Mencken and the Debunkers* (Athens: University of Georgia Press, 1984).

90. Louis D. Rubin, Jr., "'If Only Mencken Were Alive . . . ,'" in *The Comic Imagination in American Literature*, ed. Louis D. Rubin, Jr. ([Washington, D. C.]: Forum Series, 1974), 240–42.

91. Mary Miller Vass and James L. W. West III, "The Composition and Revision of Mencken's *Treatise on the Gods*," *Publications of the Bibliographical Society of America* 77 (Fourth Quarter 1983): 447–61.

1: Intimate Impressions and Insights

On H. L. Mencken

George Jean Nathan*

In the monthly department, "Répétition Générale," which we jointly conduct in *The Smart Set Magazine*, there was some months ago incorporated the following paragraph:

> When one of us, in the course of his critical writings, indulges himself in polite words about the other, it is a common antic of the newspaper literary supplement professors to observe that this encomium is merely by way of mutual log-rolling, that it is based upon no sounder critical ground than our friendship for each other and our commercial alliance, and that it is perhaps not honestly believed in by either the one or the other. This, of course, is idiotic. We are friends and partners, not because we admire each other's beauty, or each other's conversation, or each other's waistcoats or wives, but because we respect each other professionally, because each to the other seems to know his work in the world, and how to do it, and how to do it—it may be—just a little bit better than the next nearest man. This obviously, is the soundest of all bases for friendship. It is not friendship that makes men approve one another; it is mutual approval that makes them friends.

Let me add a word about Mencken in particular. I respect him, and am his friend, because he is one of the very few Americans I know who is entirely free of cheapness, toadyism and hypocrisy. In close association with him for more than twelve years, I have yet to catch him in a lie against himself, or in a compromise with his established faiths. There have been times when we have quarrelled and times, I dare say, when we have hated each other: but when we have met again it has been always on a ground of approval and friendship made doubly secure and doubly substantial by the honesty of his point of view (however wrong I have held it), by the wholesomeness of his hatred, and by his frank and ever self-doubting conduct at our several Appomattoxes.

Perhaps no man has ever been more accurately mirrored by his writings than this man. He has never, so far as I know, written a single line that he hasn't believed. He has never sold a single adjective—and there

*Reprinted by permission of the publisher from *The Borzoi, 1920* (New York: Alfred A. Knopf, 1920).

have been times when opulent temptations have dangled before him. And on certain of these occasions he could have used the money. There may be times when he is wrong and when his opinions are biased—I believed that there are not a few such times—yet if he is wrong, he is wrong honestly, and if he is biased, he neither knows it in his own mind nor feels it in his own heart. He is the best fighter I have ever met. And he is the fairest, the cleanest, and the most relentless.

But does he accept himself with forefinger to temple, with professorial wrinkles, as an Uplifting Force, a Tonic Influence? Not on your ball-room socks! No critic has ever snickered at him as loudly and effectively as he snickers at himself. "What do you think of your new book?" I usually ask him when he has finished one. And his reply generally is, "It's got some good stuff in it—and a lot of cheese. What the hell's the use of writing such a book, anyway? My next one . . ."

Life to him is a sort of Luna Park, and he gets the same sort of innocent, idiotic fun out of it. He would rather drink a glass of good beer than write; he would rather talk to a pretty girl than read; he would rather wallop the keys of a piano than think; he would rather eat a well-cooked dinner than philosophize. His work, which so clearly reflects him spiritually, represents him equally clearly in helpless revolt against his corporeal self.

This, a snapshot of Henry Mencken, for ever applying the slapstick to his own competence, constantly sceptical of his own talents, and ever trying vainly to run away from the pleasure that his temperament rebelliously mocks. I am happy to know him, for knowing him has made the world a gayer place and work a more diverting pastime. I am glad to be his partner, his collaborator, his co-editor, his drinking companion, and his friend. For after all these many years of our friendship and professional alliance, there is only one thing that I can hold against him. For ten years he has worn the damndest looking overcoat that I've ever seen.

H. L. Mencken   Elizabeth Shepley Sergeant*

Coming toward me, very swiftly, as I walked in the direction of Fifth Avenue on Forty-fourth Street, I saw a rather short, stocky figure of a man whose blue eyes shone ahead of him like a sort of searchlight. He leaned a little forward, stooping his shoulders, as if to hasten his pace, and he was strongly careened to the right: a boat under full sail. But what bore him down and forward was not a spanking breeze; it was an obviously weighty traveling bag, suspended from a long and almost simian arm. This pedestrian seemed more alertly intent on his way and his business than any other man within range; those china-blue eyes were not preoccupied with Forty-fourth Street at all, but with some inner objective toward which they were

*From the *Nation* 124 (16 February 1927): 174–78. Reprinted by permission of the *Nation*.

heading. It struck me with a shade of surprise that a prosperous bourgeois American should be carrying his own handbag instead of voyaging in a taxi. So, as he passed, I took rather special notice of a short, square, pleasant, determined face. The man was in his prime, yet there was something boyish about him. He belonged to the business world, yet there was something of the thinker in his mien. He was very much at home in New York—indeed, I thought I had seen him before myself—yet he had the air of a visitor. A provincial professor, of some very living subject, on his way to a congress? I fear I have spoken an insult. For the man I had noted was H. L. Mencken, on his way from Hollins Street, Baltimore, via the caves of the Heckscher Building, to the Hotel Algonquin.

I tracked him down at last, you see, in Alfred Knopf's waiting-room. I sat somnolently on a deep couch; in the shaded light Mencken was dismissing, very kindly, a young aspirant who would have liked to be told exactly how to write his article for the *American Mercury*. Mencken knows his influence with the youth of the age, and it has reached his ears that the writers in his magazine are prone to imitate him. He explained that he had now made it a rule to know nothing about any article until it reached his desk in finished form. So dismissing, he collided with a tall glass vase of red flowers. The vase fell over; young ladies with bobbed hair came running at the crash. Mencken was for a moment aghast. He made sounds and gestures of compunction and dismay. Then he came to himself. "Anyhow it was an ugly vase," he said, with that blue-eyed laugh which has something remote and mirthless about it, vanishing in the direction of his private lair while the secretaries picked up the pieces.

But he does not wish to be thought of as a "slayer," so he told me, very earnestly, on another occasion, in his rooms at the Algonquin, after an absinthe cocktail had been dispensed, and a perfect bottle of Moselle placed handy, and a well-chosen jellied bird—this befell on a hot summer day—set on the board. He need not have said it, for even in these impersonal hotel rooms he moves in an atmosphere of amenity. Only a gentle host, in the old-fashioned sense, a host who is also an artist—and surely artists are seldom slayers at bottom—could take so much trouble about gastronomy and vintages. I had expected to meet an artist and an epicure, but I was hardly prepared for the sentimentalist—the solid, Germanic sentimentalist—who emerged when he talked of Baltimore, its stable and familiar scenes: the red brick house with white trimmings, where he had lived for forty-odd years; the quiet domestic life that has gone on there; the classical orchestral music that is produced by the Saturday Night Club, where, with a group of tried old friends, doctors and professors, Mencken plays the second piano part. Even when Mencken is "slaying," it is, I think, to the great roll of the Eroica. In his daily friendly intercourse one hears another, less fateful, more fitful strain of music. From the moment of this first real talk I have associated with our most terrible and earth-shaking critic a word which he often uses in his writing, though few remember it when they, in turn, come to criticism of him. It is "charm." Like a lost flower, charm is carried away on the flood of his invectives.

When these invectives began, I felt confronted not by the sword of the slayer but by a mighty tide—a literal flood-tide of speech, rolling in, wave after wave, rising to a crest, subsiding, rising again, from the inexhaustible Great Lake of Mencken's absorbed and all-inclusive knowledge of what some might call (not he) the "folkways" of his country. The American scene, the American lot, the common American life, the faulty and fictitious American democracy. I speak of a Great Lake rather than of an ocean, for the waves were America-bound—except, perhaps, when he commended the fine tyrannical government of Frederick the Great—and they had, to my disaffected Puritan eye, used to the rocky northern seaboards, something a little featureless and uniform in their variety. Votes, senators, common decency, Bryan, Doctor Coolidge, boobs and yokels, button manufacturers, comstocks, wowsers, snouting and preposterous Puritans, "made for satirists as catnip was made for cats." H. L. Mencken rolled them all on the beach—on his tongue—like so much wreckage, for my fascinated eyes.

But suddenly a word was spoken that had another echo. It was LIBERTY. When that simple word resounds about Mencken's head, the waves of fluent speech recede. You see him, in the midst of a silence, posing with rapt blue eyes for the picture of a revolutionist of '48, or of an adolescent who has just won a contest with an autocratic father. To use another image, it is as if the traffic signals had changed, and a new light of faith had come out in a doubter's face. This abstract good, this Liberty, is what my Algonquin host was in need of. A fig for wine, women, and song! As Diogenes searched for an honest man, so does the editor of the *Mercury* search for a free Americano. . . .

A journalist cited to me, apropos of the two Menckens—the comedian of youth, whose tone is not so different, except that it is mature, from that of the Harvard *Lampoon* or any similar college paper, and the sardonic and solemn critic and pamphleteer of our life and letters who has made himself a great national force—the story of the man who went into a restaurant and first consumed a meal of sausage and sauerkraut: that was for his tape worm. Then he ordered the meal of an epicure that was for himself. This solid and sentimental family man of Baltimore, argues my friend, the Mencken who believes in monogamy and proclaims that women should nurse their babies, and is sure that marriage is not a licensed week-end; this puritanical skeptic, with his bookish and even scholarly tastes and his need of a familiar solitude in which to formulate in highly wrought phrases his scheme of fatalistic valuations—he is doubled by a discursive and immensely curious journalist, a man of broader ways and humors, who must keep in touch with the worst that is known and thought in his country in order to ply the trade he entered upon as soon as he could escape from the family cigar factory: the trade of destructive and ironic critic of his day and hour. . . .

A non-Anglo-Saxon American—that is, a non-Puritan, a man of European rather than of British lineage. There is, as he says, undeniably

> a difference in their primary instincts, in their reactions to common stimuli, in their ways of looking at the world, and that difference has, of late years, come to the estate of conflict, with the "Anglo-Saxon" striving to keep what he has—his point of view, his cultural leadership, his political hegemony—and the non-"Anglo-Saxon" trying to take it away from him. . . . To admit the conflict is to admit his clear right, nay, his bounden duty to battle for his side, passionately, desperately, and with any weapon at hand.

When I spend two or three hours with Mencken I become subtly aware that he is the descendant of gregarious, agnostic, scholarly, musical, extraverted Germans, saturated for centuries in the common life of the cafe and the marketplace and the popular classical concert, while I descend from lonely New England farmers and doctors and divines who meditated on eternity and morality and the state of their souls as they pursued their introverted and difficult lives. Mencken, though so much of a romantic Nietzschean individualist, hates and loathes his solitude as a writer, rages against it as he rages about his amenities, and worries not at all about his soul. Theoretically he loves to stand alone, a superior individual whose mission it is to resist and survive. Practically and actually he is a very gregarious human who enjoys a drummer or a Babbitt much better than a cultured man, studies his customs and his ideas and even his speech—remember that remarkable work *The American Language*—with close attention, though he cannot endure being governed by his opinions. . . .

Henry had intentions of his own about his career. . . .His time in the factory was brief. [When] his father died, he took over the headship of the family, and once and for all settled down to live with his mother, and got an assignment on the Baltimore *Morning Herald*.

By 1903, he was city editor. By 1905, at the age of twenty-five, he was editor-in-chief. The next year he moved to the more famous *Sun*, where he stayed until 1917. His most notable work there was done for his free-lance column—the origin of the "Maryland Free State," of which he is so justly proud. He became literary critic of the *Smart Set* in 1908, to Nathan's dramatic critic; and thus began his long and affectionate association with the new literature and the new authors, like Dreiser, whom he helped so materially to show their heads above the walls of Puritan prejudice . . .

Add to this bare chronicle a vast number of allied activities in the field of critical letters, including the publication of many books, and you have a career multifariously active, aggressively successful, robust and exuberant; undoubtedly one of the most significant careers of contemporary America.

Here is a vigorous trained mind, with sensitive literary and artistic perceptions and strong scientific interest, propelled by a temperament at once
ruthless, fearless, and militant. Mencken disclaims idealism, scholarship,
evangelism, yet he is really a sort of sadistic evangelist, a Puritan with a
scalpel instead of a Bible, who is all the people he condemns. "It is difficult," he admits, "for an American to contemplate an American without
something comparable to moral indignation."

Mencken's indignation and his isolation grow with the years. When he
had gathered about himself a fairly numerous group of creative literary
spirits—about his earlier self, the critic as artist, who smashed the old idols
of wholesomeness and respectability—he turned away from them. They no
longer needed him. Their cause was won. The parlous state of the democratic state called him to new and more bitter social action. The *American
Mercury* takes less interest in the arts than the *Smart Set* of old, and more
in social phenomena. The partnership with Nathan, which belonged to the
aesthetic years, was here dissolved, and one finds the social critics, the historians, the doctors, and scientists taking the floor. Mencken admits that
he can scarcely now read a current novel. "He will be Mayor of Baltimore
in five years," remarked Nathan sagely. . . .

Take it as a joke or a prophecy, but be assured that *Notes on Democracy,* that fierce, surgical diagnostic and dissection of our democratic
scheme—"I am not engaged in therapeutics but in pathology"—is regarded
by the author as his most important work. It is based on the theory that
men are not alike, that politics is not soluble by the seraphic intuition of
the boobs,

> that the world is a vast field of greased poles flying gaudy and seductive
> flags. Up each a human soul goes shinning, painfully and with many a
> slip. Some climb eventually to high levels; a few scale the dizziest
> heights. But the great majority never get very far from the ground. There
> they struggle for a while and then give it up. The effort is too much for
> them: it doesn't seem to be worth its agonies. Golf is easier; so is joining
> the Rotary; so is fundamentalism; so is osteopathy, so is Americanism.

Democracy is the government of the envious, of those who cannot allow
their superiors—the ideally educated modern men, who have put away the
immemorial fears of the race and are sure of themselves in this world—a
chance to rule them. Democratic man hates the fellow who is having a better time than he, as the Puritan and the Prohibitionist do.

Is Mencken going by his invectives to swell the company of the governing aristocrats, as he undoubtedly swelled the company of the free writers? Is he, by his words of scorn, bringing out of their holes men of "common decency" who do not buy votes or office, or compromise with ideas
for jobs? He seems to doubt it.

> The free man is one who has won a small and precarious territory from
> the great mob of his inferiors, and is prepared and ready to defend it and

make it support him. All around him are enemies, and where he stands there is no friend. He can hope for little help from other men of his own kind, for they have battles of their own to fight. He has made himself a sort of god in his little world, and he must face the responsibilities of a god, and the dreadful loneliness.

The passage, as much as any in Swift's satires, seems to spring from a tragic source.

Mencken, it is well known, is a dominating contemporary influence in our universities. Yet he is not, in any daily human sense, close to the young. He still stands on a table of isolation, above these young collegians who stretch out their hands to him. Life, says Horace Walpole, is a comedy to those who think, a tragedy to those who feel.

It is easy to see whence the legend of Mencken the slayer arose. Straight from the books. Looking toward the human being I see a man with bright blue eyes and a gentle mouth, listening to a strain of music and surrounded by old and even elderly friends—mostly doctors and musicians and journalists, the happiest boon companions Baltimore has to offer. Mencken's friends know him as a man of originality, "hence of genuine charm." A man with a wine cellar. A man extraordinarily free. A man who has had a rare time in that silent study which is his tomb and his solace, charging innocent words with his own powerful brand of dynamite and arranging them in his own dangerous pattern. They know him as a man who likes to do a good turn to the very underdogs he affects to despise, and who would ill endure himself the iron rule of a Kaiser or a Mussolini. They know him as a romantic adventurer in the field of sex who feels love to be the business of the cool of the evening. They know him as one who has furnished more ideas to other men than any other living American critic. Perhaps he has failed to live up to the traditions of his substantial, patriarchal tribe, good citizens of the Free State, by remaining a bachelor. But the descendants of an original and generous artist are not always children of flesh and blood. They are sometimes, like Mr. Babbitt—Mr. Boob—the children of other men's brains.

Henry L. Mencken (1880–1956)   Gerald W. Johnson*

H. L. Mencken's *Prejudices*, especially the first three volumes, his *American Mercury* 1924–1934, his *American Language* with its supplements, and his *Days*, in form an autobiography but in fact a social history of extraordinary color and texture, constitute a body of work commanding the respectful attention of the literary world. As critic, as editor, as philologist, and as historian the man made original and arresting contributions to

*From the *Saturday Review* 39 (11 February 1956): 12–13. © 1956, *Saturday Review* magazine. Reprinted by permission.

the national letters; and a writer who has scored in four separate fields is sufficiently unusual to deserve careful scrutiny and analysis. His passing may be relied on to draw all pundits to their typewriters or dictaphones.

But there was also a character known as Henry Mencken to a relatively small circle in Baltimore and to an even smaller group outside the city; and he was, at least in the opinion of this writer, more remarkable than the H. L. Mencken known to everybody. His passing on January 29 also deserves notice, not in the style of literary analysis, but in the plain speech of the unschooled, in which he was as expert as he was in the language of the Academy.

This man was conspicuously kindly and polite. The information may come as a stunning surprise to those who are familiar only with the roaring invective of which H. L. Mencken was master and the acid wit in which he barbecued heroes and demigods of all sects and fashions; but I refer, not to H. L. Mencken, the public figure, but to Henry Mencken, citizen of Baltimore. He was fully aware of this distinction and drew it sharply himself; as far as he could, he screened Henry Mencken from the observation of press and public, while thrusting H. L. Mencken to the fore.

He once told a friend that when he went into the Stork Club in New York and the diners stared and then turned to whisper to each other, he thought it was swell; but when the same thing happened in Miller's Baltimore restaurant he found himself perspiring and acutely uncomfortable. For that reason he commonly avoided the big places, especially when dining alone. What café society calls "a celebrity" appeared to his realistic eye merely as a curiosity, and he hated the idea of being a curiosity in his home town.

But he was, of course. No such vivid personality could live anywhere without being something of a curiosity, no matter how sedulously he might avoid outward eccentricity. Mencken avoided it. He was of medium height, five feet eight or nine, but stocky enough to look shorter. Clean-shaved and conservatively dressed, with no oddities of posture or gait, he should have merged imperceptibly into a street crowd. But he didn't. He stuck out, for reasons almost impossible to capture and fix in words. The best one can say is that he stood and walked and talked like other men, only more so. He was conspicuously normal.

Into that medium-sized body was packed the vitality of twenty ordinary men. He was surcharged, and the fact was evident in whatever he did, even in the way he put his foot down in walking, or the flip of a hand when he returned a greeting. It was revealed in an immense capacity for work, and in a correspondingly immense capacity for enjoyment. This enraged ascetics, of course, and they called him a sensualist which, in the way they meant it, was nonsense.

But in another way, a quite extraordinary way, perhaps the charge had something in it. Henry Mencken's perceptions were keen, as are those of any man who is intensely alive; to observers it seemed that he could extract more, and more profound, pleasure out of one seidel of beer than most men could from a gallon; certainly he could extract energy and encouragement from apparent defeat; and certainly he could detect and savor lusty humors in situations which to most men meant only tragedy and despair. In seventy-five years he not only outlived the rest of us, he lived far longer; one is tempted to assert that he lived like Noah and Seth and Enoch, those Old Testament ancients.

This gave him a towering advantage over the majority of those with whom he came in contact, and as a rule the man who enjoys a towering advantage is a hateful fellow. The marvel of Henry Mencken is that he was nothing of the sort. H. L. Mencken was hated. Every opprobrious term in the vocabulary of billingsgate was hurled at him, and even honorable terms were applied to him with the force of epithets; he was called a Jew, a Catholic, and a Communist, but never by a Jew, a Catholic, or a Communist, always by their enemies. It would be difficult, indeed, to identify a man who didn't hate H. L. Mencken at one time or another and for one reason or another.

But I have yet to encounter man, woman, child, or beast of burden who knew Henry Mencken and hated him. He was too expansive, too free of envy, too obviously void of any disposition to grasp at personal advantage. Even those most captious of critics, writers who knew that he could out-write them, once they came within the magnetic field of his personality lost the capacity to hate. They could be exasperated by him, they could denounce him with fire and fury; but they had trouble doing it with a straight face.

The explanation is that Henry Mencken was an intellectual philanthropist. Occasionally he would follow some deliverance with the warning, "Now don't you write that. I mean to use it myself"; but as a rule he scattered ideas with the grand abandon, so astonishing to Darwin, of the fir-tree in scattering pollen.

Incidentally, the writers who knew Henry Mencken were few. Every semi-literate scribbler in the country knew H. L. Mencken, of course, and those who had met him in the flesh must have numbered thousands; but in Baltimore his intimates, outside the group closely associated with him on the Baltimore *Sun*, included relatively few writers. True, he married the novelist, Sara Haardt, but there was a touch of the Pygmalion complex in that. Mencken had done a great deal toward pruning and strengthening her literary style when she was an aspiring youngster and he was probably a bit in love with his own creation. But this factor was only a touch; the charming lady from Alabama had plenty to account for the romance without seeking explanations in the subconscious. One of her charms was her extraordinary wisdom in being not merely tolerant but gracious to any odd fish that Henry chose to bring to the house.

And odd they certainly were! All the human flotsam and jetsam of the seven seas of literature eventually washed up on the big brownstone steps of the Cathedral Street house—this was during Mencken's married life, tragically brief, as Sara died within a few years—and it included as H. L. M. once said of the lady drys, "some specimens so dreadful that one wonders how a self-respecting God could have made them." But these were at most friends of H. L. Mencken, more often mere acquaintances, and all too often complete strangers brazen enough to walk in uninvited.

The friends of Henry Mencken were odd, but in a different sense— odd in that they didn't match, could not be listed in any one category. Status of any sort, social, economic, intellectual, or other was irrelevant. They were so different that one can think of but a single characteristic that they possessed in common—they were all vibrantly alive. Whether it was Max Broedel, the anatomical artist, who rarely had a cent, or Harry C. Black, principal owner of the *Sun*, who had dollars and some millions of them; whether it was Raymond Pearl, the biologist and one of the great brains of Johns Hopkins, or William Woollcott, the mucilage manufacturer, who loudly proclaimed that he had no brain at all (although he was a finer wit than his famous brother, Alexander); whether it was a barber or a governor, any man to whom Henry Mencken took a liking was one who savored life, sometimes with a wry face, but definitely.

In the office of the *Sun* H. L. Mencken could work with anybody, although there were some who tried him to the limit. But Henry Mencken's close associates again were various: Paul Patterson, the publisher, diplomatic but as refractory as basalt; Henry Hyde, veteran star reporter, as stately as Mencken was ebullient; the two Eds, Murphy, managing editor, and Duffy, cartoonist, explosive Irishmen; and the Owens pair, John and Hamilton, chief editors, distant cousins and distantly Welshmen. They were all experts, but there were other experts around the place who maintained polite relations with H. L. Mencken, yet never caught a glimpse of Henry. Those who did had something more than *expertise;* they had zest and a fine appreciation of the flavor of life even when—perhaps especially when—it displeased them.

To us smaller fry in the organizaton he was consistently genial and consistently helpful, although he could be sardonic. To me one day he observed, blandly, "He is a great cartoonist, but in politics, of course, Duffy is an idiot." Since Duffy's politics and mine were identical I got it, all right.

The newspaper man, however, was not Baltimore's Henry Mencken. That character was never to be found in public places, but only in private houses, or semi-private apartments such as the upper room over Schellhäse's restaurant, where he led the Saturday Night Club in wild forays in the realm of music, sometimes murderous enterprises such as playing the nine symphonies of Beethoven in succession—they finished at dawn— sometimes elaborate buffooneries such as orchestrating for ninety instruments Willie Woollcott's ribald ditty about the 100 per cent American; or alone at home devising preposterous communications and mementos. I had on my desk for years a three-pound chunk of rock sent through the mails at terrific expense with a preternaturally solemn document certifying it as an authentic madstone.

But the unforgettable Henry Mencken, the man who really altered the lives of the relatively few who knew him, was Mencken sitting at ease after the day's work was over, with a cigar in his mouth, a seidel in his hand, and around him a small group who were equal to the rapier play of his wit—Woollcott, Pearl, Gilbert Chinard, a very few others. In such surroundings Henry Mencken talked better than H. L. Mencken ever wrote— lightly, ironically, extravagantly, but with a flashing perception that illuminated whatever it touched, and it touched everything. A display of intellectual pyrotechnics it was, certainly, but like any fine fireworks display it created in an ordinary place on an ordinary night a glittering illusion; momentarily, at least, life sparkled and blazed, and the knowledge that it can ever sparkle and blaze is worth having. In fact, it is one of the best things a man can have.

It was not optimism. Henry Mencken, like H. L. Mencken, was a pessimist; but his pessimism was more invigorating than the gurgling of any male Pollyanna. "The trouble about fighting for human freedom," he remarked once, "is that you have to spend much of your life defending sons-of-bitches; for oppressive laws are always aimed at them originally, and oppression must be stopped in the beginning if it is to be stopped at all." It is hard to imagine anything more dismal, but I do not believe it will sap the courage of any fighting character.

Mencken would have disliked being compared to pietistic Samuel Johnson, but he played a very similar role in his own city. The difference was that Johnson always and Mencken never took himself too seriously; nevertheless, each was not only witty, "but the cause that wit is in other men." Nor did it stop with wit. They caused a zest for life to be renewed in other men, they touched the dull fabric of our days and gave it a silken sheen. Boswell, greatest of biographers, recognized but never could translate into words the quality that made contact with his hero a milestone in every man's life; and if Boswell could not do it for Johnson, what hope is there that any lesser person can do it for Mencken? One may only record the fact and pass on.

Nevertheless, it is true that when Mencken died there were those in Baltimore who were not much interested in what the world had lost—the incomparable reporter, the critic, the philologist, the social historian, H. L. Mencken. They were too much occupied in lamenting their own loss—Henry Mencken, the unique, who, deriding them exalted them, in threatening them encouraged them, in prophesying death and doom gave them a new, strong grip on life. The man who really knew him will do far more living in the same number of days than he would have done without that contact. If there is a finer gift that a man can bestow upon his friends, I cannot name it. They mourn with cause.

2: *From Local Prominence to National Fame, 1905–1918*

An Interpretation of Shaw
[Review of *George Bernard Shaw: His Plays*]

Mr. Henry L. Mencken, an author of whom the reviewer is lamentably ignorant, is under the impression that some persons may be too much occupied with other matters to read in full the plays of George Bernard Shaw, and he has obligingly, if not altogether fairly, offered them the scenario of each play, filled out with his own interpretation. The first sentences of his outline of *Candida* are submitted that the true Shawite may judge of the reliability of the author's interpretation:

"*Candida*," says Mr. Mencken, "is a latter day essay in feminine psychology after the fashion of *A Doll's House*, *Monna Vanna*, and *Hedda Gabler*. Candida Morell, the heroine, is a clergyman's wife, who, lacking an acquaintance with the philosophies and face to face with the problem of earning her daily bread, might have gone the muddy way of Mrs. Warren. As it is, she exercises her fascinations upon a moony poet, arouses him to the mad dog stage of passion, drives her husband to the verge of suicide— and then, with bland complacency and unanswerable logic, reads both an excellent lecture, turns the poet out of doors, and falls into her husband's arms, still chemically pure. It is an edifying example of the influence of mind over matter."

Mr. Mencken has read Huneker, William Archer, Cunningham Graham, and the other epigrammatic critics, and having something of a turn for epigram himself he has made a readable book and one likely to further the stirring habit of disputation. He regards Mr. Shaw as an indubitable searcher for truth. The drama, he points out, is the record of conflict. Shaw's conflicts are between the orthodox and the heterodox. "Darwin," says Mr. Mencken, "made this war between the faithful and the scoffers the chief concern of the time, and the sham-smashing that is now going on in all the fields of human inquiry might be compared to the crusades that engrossed the world in the middle ages. Every one, consciously or unconsciously, is more or less directly engaged in it, and so, when Shaw chooses conspicuous fighters in this war as the chief characters of his plays, he is

39

but demonstrating his comprehension of human nature as it is manifested today."

This is quite self-evidently true. Mr. Shaw has been trying to help men and women to understand themselves. He has invited them to come out from behind their own hypocrisy and stand in the open and fight for what they are secretly and actually thinking. The only difficulty is that in presenting a type a dramatist labors under the disadvantage that each man, conscious of the variant instincts, impulses, dreams, and principles of his own personality, finds the coincidence between himself and the depicted character too slight to admit of genuine sympathy of a subjective sort. While, on the other hand, Mr. Shaw's manifest coldness toward the creations of his extraordinary fancy causes the public, also, to regard with alien eyes these odd specimens of humanity whom he has caught and speared to his paper for the scientific scrutiny of the pessimistic.

The real trouble with Shaw is, cognizant of almost everything though he is, he has failed at the last to be cognizant of what is best in men and women. He has counted in almost everything except such little matters as simplicity, ideality, direct, instinctive sacrifice, and genuine, natural affection. It is by these things that the greater part of humanity moves, and for them the complex play of ulterior motives and unconfessed temptations is no more than the dancing of phosphorus over the water. It is there for an hour, giving to the familiar scene a curious unreality and lending an evil enchantment of its own, but presently it is gone and the wholesome sea lies under the morning sun taking and giving of the fair elements of life. The deeps are not disturbed. When Mr. Shaw becomes aware of these deeps in the human soul and pays to humanity the tribute which it really deserves he will be better understood.

Mr. Mencken has, however, shown more of a sense of fitness than to make such trite remarks as those above. He has brought a satirist's comprehension to a greater satirist's work. The book is worth adding to the shelf of Shawana—if one has such a thing.

An Account of Nietzsche
[Review of *The Philosophy of Friedrich Nietzsche*]

Anonymous*

In this volume, *Friedrich Nietzsche*, by Henry L. Mencken, (Luce & Co.), we are given in the introduction a clear notion of the writer's own attitude toward the great German, as well as some conception of his fitness to write upon and to translate him. It is evident that Mr. Mencken possesses the requisite sympathy, and withal a certain clear, forceful, even ar-

*From the *New York Times Book Review*, 15 February 1908, 90.

dent style, a keen and thoroughgoing intellect, knowledge of men, and a sense of humor. He is not hampered by prejudice nor dismayed by traditions, and he is able to leave out inessentials without destroying the harmony of what remains. He has made a good book and gives us a pretty fair conception of just what Nietzsche was and what he stood for.

In the sketch given of the philosopher's life we get an impression as of a sick and fretful eagle confined in a barnyard, maddened by its senseless chatter, with a far eye on rocky, desolate heights, tearing with fierce beak and claws at the prized and awe-inspiring erections with which the sleek fowls have been fenced in and guarded from the real world without. "Is it true?" was Nietzsche's one question to everything life or man opposed to him. A terrible sincerity held him in its grasp, an intolerance of the least sham, the slightest cowardice. He would not be happy at the price of truth, or what he conceived to be truth. He died at the age of 56, after several years of insanity, nursed and coddled like a little child—gentle, docile, saying to the sister who devoted herself to him: "You and I, my sister—we are happy!"

The succeeding chapters, under such heads as "The Superman," "Truth," "Christianity," "Women and Marriage," etc. give us the structure made by Nietzsche to express his conception of the universe, and his idea as to how this universe should be and could be improved.

Whether one agrees with any or all of his conclusions is not here to the point. The important thing is that Mr. Mencken has given us in this book, easily held in the hand and written for the layman without mysteries and involutions, the opportunity of seeing just what Nietzsche thought and wrote, and the privilege of making up our individual minds as to the truth and value of this thought. He also quotes from many of the German's critics, and seeks to define his value as a teacher.

Fanfare [Review Essay on A Book of Prefaces]   Burton Rascoe*

When Henry L. Mencken unpacks his idiomatic brasses, tunes up his verbal strings, and gets in readiness his phrasal woodwinds to orchestrate a fugue in damnation or in praise of man, god, or novel, his all too meager audience cancels all other engagements, to be on hand at the initial presentation. The result, his audience knows, will be an experience of pure enjoyment. His musicianship is unfailing. His program is unsatisfactory only in its impermanence. Though the theme he proposes is invariably Mencken—Mencken apropos of this or that—he gives it infinite and intricate varia-

*From the *Chicago Tribune*, 11 November 1917, part 8, p. 7. Reprinted by courtesy of the *Chicago Tribune*.

tions. He is, indeed, a contrapuntist in letters of the stature of Bach in music.

It is, then, as an artist in words that Mr. Mencken is first to be considered. That he has inscribed on the lintel of his doorpost "Critic" is of small moment (though critic, he is, I should say, of a penetration and intelligence surpassing that of most of the august sciolists who hold forth in our journals of critical platitudes). He has the true mark of the word artist: an aptitude for connotation. The baldly obvious, the commonplace in expression are to him anathema. In the employment of hackneyed, lifeless similes, shopworn nouns and adjectives, he sees a dull intellect plodding pathetically along, redeemed only if it express with dubious clarity a new or vital idea. Knowing the style is the man and that any one who has something definite to express gives to it naturally a form that commands attention in itself, he respects the manner above the content, cultivates the nuance in his own compositions, and holds it in reverence in the work of others.

He is distinctly "aware." He dwells in no ivory tower, aloof and austere. The whole process of daily life in this republic, its utter seriousness over fallacies and foibles, its flatulent popular idols, its preference in literature, politics, amusements, and moral schemes, its lusty, unpretentious *vulgus,* its self-styled intelligentsia, all furnish him with ammunition for his critical mitrailleuse. He reads everything that has bearing upon the life about him from handbills to Supreme court decisions. His vivid combinations, his apt coinage of words are traceable to a close observation and appraisement of daily affairs. Add a nimble imagination and you have the recipe of his style, the most vigorous and individual in this country.

Of that style he owes much to his early studies of Nietzsche, perhaps the greatest poet Germany has produced. It has the slash, incisiveness, and gusto of the apothegmatic *Will to Power* of the philosopher, who found an eager and sympathetic interpreter for English readers in Mencken, and whose philosophic disciple Mencken in some respects remains. It is the style of a satirist and humorist of a high order, who is equal to compact and devastating expletives such as "the jitney geniuses of Washington square" and "the kept idealists of the *New Republic.*" It moves with an irregular tempo, replete with Wagnerian dissonances. It is imagistic, colorful, dynamic.

We come now to Mencken's critical ability, to the force he exercises in American letters. It is a paradox that the destructive critic is really the only constructive critic: it is the critic who ceaselessly wields the ass's jaw bone against the host of Philistines who makes way for the chosen people. It is the iconoclast who, by shattering old idols, replaces decadence with the sap of life. Mencken is that sort of critic, creative in his incessant war upon the hokum of our day.

American literature has been, and is, singularly deficient in established critics who have anything like a rational conception of their jobs. . . . Criticism, it would seem, is either an exercise in hieroglyphics, a sermon, or a requiem high mass at 4 o'clock in the afternoon—anything except a sane, intelligent effort to get at a writer's intention and judge him as to whether he achieved it, well or ill.

This effort Mencken makes in A *Book of Prefaces*, dealing with Conrad, Dreiser, and Huneker, with an added chapter on "Puritanism as a Literary Force." It is a book of creative criticism in a sense unusual in American letters. . . .

It is a work of appraisement and appreciation by a man who can write coherently and with effect, who knows several languages and their literatures and yet is not a don, who has taste and discrimination and yet is not a prig, who can pass judgment on a writer and yet not assume that the destiny of the race is thus determined by his words, and who can be a critic and yet be human. To get the full force of his writings, of course, one must at least know the A B C's of literature, but one must also know that this is the year 1917. A pedant will miss as many of his allusions as will a parlor maid or a chauffeur.

Mencken has his share of intellectual fourflush (less, though, indeed, than have the Messrs. Brownell, More, et al.). He has a habit of uttering glib dicta regarding men about whose work it is evident he knows nothing. He has, at times, an offensive intellectual arrogance and a vainglorious trick of parading names of unfamiliar writers through the pages of his discourse, a trick that sometimes leads him into amusing errors (for instance, in A *Book of Prefaces* he refers twice to Przybyszewski, author of *Homo Sapiens*, as Przhevalski). He exhibits a naive pride in the fact that he knows the original titles of foreign works (for instance, he mentions Ibsen's A *Doll's House* under the Dano-Norwegian title *Et Dukkehjem* . . .).

He has an intolerance as definite in its way as the intolerance of the Methodism and Puritanism he fights. He has a sentimental bias for the melancholy as against the joyous temperament, a trifle lugubrious is he, even when he celebrates the caressing virtues of Pilsner. At heart he is a Puritan, as was Nietzsche and is Shaw. But a Puritan *ex ovo* is every man Bob of us born under the Stars and Stripes: mortal man inherits the sins of his fathers; if he would displace the stars with his uplifted head he must first do battle with his impeding environment.

And he has his regular fling at bourgeoisie baiting, a pastime he pleasingly alternates with badgering the "intellectuals." It is great fun for him and for his readers. With an adjective and a noun he can strip a Chautauqua pundit of every stitch of his pretentious accouterments and leave him shivering in the altogether, a pathetic and ridiculous spectacle.

He is at his best as a critic, of course, in dealing with prose literature. He has little patience with or appreciation for poetry and with characteristic impromptu he is likely to consign to the limbo of his estimates along with a hack versifier a poet of high caliber, whose methods and aims he does not immediately apperceive. It is this intolerance, these snap and final

judgments, this childish delight in an occasional display of cultural bijoute-
rie, that lessen his stature as a critic. Some of us hope that before long he
will shed these impedimenta and gain a trifle more of poise and balance,
without losing thereby his gem-like quality of phrase.

This consummation he has in a large measure achieved in *A Book of
Prefaces*. His occasional sacrifice of clear perspective to the pungent line is
here absent. He has approached Conrad, Dreiser, and Huneker with an
unwonted chastity of critical materials and given an equitable estimate and
a keen analysis of the artistic aims of these men. He inspires one with a
desire to find pleasure in their writings, or, if one is already familiar with
them, to cherish a more intimate acquaintance with their creations. This is,
of course, the mission—if he have a mission—of the critic. . . .
        Mencken has rooted lustily for Dreiser ever since the latter first ap-
peared on the literary scene. He early discerned in Dreiser a new and vital
force in American letters, a sincere and unflinching artist, pledged to present faithfully various phases of life as he had seen it. And when Dreiser
was down and gasping under the onslaught of public and professional
critics, Mencken stepped in, wielding his mighty cutlass, decapitated some
half dozen of the more weighty anthropophagites, and drove the rest to
cover. The fight is not over, but Mencken is holding them at bay and
others have enlisted in his aid. He knows Dreiser's faults, of which there
are many, and he points them out in this book, but he also knows Dreiser's
merits entitle him to high consideration.
        James Gibbons Huneker is Mencken's proctor, now become Bier-
bruder. An apt pupil, Mencken has passed the goal of his master, but on
this account he has lost none of the gratitude to the man whose value as a
cosmopolite in the midst of American provincialism is as an Edelweiss on
an Alpine cliff. To Huneker, eminently a wit, a raconteur, a dilettante, an
amateur of aesthetic experiences, Mencken attributes a certain profundity,
a scholarly erudition; but it is out of an almost filial respect and gratitude
that he does so. Huneker, the gentleman dabbler, the discursive essayist,
as full of treasurable reminiscences as a traveling salesman is of smutty stories, is not profound and has no desire to be.
        The chapter on "Puritanism as a Literary Force" deserves a thousand
words of itself. Suffice to say it is a terrific, but probably useless, denunciation of our lay and official misunderstanding of the functions of the fine arts,
a typhonic blast at our critical desuetude, a knockout blow at the solar
plexus of our stark, tyrannical Organizations with an Obsession for Vice.
That the powerful lunge will peter out as a beautiful but ineffectual gesture
is more than likely. The catharists of the country have the obtuseness of
numbers on their side and among our scant national virtues reflection is
not.
        Meanwhile an audience that is with him from the first note awaits
the next concert of the great fuguist, attentive and diverted when he

essays a rollicking scherzo like "The Artist" and "Death—A Philosophic Discussion."[1]

Notes

1. In *A Book of Burlesques* by Henry L. Mencken [John Lane Co., 1916].

H. L. Mencken [Review Essay on *A Book of Prefaces*]
Randolph Bourne*

Mr. Mencken gives the impression of an able mind so harried and irritated by the philistinism of American life that it has not been able to attain its full power. These more carefully worked-over critical essays are on the whole, less interesting and provocative than the irresponsible comment he gives us in his magazine. How is it that so robust a hater of uplift and puritanism becomes so fanatical a crusader himself? One is forced to call Mr. Mencken a moralist, for with him appraisement has constantly to stop while he tilts against philistine critics and outrageous puritans. In order to show how good a writer is, he must first show how deplorably fatuous, malicious or ignorant are all those who dislike him. Such a proof is undoubtedly the first impulse of any mind that cares deeply about artistic values. But Mr. Mencken too often permits it to be his last, and wastes away into a desert of invective. Yet he has all the raw material of the good critic—moral freedom, a passion for ideas and for literary beauty, vigor and pungency of phrase, considerable reference and knowledge. Why have these intellectual qualities and possessions been worked up only so partially into the finished attitude of criticism? Has he not let himself be the victim of that paralyzing Demos against which he so justly rages? As you follow his strident paragraphs, you become a little sorry that there is not more of a contrast in tone between his illumination of the brave, the free and the beautiful, and the peevish complaints of the superannuated critics of the old school. When are we going to get anything critically curative done for our generation, if our critical rebels are to spend their lives cutting off hydra-heads of American stodginess?

Mr. Mencken's moralism infects the essay on Conrad perhaps the least. With considerable effort the critic shakes himself loose from the clutches of his puritan enemies and sets Conrad very justly in relation to his time. "What he sees and describes in his books," Mr. Mencken says, "is not merely this man's aspiration or that woman's destiny, but the overwhelming sweep and devastation of universal forces, the great central drama that is at the heart of all other dramas, the tragic struggles of the soul of man under the gross stupidity and obscene joking of the gods." He likes Dreiser for the same reason, because "he puts into his novels a touch

*From the *New Republic* 13 (24 November 1917): 102–3.

of the eternal Weltschmerz. They get below the drama that is of the moment and reveal the greater drama that is without end." Mr. Mencken discusses Dreiser with admirable balance, and his essay is important because it criticizes him more harshly and more searchingly than many of us dare to do when we are defending him against the outrageous puritan. The essay on Huneker is perhaps the most entertaining. If "to be a civilized man in America is measurably less difficult, despite the war, than it used to be, say, in 1890" (when Mr. Mencken, by the way, was ten years old), it is to Mr. Huneker's gallant excitement that part of the credit is due.

Dreiser and Huneker Mr. Mencken uses with the utmost lustiness, as Samson used the jaw-bone, to slay a thousand Philistines, and his zeal mounts to a closing essay on "Puritanism as a Literary Force," which employs all the Menckenian artillery. Here Mr. Mencken, as the moralist contra moralism, runs amuck. It is an exposure that should stir our blood, but it is so heavily documented and so stern in its conviction of the brooding curtain of bigotry that hangs over our land, that its effect must be to throw paralyzing terror into every American mind that henceforth dares to think of not being a prude. Mr. Mencken wants to liberate, but any one who took his huge concern seriously would never dare challenge in any form that engine of puritanism which derives its energy from the history and soul of the American people. Mr. Mencken is much in earnest. His invective rises above the tone of scornful exaggeration. But his despair seems a little forced. I cannot see that the younger writers—particularly the verse-writers—are conscious of living under any such cultural terrorism as he describes. Mr. Mencken admits that the puritan proscription is irrational and incalculable in its operation. Surely as long as there are magazines and publishers—as there are in increasing numbers—who will issue vigorous and candid work, comstockery in art must be seen as an annoying but not dominating force. Mr. Mencken queerly shows himself as editor, bowing meekly under the puritan proscription, acting as censor of "a long list of such things by American authors, well-devised, well-imagined, well-executed, respectable as human documents and as works of art—but never to be printed in mine or any other American magazine." But what is this but to act as busy ally to that very comstockery he denounces? If the Menckens are not going to run the risk, in the name of freedom, they are scarcely justified in trying to infect us with their own caution.

The perspective is false that sees this persecution as peculiar to America. Was not Lemonnier prosecuted in Paris? Did not Baudelaire, Flaubert, Zola suffer? Did not Zola's publisher in England die in prison? Has not D. H. Lawrence's latest novel been suppressed in England before it had even a chance to be prosecuted here? It is England not America that has an official censorship of plays. Comstockery is not so much a function of American culture as it is of the current moralism of our general middle-class civilization. The attack must be, as Nietzsche made it, on that moralism rather than on its symptoms. But Mr. Mencken is not particularly happy in his understanding of Nietzsche. He wrote the book from which a majority of the Americans who know about Nietzsche seem to have gotten their ideas. How crude a summary it is may be seen by comparing it with the recent study of Nietzsche by another American, W. M. Salter. One wishes Mr. Mencken had spent more time in understanding the depth and subtleties of Nietzsche, and less on shuddering at puritanism as a literary force, and on discovering how the public libraries and newspapers reviewers are treating Theodore Dreiser.

Mr. Mencken's mode of critical attack thus plays into the hands of the philistines, demoralizes the artist, and demoralizes his own critical power. Why cannot Demos be left alone for a while to its commercial magazines and its mawkish novels? All good writing is produced in serene unconsciousness of what Demos desires or demands. It cannot be created at all if the artist worries about what Demos will think of him or do to him. The artist writes for that imagined audience of perfect comprehenders. The critic must judge for that audience too.

Beautifying American Literature
[Review Essay on
A Book of Prefaces]   Stuart P. Sherman*

Mr. Mencken is not at all satisfied with life or literature in America, for he is a lover of the beautiful. We have nowadays no beautiful literature in this country, with the possible exception of Mr. Dreiser's novels: nor do we seem in a fair way to produce anything aesthetically gratifying. Probably the root of our difficulty is that, with the exception of Mr. Huneker, Otto Heller, Ludwig Lewisohn, Mr. Untermeyer, G. S. Viereck, the author of "Der Kampf um deutsche Kultur in Amerika," and a few other choice souls, we have no critics who, understanding what beauty is, serenely and purely love it. Devoid of aesthetic sense, our native "Anglo-Saxon" historians cannot even guess what ails our native literature. For a competent historical account of our national anaesthesia one should turn, Mr. Mencken assures us, to a translation, from some foreign tongue—we cannot guess which—by Dr. Leon Kellner. Thus one readily perceives that Mr. Mencken's introductions to Conrad, Dreiser, and Huneker and his discourse on "Puritanism as a Literary Force" are of the first importance to all listeners for the soft breath and finer spirit of letters.

Though a lover of the beautiful, Mr. Mencken is not a German. He was born in Baltimore, September 12, 1880. That fact should silence the silly people who have suggested that he and Dreiser are secret agents of the Wilhelmstrasse, "told off to inject subtle doses of *Kultur* into a naïf and

*From the *Nation* 105 (29 November 1917): 593–94. Reprinted by permission of the *Nation*.

pious people." Furthermore, Mr. Mencken is, with George Jean Nathan, editor of that staunchly American receptacle for *belles-lettres,* the *Smart Set.* He does indeed rather ostentatiously litter his pages with German words and phrases—*unglaublich, Stammvater, Sklavenmoral, Kultur, Biertische, Kaffeeklatsch, die ewige Wiederkunft, Wille zur Macht* . . . u. s. w. He is a member of the Germania Männerchor, and he manages to work the names of most of the German musicians into his first three discourses. His favorite philosopher happens to be Nietzsche, whose beauties he has expounded in two books—first the "philosophy," then the "gist" of it. He perhaps a little flauntingly dangles before us the seductive names of Wedekind, Schnitzler, Bierbaum, Schoenberg, and Korngold. He exhibits a certain Teutonic gusto in tracing the "Pilsner motive" through the work of Mr. Huneker. His publisher is indeed Mr. Knopf. But Mr. Knopf disarms anti-German prejudice by informing us that Mr. Mencken is of "mixed blood—Saxon, Bavarian, Hessian, Irish, and English"; or, as Mr. Mencken himself puts it, with his unfailing good taste, he is a "mongrel." One cannot, therefore, understand exactly why Mr. Knopf thinks it valuable to announce that Mr. Mencken "was in Berlin when relations between Germany and the United States were broken off"; nor why he adds, "Since then he has done no newspaper work save a few occasional articles." Surely there can have been no external interference with Mr. Mencken's purely aesthetic ministry to the American people.

As Mr. Mencken conceives the aesthetic ministry, there is nothing in the world more dispassionate, disinterested, freer from moral, religious, or political significance. The "typical American critic," to be sure, is a pestilent and dangerous fellow; he is a Puritan; he is obsessed by nonaesthetic ideas; he is ever bent on giving instruction in the sphere of conduct; he is always talking about politics and morals. But, Mr. Mencken assures us, "criticism, as the average American 'intellectual' understands it, is what a Frenchman, a German, or a Russian would call donkeyism." Now, though Mr. Mencken is not a German, he has an open mind. One may even say that he has a "roomy" mind. And by that token he is quite certainly not a typical American critic. We imagine that he may fairly be taken as a representative of the high European critical outlook over "beautiful letters"—as he loves to call such finely sensitive work as that of Mr. Dreiser. He does not wander over the wide field of conduct with a birch rod; he simply perceives and feels and interprets the soul of loveliness in art—to use his own expressive phrase, he beats a drum for beauty.

One who does not fix firmly in mind Mr. Mencken's theoretical *Standpunkt* is likely to be somewhat confused by his practice. The careless and cursory reader of these *belles pages* of his will probably not, it is true, be impressed with their aesthetic purity and serenity, not at first. One's first impression, indeed, is that Mr. Mencken has as many moral and political irons in the fire as the "typical American critic"—the poor native whose blood is not so richly tinctured with Saxon, Bavarian, and Hessian elements. He has a dozen non-aesthetic standards which he incessantly employs in the judgment of books and authors. He has a "philosophical theory," "politics," "social ideas," "ideas of education," and "moral convictions," with all which a piece of literature has to square, if it is to please him. These general ideas he treats by no means as trifles; he thrusts them into one's face with peculiar emphasis and insistence. So that presently one begins to suspect that his quarrel with American criticism is not so much in behalf of beauty as in behalf of a *Kultur* which has been too inhospitably received by such of his fellow-citizens as look to another *Stammvater* than his. Of course, the true explanation is that Mr. Mencken's culture-propaganda is what a drummer (for *das Schöne*) would call his "side-line." Beauty is the main burden of his pack.

Though Mr. Mencken's *Kultur* is not German, it reminds one faintly of the German variety as described by Professor Eucken in October, 1914: "Our German Kultur has, in its unique depth, something shrinking and severe; it does not obtrude itself, or readily yield itself up; it must be earnestly sought after and lovingly assimilated from within. This love was lacking in our neighbors; wherefore they easily came to look upon us with the eyes of hatred." Mr. Mencken's culture is like this in that one must love it ere it will seem worthy of one's love. For example, his fundamental philosophical idea is, that "human life is a seeking without finding, that its purpose is impenetrable, that joy and sorrow are alike meaningless." Then there are his political notions. The good Mr. Knopf—the good and helpful Mr. Knopf—tells us that in politics our lover of beautiful letters is "an extreme Federalist." We had divined that. Mr. Mencken himself shrinkingly betrays the fact that he considers the hopes and professions of democracy as silly and idle sentimentality. Then there are his social ideas: he is for a somewhat severe male aristocracy; he firmly points out "how vastly the rôle of women has been exaggerated, how little they amount to in the authentic struggle of man." Then there are his educational ideas. The useful Mr. Knopf informs us that Mr. Mencken "attended no university." We had divined that also. Does he not explicitly declare that "college professors, alas, never learn anything"? Does he not steadily harp on "the bombastic half-knowledge of a school teacher"? Does he not note as a sign of Mr. Huneker's critical decadence the fact that he has spoken civilly of a Princeton professor? Does he not scornfully remark, "*I* could be a professor if I would"? Then there are his moral convictions. He is anti-Christian. He is for the *Herrenmoral* and against the "Sklavmoral that besets all of us of English speech." He holds with Blake that "the lust of the goat is also to the glory of God." Finally there are his national and racial feelings and convictions. He holds that the Americans are an "upstart people," and that "formalism is the hall-mark of the national culture." He holds that the Anglo-Saxon civilization excels all others as a prolific mother of quacks and mountebanks. Mr. Mencken's continuous tirade against everything respectable in American morals, against everything characteristic of American soci-

ety, and against everything and everybody distinguished in American
scholarship and letters, is not precisely and strictly *aesthetic* criticism; indeed, an unsympathetic person might say that it is not criticism at all, but
mere scurrility and blackguardism. His continuous laudation of a Teutonic-
Oriental pessimism and nihilism in philosophy, of anti-democratic politics,
of the subjection and contempt of women, of the *Herrenmoral*, and of anything but Anglo-Saxon civilization, is not precisely and strictly *aesthetic*
criticism; an unsympathetic person might call it infatuated propagandism.
But, of course, all of these things are properly to be regarded as but the
obiter dicta of a quiet drummer for beauty.

Still, for the aesthetic critic, it is a pleasure to turn from Mr. Mencken's somewhat polemical general ideas to the man himself as revealed by
the subtle and finely woven garment of his style. Though not a German,
Mr. Mencken has a beautiful style; and though he could be a professor if
he would, he has a learned style. To his erudition let stand as witnesses
the numberless choice words calculated to send the vulgar reader to a dictionary: "multipara," "chandala," "lamaseries," "coryza," "lagniappe," "um-
bilicarii," "Treuga Dei," "swamis," "gemaras," "munyonic," "glycosuria."
This is clearly the vocabulary of an artist and a scholar. As an additional
sign of his erudition, consider his discovery that Mr. Dreiser "stems" from
the Greeks; also his three-line quotation from a Greek dramatist—in the
original Greek. To prove the beauty of his phrasing and his general literary
feeling, one has but to open the book and dip in anywhere. Here, in Dry-
den's words, is "God's plenty." How gently he touches the decline of religious faith in New England; "the old God of Plymouth Rock, as practically
conceived, is now scarcely worse than the average jail warden or Italian
padrone." How nobly he lays to rest the moral faith of our fathers: "the
huggermugger morality of timorous, whining unintelligent and unimagina-
tive men—envy turned into law, cowardice sanctified, stupidity made noble, Puritanism." How adequately he interprets the spirit of our emancipa-
tors: "The thing that worried the more ecstatic Abolitionists was their
sneaking sense of responsibility, the fear that they themselves were flouting
the fire by letting slavery go." What a felicitous image of Emerson!—"a dil-
igent drinker from German spigots"; alas, poor Emerson, he left the German taproom too soon, and so remained a "dilettante" all his life. And here
are jewels three words long that on the forefinger of Belles Lettres will
sparkle forever: "professional sinhound," "blackmailing Puritan," "campaigns of snouting and suppression," "the pall of Harvard quasi-culture,"
"college pedagogues," "the gifted pedagogue," "Philadelphia, that depress-
ing intellectual slum," "pedants lecturing to the pure in heart," "a leap to
the Victorians, the crêpe-clad pundits, the bombastic word-mongers of the
Nation school," "the kept idealists of the *New Republic*," "the pious gur-
glings of Longfellow," the "giggle" and "kittenishness" of Mr. Howells,
"Rufus Wilmot Griswold, that almost fabulous ass," "the era of cuspidors,"
the "sonorous platitudes" [of Mr. Brownell], the "calm superior numskul-

lery that was Victorian," "eminent excoriators of the Rum Demon," "the intolerable prudishness and dirtymindedness of Puritanism"—"one ingests a horse-doctor's dose of words, but fails to acquire any illumination."

The sheer verbal loveliness of writing like this can never pass away. It is the writing of a sensitive intellectual aristocrat. It has the quality and tone of high breeding. It is the flower and fragrance of a noble and elevated mind that dwells habitually with beauty. Does not one breathe a sigh of relief as one escapes from the ruck and muck of American "culture" into the clear and spacious atmosphere of genuine aesthetic criticism? If, by exchanging our American set of standards for his "European" set, we could learn to write as Mr. Mencken does, why do we hesitate? Well, as a matter of fact, there is already a brave little band of sophomores in criticism who do not hesitate. These humming Ephemera are mostly preserved in the pure amber of Mr. Mencken's prose. At everything accepted as finely and soundly American, swift fly the pebbles, out gushes the corrosive vapor of a *discriminating* abuse. The prospect for beautiful letters in America is visibly brightening.

American Genius and Its Locale
James Weldon Johnson*

We have often referred to the writings of H. L. Mencken. His English is a mental cocktail, an intellectual electric shock. Anybody who habitually dozes over conventional English ought to take Mencken at least once or twice a week in order to keep the moss and cobwebs out of their brains. Mr. Mencken writes excellently on a wider range of subjects than any other one writer in the United States, and whatever his topic may be, he is always interesting. But he is at his best when he is talking about the theatre or literature or music or philosophy or feminism or criticism. On these subjects, he is an authority.

The chief charm of Mencken is that he always has a fresh point of view on even the oldest subject. If the subject is one that does not admit of a fresh point of view, Mencken does not touch it, he considers it as already finished, exhausted; as a subject to be left in the embalmed state of the tomb of literature. It is into this very pit that Mencken always avoids that so many writers fall; they do not even know when a subject is exhausted.

Mencken's style is all his own; nobody in the country writes like him. Sometimes we know that he is laughing at his readers, and sometimes we suspect he is laughing at himself. We might call him a humorous cynic, and when he is most cynical, he is most enjoyable. He is the cleverest writer in America today.

*From "Views and Reviews," *New York Age*, 20 July 1918, editorial page.

But those who look for cleverness in Mencken are missing the best part of him; the best part of Mencken is truth. He gets at truth because he is devoid of the sentimental and mawkish morality that seems to be the curse of everyone who writes in the English language. In other words, he is free and is therefore not afraid to write the truth. Many a writer is sincere enough, but bound by so many conventions that he cannot write the truth. Mencken pays no regard to traditions and conventions as such; he has absolutely no respect for them merely on account of their age.

The other day we picked up an article headed, "Mr. Cabell of Virginia." The article was by H. L. Mencken. Of course we were at once interested in Mr. Cabell because Mr. Mencken was talking about him. The article was a critical estimate of Mr. Cabell's work as a novelist. We know very little about that work, never having read any of Mr. Cabell's books; but Mr. Mencken puts high value on him, and we have made up our mind to read at least one of those books at first opportunity. The critic gives as one of the reasons why Cabell should be read the following: "he is the only indubitably literate man left in the late Confederate States of America." Then he goes on to say:

> Let the last consideration engage us first. What I mean to say is that Cabell is the only first-rate craftsman that the whole south can show. In all that vast region, with its 30,000,000 or 40,000,000 people and its territory as large as half a dozen Frances or Germanys, he is the only author worth a damn—almost the only one who can write at all. The spectacle is so strange that I can't keep my eyes from it. Imagine an empire as huge as the Holy Roman, and with no more literature than Pottstown, Pa., or Summit, N. J.—not a poet, not a serious historian, not a critic good or bad, not a dramatist dead or alive, and but one novelist!

Then Mr. Mencken takes up the question of the lack or rather the absence of literary men and women in the south, and says:

> The causes of this paucity I have hitherto discussed and guessed at. Perhaps the soundest theory is that which holds that the civil war destroyed the whole civilization of the region and well-nigh exterminated the civilized southerner. The few who survived came north, leaving the soil to the Ethiop and the poor white trash. The latter now struggle for possession in the manner of dogs and cats, with the odds increasingly in favor of the black. Of the two, he alone shows any cultural advance; he begins to produce artists, and even sages. But the poor white trash, now politically dominant in all the southern states, produce only traders, schemers, politicians and reformers—in brief, bounders.

There is an interesting question raised here. Why is it that the south produces no first-rate literature? As Mr. Mencken says, this whole wide region with "not a poet, not a serious historian, not a critic good or bad, not a dramatist dead or alive." We think we can shed a little light on this question. Mr. Mencken thinks the condition may be due to the fact that "the civil war destroyed the whole civilization of the region and well nigh exterminated the civilized southerner." But why should not the poor white trash produce something? Is it possible that they can be so innately inferior to the southern aristocracy? Were they any more handicapped than the "Ethiop," who, Mr. Mencken says, "alone shows any cultural advance."

We do not think that the destruction of the old southern civilization or any innate inferiority of the poor white trash is the reason; the real reason is that the white south of today is using up every bit of its mental energy in this terrible race struggle. All of the mental efforts of the white south run through one narrow channel; the life of every southern white man as a man and a citizen, most of his financial activities and all his political activities, are impassably limited by the ever present "Negro problem." All of the mental power of the whole south is being used up in holding the Negro back, and that is the reason why it does not produce either great literature or great statesmen or great wealth. That is, the white south is less intensely interested in forging ahead than it is in keeping the Negro from forging ahead. Witness: in Alabama there is opposition to a compulsory education law because under it Negro children would be compelled to go to school.

On the other hand, the Negro is not using up any of his strength in trying to hold anybody back, he is using every ounce of it to move forward himself. His face is front and toward the light; when the white man tries to force him back he, the white man, turns from the light and faces backward. Unless the white people of the south rightabout on this question, the Negro will in the long run outdistance them in the higher and finer achievements.

3: Heyday in the Twenties, 1919–1929

The Living Speech [Review of *The American Language*]

F[rancis] H[ackett]*

Never has the flourishing personality of H. L. Mencken been so happily exercised as in this big book on the living speech of America. In Mr. Mencken there is something of the pedant and something of the anarchist. This book is compounded of both. It is the benign pedant, voracious and systematic and indefatigible, that has accumulated and organized the large mass of material that has gone into the volume; and it is the anarchist that has breathed fire into it. This anarchist, however, is not of the sallow kind. He is jocund and expansive, a Samson in girth and a Samson to send torches among the Philistines. He delights in raciness and has no fear of the grossest barbarism, yet he is cheerfully contemptuous of what he calls the "yokelry" and the "stupid populace" and the "gaping proletariat." He believes in a law at least to the extent of ascertaining it. He uses the tools of pedantry to give himself mastery. But he steers between the populace, on one hand, and "Prof. Balderdash," on the other. The result is a work which it is a platitude to call refreshing but which is actually refreshing in the deep sense as well as the obvious.

H. L. Mencken is a pioneer. He turns on the language we habitually use the mind and the imagination of a fresh inquirer, an inquirer whose sophistication cannot be seriously questioned yet an inquirer who is not indentured to sophistication. And out of that fresh inquiry we are enabled to form a new view of our own spoken and written language. Mr. Mencken untiringly helps us to comprehend much that is obscure and irregular in the shifting courses of American expression. The living speech is a Mississippi which cannot easily be charted, but Mr. Mencken is a pilot who knows the new channels as well as the old, who steers us with the true current of the living stream. Many of us have no serene conviction in the matter of new idiom and new spelling and new locution. We grope rather blindly among the tendencies we are favoring and the tendencies we are resisting. We respond and we draw away, but we do not rationalize. Mr. Mencken comes titanically to our aid. Necessarily disregarding the prudes and the scholastic rhetoricians, he has opened his mind to receive every

*From the *New Republic* 19 (31 May 1919): 155–56.

conceivable kind of data respecting the language now in use among the people of America, and with these usages to argue from he has created at least the beginning of an American rationale.

This does not mean that *The American Language* is sentimental radicalism. It is true that Mr. Mencken is hyperbolic at the beginning. He talks of the English dialect and the American dialect and he quotes someone who dwells on "the growing difficulties of intercommunication." Also he enjoys showing the enormous difference between unsophisticated American and sophisticated English, and he rather gleefully foreshadows the day when "me see she" will be common and therefore sound American usage. Without a parallel investigation of unsophisticated usages in English, I do not see how one can rest with such a conclusion. It is amusing to hurl the stink-pot of popular Americanisms among the grammarians, but Whitechapel and the Mile End Road and the Coombe and the rookeries of Glasgow could furnish similar weapons. The erosions of inflected speech are nominally more significant in America because language has a "general uniformity throughout the country," but it is one thing to produce the evidence of a common illiteracy, another thing to prove that the illiteracy is destined to supplant the corresponding literacy. "It is useless to dismiss the growing peculiarities of the American vocabulary and of grammar and syntax in the common speech as vulgarisms beneath serious notice." Yes, if the "peculiarities" are definitely growing: but the actual repetition of a misuse from mouth to mouth is only one factor in deciding its eventual triumph. Does the misuse "work"? That is the qualitative test which must be met by such lazy and illogical locutions as "me see she."

But the great distinction of Mr. Mencken's book is his "the bee stang him" pragmatic method. "There are few forms in use," he quotes Lounsbury, "which, judged by a standard previously existing, would not be regarded as gross barbarisms." This extreme statement Mr. Mencken stupendously vindicates. In all the luxurious minutiae of his inquiry there is an impartial and scholarly use of evidence, yet his work cannot help serving as an antidote to snobs and snobbishness. "The attempt to make American uniform with English has failed ingloriously; the neglect of its investigation is an evidence of snobbishness that is a folly of the same sort." These and simpler snobbishnesses are constantly corrected in his pages. Everyone knows the superior smile with which people who have the right shibboleth glance at one another when an outsider commits himself in their hearing— yet how often the right shibboleth is the index to the silliest kind of group complacency. Mr. Mencken exhibits many barbarisms such as "to ambition," "to compromit," "to happify." Right alongside them he prints words elevated to the peerage that were once similarly humble commoners. To advocate, to progress, to oppose, to derange, to appreciate (in value), lengthy, dutiable, reliable, bogus, influential, presidential—these were plebeians to start with, equally "bad form" and equally disdained. The same formalism is to be found in spelling, of course, and very often today an inherited American barbarism is cherished by the very person who shudders at a more recent one. In grammar, as Mr. Mencken says, there is also "a formalism that is artificial, illogical and almost unintelligible—a formalism borrowed from English grammarians, and by them brought into English, against all fact and reason, from the Latin." His list of popular conjugations, partly derived from Professor Ring Lardner, is a perfect museum of barbarism. It is also an extraordinary exhibition of professional zeal.

The great value of *The American Language* is indeed, its sagacious thoroughness. It covers every sort of American idiosyncrasy in idiom, in spelling, in pronunciation, in grammar, in slang. To do so with piquancy was natural to Mr. Mencken, but the delight of the volume is its workmanship. And Mr. Mencken is not less marvelous in his ingenious generalizing than in his inexhaustible information.

He is not omniscient. He himself uses the archaic form 'round instead of round. He is surely not right in saying that the English vegetable marrow is the same thing as squash. He leaves out the American "ride" as an equivalent to the English "drive" (motor-ride). He says the English call a napkin a serviette and a coal-scuttle a coal-hod. Few English do. He says "diggings" is American for "habitation" whereas it is frequent English for "lodgings." Words like frisk and punk and sump and go-cart might be included to illustrate certain Americanizations. There are various Vanity Fair and Condé Nasty contributions to American—"undies" for underwear—that deserve to be noted.

But if a few unconsidered trifles have escaped Mr. Mencken, think of what he has captured and mounted. " 'I like a belt more looser 'n what this one is.' 'Well, then, why don't you unloosen it more 'n you got it unloosened?' " To have an ear for this kind of speech, to preserve and diagnose it, is to do more than study the fauna and flora of language. It is to set the foundations for a more salient national literature. For what Mr. Mencken says at the end of his fascinating and inspiring book is surely true; the American dialect is now apprehended "as something uncouth and comic. But that is the way that new dialects always come in—through a drumfire of cackles. Given the poet, there may suddenly come a day when our theirns and would'a hads will take on the barbaric stateliness of the peasant locutions of old Maurya in *Riders to the Sea*. They seem grotesque and absurd today because the folks who use them seem grotesque and absurd. But that is a too facile logic and under it is a false assumption. In all human beings, if only understanding be brought to the business, dignity will be found, and that dignity cannot fail to reveal itself, soon or late, in the words and phrases with which they make known their high hopes and aspirations and cry out against the intolerable meaninglessness of life." Beautifully said, and this is the flame which Mr. Mencken guards savagely from demons.

American Literature or Colonial?   Ernest A. Boyd*

As the United States increasingly produce writers whose work is a vigorous assertion of their national identity, the clashes become more frequent between these original personalities and the professorial guardians of colonial precedents and traditions. An Irish critic can at once foresee the time when Americanism versus anglicisation will be the subject of literary, as it has been of political, debate. American literature has begun, as Anglo-Irish literature did, by half-deliberate, half-unconscious imitation of English models. There are many signs that it is now entering into the final phase which precedes emancipation. As each heretical talent is revealed, louder are the agonised protests of the mandarins, whose duty it is to guard intact the glorious heritage of colonialism. As to so many other reactionaries, the war was a godsend to these intellectual satraps, who were enabled to lynch their opponents in the name of patriotism. The dispute was skilfully sidetracked into an appeal to the unreason of mere jingoism.

This process was, of course, greatly assisted by the general mobilization of the *intelligentsia* in the belligerent countries, and the conscription of brains has had everywhere an effect as devastating as the conscription of bodies. It has produced a vast horde of kept newspapermen and subsidized intellectuals, who have exchanged whatever independence of mind the Almighty endowed them with for various more profitable assets in these strangely democratized times. Therefore, whenever colonial inquisitors were faced with a troublesome phenomenon, they had merely to shout for the guards, and straightway the offender was flung into the dungeons reserved for the Germano-Hibernian-Bolshevik bogeymen. Whereupon the doctors and saints of literature returned to their meditations upon the moral giants of Anglo-Saxondom, or resumed their treatises on the philosophy of Mr. Ralph Waldo Trine, "in tune with the Infinite." Moreover, as the virtuous were rewarded by journalistic and kindred missions to Europe, they carried to Old England the glad tidings of the colonial evangel, recommending to inquirers only the safest and sanest imitators. In return, the Mother Country exchanged the visits in the persons of those best qualified to maintain this tradition of solidarity. In this fashion the dreadful spectacle of American literary independence was not allowed to offend the susceptibilities of the best society on both sides of the Atlantic. . . .When will American criticism have the courage to base the claims of contemporary American literature on those works which are essentially and unmistakably American?

Those, as a rule, are by far the best and most original books written in the United States. For the most part, they are unknown in England. Eleven years ago, James Branch Cabell's *Chords of Vanity* strayed into the catalogue of a London purveyor of best sellers, but his name is unfamiliar

*From the *Freeman* 1 (17 March 1920): 13–15. Copyright 1920–24 by The Freeman, Inc. Copyright 1924 by B. W. Huebsch. Courtesy of Viking Penguin Inc.

even to the subconscious consumers of the fiction of the circulating libraries. No English edition of Sherwood Anderson's *Winesburg, Ohio* exists. The poetess whose line, "Laugh and the world laughs with you" has elicited an unnecessary testimonial from the author of *The Advance of English Poetry*—the adjective is significant—is a household name to thousands who will never hear of Lizette Woodworth Reese or Carl Sandburg. Verse, however, stands more chance of securing its relatively limited hearing, owing to the interchange of non-academic news between London and New York and Chicago. But the superb essays of H. L. Mencken, the dramatic criticism of George Jean Nathan, enthusiastically praised by the few Europeans who have read them—when will they displace the chaste prose of Messrs. Lyon Phelps, Elmer More or Brownell? No doubt when Dreiser is as well boomed by the literary liaison-officers of Anglo-Saxondom as are Ellen Glasgow, Gene Stratton Porter and Robert W. Chambers!

Whenever an American writer of the first rank does reach the discriminating foreigner there is usually no hesitation to recognize real worth. Dreiser's *Sister Carrie* was estimated as it deserved by the London press in the first year of its existence. The *Athenaeum* has only recently endorsed the praise of Mencken by the *Mercure de France*. At the same time, even if the result is the publication of the latter's work in an English edition, he may not be more often mentioned than Dreiser, whose books are available, but are discreetly passed over by artisans of the Anglo-American literary alliance. Owing to technical publishing reasons, in some measure, a considerable number of important American books languish more or less obscurely in the lists of London publishers. Some years ago, Grant Richards did a great deal of pioneering work in this connection, introducing American writers outside the ordinary category of importations, such as Frank Norris, Mary MacLane and others. But the mere existence of English editions, needless to say, does not ensure any general realization of the significance of an American author. And it is just here that the conspiracy of silence, or abuse, employed by the colonials, achieves its real purpose.

Precisely to the degree that an American book is independent of the Anglo-Saxon conventions and prejudices is it likely to lack the support which will make it at once famous and successful. Suppose an Englishman who was interested by *Sister Carrie* in 1900 had tried to keep track of the author's name. For many years it was impossible, and when Dreiser resumed novel-writing, the only thing one heard was that he was wicked and intolerable, until finally the war provided the innuendo of association with the devilries of the Wilhelmstrasse. Then the moral arbiters of the world had their chance of consigning all the ungodly, de-colonialized literature into the limbo of Nietzsche, Wagner and similar emissaries of Satan. Instead, the effusions of Miss Mildred Aldrich, the homilies of Dr. Woodrow Wilson, and the inventor of "Dere Mabel" were gathered to the greater glory of the Anglo-Saxon God. Patriot-authors went out to the North American colonies, to collect the dollars not yet lent to the Mother Country, and all the professors of English literature felt that their efforts had not been in vain. With what tearful pride they saw their intellectual children accepted as worthy to nestle on the bosom of dear old grandma Britannia. Even Dr. Stuart Sherman could afford to poke a little heavy fun at those unregenerate American writers who are not of the elect, whose Americanism is not sufficiently British to satisfy the colonial mind.

Once the issue is frankly raised between American and colonial literature, it will be impossible to obscure the conflict by moral vapourings and impassioned appeals against the subtle evil of hyphenation. Allusions to the Germania Maennerchor and Sinn Fein will not disguise the fact that it is precisely this reprehensible, un-Presbyterian literature which is most national. That is to say, only an American could have written *Prejudices* and *A Book of Prefaces*. Wherever the English language is spoken Dreiser and Sherwood Anderson will be at once recognized as non-British, as unmistakably as Synge or Yeats. Mencken, indeed, is so quintessentially the critical mind of America, as distinct from the colony, bold alert, independent, vigorous and idiomatic, that there is a danger of his being incomprehensible in parts to foreigners unacquainted with America. Such an obstacle to the widespread popularity of American literature in England would be a natural and welcome barrier, preferable to the present intellectual blockade by the colonials. After all, no writer complains if his works are only fully appreciated and understood by his compatriots. Anatole France does not compose with one eye on the Calvinists of Geneva, or the foreign professors of French literature. Literature is primarily for home consumption. When America realizes the individuality and superiority of her own national literature, other countries will be glad to try to understand the secrets of her genius. Attention will no longer be diverted to the model pupils of the colonial professors.

American Literature and
the Tart Set   Percy H. Boynton*

It appears that the welfare of the nation is threatened by a new menace; and the danger is clearly ominous, for the enemy is under attack from both flanks. According to the reactionaries the college professor is undermining the foundations of society. He is talking about truth and the open mind. He is trying to base his opinions on the facts. And he has the effrontery to say what he thinks about politics and international affairs, and even about the market. Wherefore some of the timorous abuse him, and the rest try to save the State by feeding him into contentment.

At the same time he is assailed from the left wing for the reason that

*From the *Freeman* 1 (7 April 1920): 88–89. Copyright 1920–24 by The Freeman, Inc. Copyright 1924 by B. W. Huebsch. Courtesy of Viking Penguin Inc.

he is already content. He is, says Mr. Boyd, in the first issue of the *Free-man*, a "professorial guardian of colonial precedents," an "intellectual satrap," a "colonial inquisitor," a "doctor and saint of literature," a pedagogue, a professor. This is mildly stimulating to the professor, who is not used to being taken seriously either for better or for worse. A gentle mauling relieves the monotony of his cloistered repose. What the reactionaries say fails to rouse in him anything but a hope that they are telling the truth—that if he is not red he is at least visibly tinged with pink. And what the newly wise say—the tart set—gratifies him by its proof that they are aware of him at all.

The tart set are just now making him the new burden of an old song; the song, begun in Revolutionary days, that American literature ought to be national, and that American writers and critics ought to be independent of old-world standards. It has echoed down the generations from Freneau to Whitman, and from Whitman via Hamlin Garland to the opening number of the *Freeman*. One of the features that proves the genuine vitality of this wholesome truth is that it has always been chanted as though it had just been revealed. One of the features that makes it pleasantly fresh today is that it is being stridently pealed forth by a chorus of young Americans whose composite derivation is obvious and recent, and whose acquaintance with the country as a whole has seldom taken them west of Tenth Avenue. And incidentally they are varying the harmony by building it over a kind of anti-academic counterpoint.

The tart set are amiable incarnations of the paradox they piously pursue. "It is precisely because," they say; and then they utter Chestertonic platitudes that are of all things unprecise, because they are sweeping expressions of temperament whose sole charm is their reckless unprecision. They preach the gospel of joy, frowning as desperately the while as the fiercest of boy bandits or the grimmest of the puritans against whom they inveigh. They must be supposed to laugh sometimes—it is inconceivable that they shouldn't; but the thought of laughter always reduces them to indignation at those who do not laugh. They can't enjoy the circus for the thought of those who have stayed at home. Their tone is that of a young man who doesn't really care for whiskey, but who drinks in bold defiance of his maiden aunt's prejudices. Indeed they devote themselves so intently to berating the living and blasting the dead that it is hard to find out what they really endorse; but on a second or third reading the fact appears. They endorse Each Other; and they revere their high priest, Mr. Mencken.

Far be it from any pedagogue to paint the lily by discoursing in general on the virtues of Mr. Mencken. He is without doubt "bold, alert, independent, vigorous, and idiomatic;" he is also without doubt what follows in the train of these characteristics: versatile, prolific, and uneven. It is better to accept him as "quintessentially the critical mind of America," and to contemplate him in the light of his *Book of Prefaces*, and his characteristic last word therein on Puritanism.

Nothing clarifies life so much as the experience of seeing only one thing at a time. It is at the base of most passion and most achievement. It accounts for love and murder and war-heroism and high finance and the grim zest of the reformer. It also accounts for the word "precisely," and for freedom of generalization that would be splendid if it weren't funny. The tart set hate the Puritan, and whenever they uncork the vials of their wrath (where they keep him always in pickle) he spreads out, genii-like, till he clouds the heavens. The rest is easy, and the result is shrill and prolonged outcries of which Mr. Mencken gives an example in a commentary on the Puritanism of the South. It is two and a half pages long; it begins with, "It is, indeed, precisely," and it ends with, "The only domestic art this huge and opulent empire knows is in the hands of Mexican greasers; the only native music it owes to the despised negro; its only genuine poet was permitted to die up an alley like a stray dog." In the intervening paragraph the sole defects of the South that are not charged against the heaven-darkening spectre, are the evils of the one-crop system and the high temperature of Yuma, Arizona.

If people do not talk too hard it is measurably true that "what they don't know won't hurt them"; but when they do talk too hard they serve themselves an ill turn by an avoidable betrayal of their ignorance. Thus, when Mr. Mencken states that "Our great humourists, including even Mark Twain, have had to take protective colouration, whether willingly or unwillingly, from the prevailing ethical foliage, and so one finds them leveling their darts, not at the stupidities of the Puritan majority, but at the evidence of lessening stupidity in the anti-Puritan minority," he makes the interesting revelation that he does not understand *Innocents Abroad* or "The Man that Corrupted Hadleyburg" or *Joan of Arc*, and that he has not read Mark Twain's War Prayer, or his protest at the indignity done to the remains of George Holland, or the controversy with Dr. Ament on the Boxer indemnities.

When Mr. Mencken comes to Whitman he dismisses him as "clearly before his time." The inference is that Mr. Mencken does not wish to admit his admiration for Walt because he is resolved to be unhappy at all American literature. And the implication is that possibly he does not care to acknowledge, or perhaps he does not know, that Whitman was the greatest Puritan of them all. Says Mr. Mencken, bitterly, "It needed no official announcement to define the function and the office of the republic as that of an international expert in morals, and the mentor and exemplar of the more backward nations." To which Whitman might have replied, had the years spared him: "It is *precisely* on this account that I once wrote,

> Have the elder races halted,
> Do they droop and end their lesson, wearied, over there beyond the seas?
> We take up the task eternal, and the burden, and the lesson,
>   Pioneers, oh pioneers.

But Mr. Mencken's finest gesture is anent Emerson and the *Dial*. He has recently disposed of Emerson as "vague and empty" when (in Tassin's volume on *The Magazine in America*) he comes on the old quarterly and applauds a passage on freedom of thought from its salutatory in 1840. Yet times have changed, he says, and "As for the *Dial* it was till lately, the very pope of orthodoxy, and jealously guarded the college professors who read it from the pollution of ideas." There is a nice humor (or humour, as Mr. Mencken would spell it) in this. For Mr. Mencken does not seem to know that Emerson wrote the salutatory which pleases him; that Emerson was promoter and one time editor of that Boston *Dial* discontinued in 1844; or that Cincinnati boasted another short-lived *Dial* before the war; or that the modern conservator of professorial innocence was not established until 1880. The reason for this ignorance, moreover, is not to be laid at the door of Tassin. It arises from the fact that to the tart set anything so remote as 1880 belongs to the dim and misty past. . . .

After all, Mr. Mencken and his associates appear to a mere "professorial guardian of colonial precedents" to be a kind of recrudescence of the New York Bohemians of seventy years ago. They were very aggressive, very unconventional, and very clever. They were so amiable that even that valiant conservative, William Winter, loved them in spite of his convictions. They achieved little in permanent literature, but a good deal in contemporary journalism. And they helped to retrieve the balance of the times. Their "prince," Henry M. Clapp, was certainly a man of less substantial performance than Mr. Mencken, but he was not inferior in his hatred of the Puritans. "Whenever I think of Boston," said Henry Clapp, "it makes me as ugly as sin!"

[Review of *Prejudices: Second Series*]

H[unter] T. S[tagg]*

It is slowly dawning upon the reading public that earth and the spacious firmament on high contain literally nothing of interest upon which H. L. Mencken has not a more or less well formed opinion: also, what is more, that before he is finished he will have expressed that opinion. This is a happy prospect menaced by only one cloud—the danger that Mr. Mencken may develop into what he so heavily belabors Mark Twain for having been in his secular character, "premier clown," "public entertainer, not unrelated to Coxey, Dr. Mary Walker and Citizen George Francis Train." Already for many of us it has become more fun to be insulted by Mr. Mencken than cosseted by another.

*From the *Reviewer* 1 (15 February 1921): 25–27. Reprinted by permission of *Southwest Review*.

But let us not borrow trouble from the future. As yet the sane, sound critic predominates over the poseur; Mencken's unrivalled facility for spreading fury wherever he treads is still an incident of his art and not its electric sign-board, as his newest book will prove, and it is always worth while getting angry. Each reader may be sure that every line which does not enrage him personally reaches the soft places of some other reader, who will join him in denouncing the author as a Hun, not because of the persistence with which he employs German words (that's merely his sense of humor) but because that epithet is still the shortest we have carrying the most opprobrium. In his first series of *Prejudices* Mencken confined himself to excessively penetrating estimates of various writers and the wares of our popular magazines, but in the present volume he embraces a wider range of criticism. The field of literature cannot contain him. He expresses original views—welcome to a few, abhorrent to many—on the Roosevelt legend; also, in the same paper, a brief and less original summary—welcome to many, abhorrent to a few,—of the character and attainments of President Wilson. He locates in a fascinating and novel fashion the true seat of that aberration known as the Divine Afflatus. He scientifically examines that popular virtue Gratitude, takes a side glance at the Cult of Hope, Prohibition, all the Allied Arts, including the decoration of the face, and finally Love. Mencken on Love is without a shadow of a doubt the most remarkable thing ever known in letters. None can afford to miss it.

Nevertheless the best of the book, the real worth of it, is not to be found in these delightful papers but in the first and the third, "The National Letters" and "The Sahara of the Bozart" respectively. The rest of it is well worth reading, as Mencken is always well worth reading, whether for laughter, anger, both or neither, but it is there that the unwelcome suggestion of the possible fate of our best literary critic rises. In "The National Letters," however, he is on his own ground, where sincere feeling, deep concern and wide knowledge cannot be obscured by glittering perversity, capriciousness and pugnacity of manner. As the title of this essay indicates it is a survey of the condition in which American literature finds itself today and the causes which have produced that condition. It is the survey of a telescopic eye and an uncompromising judgment, written in a style that is a joy to read for its own sake in this day of shoddy, inflexible prose. It is severe—cruelly so—but none too severe to meet the occasion as most readers will admit. True, not being omnipotent, Mencken may now and then be guilty of slight injustice, but all the same on the subject of the national letters he offers his best and we have no one at present who can surpass it.

In the South it is the third paper, "The Sahara of the Bozart," which will prove the most arresting, for the South is the Sahara of the Bozart. "Consider," says Mencken, "the present estate and dignity of Virginia—in the great days indubitably the premier American state, the mother of Presidents and statesmen, the home of the first American university worthy of the name, the *arbiter elegantiarum* of the western world. Well, observe Virginia to-day. It is years since a first rate man, save only Cabell, has come out of it." Of the South at large he writes: "In all that gargantuan paradise of the fourth-rate there is not a single picture gallery worth going into, or a single orchestra capable of playing the nine symphonies of Beethoven, or a single opera house, or a single theater devoted to the production of decent plays. . . ." Yet "down to the middle of the last century, and even beyond, the main hatchery of ideas on this side of the water was across the Potomac bridges. The New England shopkeepers and theologians never really developed a civilization; all they ever developed was a government. . . . But in the South were men of delicate fancy, urbane instinct and aristocratic manner—in brief, superior men—in brief, gentry. . . . It was there that nearly all the political theories we still cherish and suffer under came to birth. It was there that the crude dogmatism of New England was refined and humanized. It was there, above all, that some attention was given to the art of living—that life got beyond and above the state of infliction and became an exhilarating experience. . . . . The Ur-Confederate had leisure. He liked to toy with ideas. . . .He had that vague thing we call culture."

Mencken has a great deal more than this to say of the South, some of which, as in the other essays, is unjust, some merely unsound, as the sincerest of generalizations from facts gathered by hearsay are apt to be. But the main outline of his argument, the outstanding deductions, are so true that it were petty to cavil at the weaknesses. Moreover the genuinely progressive Southerner will forgive him anything for the fresh view he directs upon the too generally disregarded question of interbreeding in its relation to the intellectual life of the new South. Nevertheless, if this book is read in these regions, as we trust it will be, it would be but discreet of Mr. Mencken to inhabit exclusively the North for the next two or three years. He would not be popular here. We, ourself, deserve nothing less than an autographed copy of his book for this unbiased judgment of it, for it riled us not a little, too.

H. L. Mencken   Edmund Wilson*

I

A man has withdrawn from the tumult of American life into the seclusion of a house in Baltimore. He is unmarried and has surrounded himself with three thousand books. From this point of vantage he watches the

*From the *New Republic* 27 (1 June 1921): 10–13.

twentieth century with detached and ironic dismay. A not ungenial materialist, he reflects that all human activities are, after all, mainly physical in origin: inspiration is a function of metabolism; death is an acidosis; love is a biological phenomenon; idealism is insanity. But the body is capable of much enjoyment; why worry about its obvious supremacy? As long as there is Chicken à la Maryland and plenty of liquor from the boot-leggers, as long as it is possible to read Conrad and hear Bach and Beethoven occasionally, why should a man of aristocratic temperament be particularly disturbed about anything? Let the capitalist exploit the wage-slave and the wage-slave blow up the capitalist; let political charlatans and scoundrels pick the pockets of the Republic; let the women run the men to ground and the men break their hearts for the women; let the people go off to the wars and destroy each other by the billion. They can never rob Mencken of his sleep nor spoil a single dinner for him. Outside, it is all a question of Christianity and democracy, but Mencken does not believe in either, so why should he take part in the brawl? What has he to do with the mob except to be diverted by its idiocy? He may occasionally attend a political convention to gratify a "taste for the obscene" or entertain his speculative mind by predicting the next catastrophe, but, on the whole, the prodigious din and activity and confusion of the nation roars along without touching him particularly; it is all to him "but as the sound of lyres and flutes." . . .

Something like this is the comic portrait which Mencken has painted of himself; he has even pretended that it is the character in which he prefers to be accepted. But there is, behind this comic mask, a critic, an evangelist and an artist; there is a mind of extraordinary vigor and a temperament of extraordinary interest, and neither of these has ever yet been examined as seriously as it should have been. Mencken has been left far too much to the rhapsodies of his disciples and the haughty sneers of his opponents. Indeed, he has assumed such importance as an influence in American thought that it is high time some one subjected him to a drastic full-length analysis. The present writer has only space for the briefest of suggestions.

II

The striking things about Mencken's mind are its ruthlessness and its rigidity. It has all the courage in the world in a country where courage is rare. He has even had the fearlessness to avoid the respectable and the wholesome, those two devils which so often betray in the end even the most intelligent of Americans. He fought outspokenly against optimism, Puritanism and democratic ineptitude, at a time when they had but few foes. It is well to remember, now that these qualities have become stock reproaches among the intelligentsia, that it was Mencken who began the crusade against them at a lonely and disregarded post and that we owe to him much of the disfavor into which they have recently fallen,—and also that it was Mencken who first championed the kind of American literary activity of which we have now become proudest. But the activity of his mind is curiously cramped by its extreme inflexibility. In the first place, as a critic, he is not what is called "sympathetic." His criticisms deal but little with people from their own point of view: he simply brings the other man's statements and reactions to the bar of his own dogma and, having judged them by that measure, proceeds to accept or reject them. Though one of the fairest of critics, he is one of the least pliant.

In the second place, in spite of his scepticism and his frequent exhortations to hold one's opinions lightly, he himself has been conspicuous for seizing upon simple dogmas and sticking to them with fierce tenacity. When he is arguing his case against democracy or Christianity, he reminds one rather of Bishop Manning or Dr. Straton than of Renan or Anatole France. The true sceptics like Renan or France see both the truth and weakness of every case; they put themselves in the place of people who believe differently from themselves and finally come to sympathize with them,—almost, to accept their point of view. But Mencken, once having got his teeth into an idea, can never be induced to drop it, and will only shake his head and growl when somebody tries to tempt him with something else.

Thus, in 1908, when he published his admirable book on Nietzsche, he had reached a certain set of conclusions upon society and ethics. Humanity, he had come to believe, is divided into two classes: the masters and the slaves. The masters are able and courageous men who do whatever they like and are not restrained by any scruples save those that promote their own interest; the slaves are a race of wretched underlings, stupid, superstitious and untrustworthy, who have no rights and no raison d'être except to be exploited by the masters. To talk of equality and fraternity is the most fatuous of nonsense: there is as much difference in kind between the masters and the slaves as there is between men and animals.

Therefore, Christianity is false because it asserts that all souls are worth saving and democracy is a mistake because it emancipates the slaves and tries to make them the masters. It is absurd to try to correct the evolutionary process which would allow the fittest to survive and the weaklings and fools to go under. "I am," Mr. Mencken has said, "against the under dog every time." But things are getting more and more democratic and consequently worse and worse. What we need is an enlightened aristocracy to take charge of society. But there has never been any such aristocracy and we are certainly not going to produce one. In the meantime, one can but curse the mob and die at one's post.

I have not space here to criticize these views—to ask, for instance, when he says he thinks the strong should be allowed to survive at the expense of the weak, whether he means the strong like Jack Johnson or the strong like Nietzsche and Beethoven. I must assume that the confusion of thought is apparent to the reader and go on to point out that Mencken has been upholding these theories without modification since 1908 at least. He has cherished them through the European war and through the industrial war that has followed it. (Quite recently they have led him into the absurdity of asserting that it would have been a good thing for America if the war had continued longer, because this would have stamped out "hundreds of thousands of the relatively unfit." The men who were left at the end of the war in the French and German armies, were, he adds "very superior men.") And, in consequence, it seems to me that he has cut himself off in an intellectual cul-de-sac.

He has much to say to America that is of the first usefulness and importance: he has no peer in the brilliance and effectiveness of his onslaught upon political ignorance and corruption, upon Y. M. C. A.'ism and popular morality, upon the cheapness and sordidness of current ideals. But, though the moral strength which gives him courage is drawn partly from his Nietzschean principles, these principles so close his horizon as to render his social criticism rather sterile. In the matters of politics and society he can do nothing but denounce. He has taken up a position in which it is impossible that any development should please him. He detests the present state of affairs, but he disbelieves in liberalism and radicalism, and any change in their directions would presumably only make him detest the world more. He really hates repression and injustice, but he has long ago repudiated the idea of human rights to freedom and justice and he consequently cannot come out as their champion.

There have, however, been a few signs of late that he feels his old house too small: in his recent discussion of Mr. Chafee's book on free speech, he reached a pitch of righteous indignation at which he has scarcely been seen before. "In those two years," he cried, "all the laborious work of a century and a half—toward the free and honest administration of fair laws, the dealing of plain justice between man and man, the protection of the weak and helpless, the safeguarding of free assemblage and free speech—was ruthlessly undone." This is obviously in direct contradiction to the faith he has previously professed. What has one who is "against the under dog every time" to do with "the protection of the weak and helpless"? He has told us again and again that we should let the weak and helpless perish.

The truth is that in the last few years Mencken has entered so far into the national intellectual life that it has become impossible for him to maintain his old opinions quite intact: he has begun to worry and hope with the American people in the throes of their democratic experiment. I know that this is a terrible statement; it is as if one should say that the Pope had begun to worry and hope with the western world in its attempt to shake off creed; but I honestly believe it is true. This phenomenon seemed to make its appearance toward the last page of *The American Language;* and if it does not come to bulk yet larger we shall have one of our strongest men still fighting with one arm tied behind his back.

III

So much for the critic; but what of the evangelist and artist? For Mencken, in spite of all his professions of realistic resignation, is actually a militant idealist. Most Americans—even of fine standards—have long ago resigned themselves to the cheapness and ugliness of America, but Mencken has never resigned himself. He has never ceased to regard his native country with wounded and outraged eyes. The shabby politics, the childish books, the factories turning out wooden nut-megs have never lost their power to offend him. At this late date, he is, I suppose, almost the only man in the country who still expects American novelists to be artists and American politicians gentlemen.

And his expression of his resentment is by no means temperate or aloof. It is righteous indignation of the most violent sort. His denunciations are as ferocious as those of Tertullian or Billy Sunday. It is in purpose rather than in method that he differs from these great divines. (See especially his excommunication of the professors in the essay on "The National Letters.") In his exhortations to disobey the rules of the current American morality he has shown himself as noisy and as bitter as any other Puritan preacher.

And this brings us to what is perhaps, after all, the most important thing about Mencken, the thing which gives him his enormous importance in American literature today: it is the fact that here we have a genuine artist and man of first-rate education and intelligence who is thoroughly familiar with, even thoroughly saturated with, the common life. The rule has been heretofore for men of superior intelligence, like Henry Adams and Henry James, to shrink so far from the common life that, in a country where there was practically nothing else, they had almost no material to work on, and for men who were part of the general society, like Mark Twain, to be handicapped by Philistinism and illiteracy; but in the case of Mencken we have Puritanism and American manners in a position to criticize itself. For in his attitude toward all the things with which Puritanism is supposed to deal Mencken is thoroughly American and thoroughly Puritan. If he were what he exhorts us to be in regard to the amenities and the pleasures he would never rage so much about them. His sermons would be unintelligible, I should think, to a Frenchman or an Italian. Nobody but a man steeped in Puritanism could have so much to say about love and yet never convey any idea of its beauties or delights; poor Aphrodite, usually identified in his pages with the whore and the bawdy-house, wears as unalluring a face as she does in the utterances of any Y. M. C. A. lecturer; no one else would confine himself to a harsh abuse, on principle, of the people who have outlawed love. Nobody else would express his enthusiasm for the innocent pleasures of alcohol in such a way that it sounded less like a eulogy than like an angry defiance. He is an unmistakable product of Puritan training and environment. Horace or Anatole France, who really represent the sort of civilizaton which Mencken admires, would never be so acutely conscious of the problems of love and art and wine; they would take them easily for granted and enjoy them as a matter of course. But Mencken, who was born an American, with the truculent argumentative mind of the Puritan, can never enjoy them as a matter of course, as even some Americans can do, but must call down all the dark thunders of logic to defend them, like any Milton or Luther.

And he is saturated with the thought and aspect of modern commercial America. He is, we feel, in spite of everything, in the long run most at home there; are we not told that once, when walking in Paris in the spring, he was annoyed by the absence of a first-class drug-store? Instead of taking refuge among remote literatures, like Mr. Cabell and Mr. Pound, he makes his poetry of the democratic life which absorbs and infuriates him. He takes the slang of the common man and makes fine prose of it. He has studied the habits and ideas and language of the common run of his countrymen with a close first-hand observation and an unflagging interest. And he has succeeded in doing with the common life what nobody else has done,—(at least with any authentic stamp of literary distinction): he has taken it in all its coarseness and angularity and compelled it to dance a ballet, in which the Odd Fellow, the stock-broker, the Y. M. C. A. Secretary, the Knight of Pythias, the academic critic, the Methodist evangelical, the lecturer at Chautauquas, the charlatan politician, the Vice Crusader, the Department of Justice, the star-spangled army officer,—and the man who reveres all these, with all his properties and settings: the derby hat, the cheap cigar, the shaving soap advertisement, the popular novel, the cuspidor, the stein of prohibition beer, the drug store, the patent medicine, the American Legion button,—join hands and perform, to the strains of a sombre but ribald music, which ranges from genial boisterousness to morose and cynical brooding.

Take the following passage, for example, from a sort of prose poem:

> Pale druggists in remote towns of the hog and cotton belt, endlessly wrapping up Peruna. . . . Women hidden away in the damp kitchens of unpainted houses along the railroad tracks, frying tough beefsteaks. . . . Lime and cement dealers being initiated into the Knights of Pythias, the Redmen or the Woodmen of the World. . . . Watchmen at lonely railroad crossings in Iowa, hoping that they'll be able to get off to hear the United Brethren evangelist preach. . . . Ticket-choppers in the Subway, breathing sweat in its gaseous form. . . . Family doctors in poor neighborhoods, faithfully relying upon the therapeutics taught in the Eclectic Medical College in 1884 . . . Farmers plowing sterile fields behind sad

meditative horses, both suffering from the bites of insects. . . . Greeks tending all-night coffee-joints in the suburban wildernesses where the trolley-cars stop. . . . Grocery clerks stealing prunes and gingersnaps and trying to make assignations with soapy servant-girls. . . Women confined for the ninth or tenth time, wondering hopelessly what it is all about. . . . Methodist preachers retired after forty years of service in the trenches of God, upon pensions of $600 a year. . . . Wives and daughters of Middle Western country bankers, marooned in Los Angeles, going tremblingly to swami seances in dark smelly rooms. . . . Chauffeurs in huge fur coats waiting outside theatres filled with folks applauding Robert Edeson and Jane Cowl. . . . Decayed and hopeless men writing editorials at midnight for leading papers in Mississippi, Arkansas and Alabama. . . .

One recalls the enumeration of another set of visions:

> The pure contralto sings in the organ loft,
> The carpenter dresses his plank, the tongue of his foreplane whistles its wild ascending lisp,
> The married and unmarried children ride home to their Thanksgiving dinner,
> The pilot seizes the king-pin, he heaves down with a strong arm,
> The mate stands braced in the whale-boat, lance and harpoon are ready,
> The duck-shooter walks by silent and cautious stretches,
> The deacons are ordained with cross'd hands at the altar,
> The spinning girl retreats and advances to the hum of the big wheel,
> The farmer stops by the bars as he walks on a First-day loaf and looks at the oats and rye. . . .
> The young fellow drives the express-wagon (I love him, though I do not know him),
> The half-breed straps on his light boots to compete in the race,
> The Wolverine sets traps on the creek that helps fill the Huron,
> The clean-hair'd Yankee girl works with her sewing machine or in the factory or mill,
> The Missourian crosses the plains toting his wares and his cattle. . . .

This was the day before yesterday, and Mencken is today. Is not Mencken's gloomy catalogue as much the poetry of modern America as Walt Whitman's was of the early Republic? When the States were fresh and new and their people were hardy pioneers, we had a great poet, from whose pages the youth and wonder of that world can reach us forever; and now that that air is soured with industry and those pioneers have become respectable citizens dwelling in hideously ugly towns and devoted to sordid ideals, we have had a great satirist to arouse us against the tragic spectacle we have become. For Mencken is the civilized consciousness of modern America, its learning, its intelligence and its taste, realizing the grossness of its manners and mind and crying out in horror and chagrin.

H. L. Mencken [Review Essay on
Notes on Democracy]   Walter Lippmann*

Here in two hundred pages is Mr. Mencken's philosophy. Here are
the premises of that gargantuan attack upon the habits of the American nation which has made Mr. Mencken the most powerful personal influence
on this whole generation of educated people. I say personal influence, for
one thing this book makes clear, and that is that the man is bigger than his
ideas.

If you subtract from this book the personality of H. L. Mencken, if you
attempt to restate his ideas in simple unexcited prose, there remains only
a collection of trite and somewhat confused ideas. To discuss it as one
might discuss the ideas of first rate thinkers like Russell, Dewey, White-
head, or Santayana would be to destroy the book and to miss its importance. Though it purports to be the outline of a social philosophy, it is really the highly rhetorical expression of a mood which has often in the past
and may again in the future be translated into thought. In the best sense
of the word the book is sub-rational: it is addressed to those vital preferences which lie deeper than coherent thinking.

The most important political books are often of this sort. Rousseau's
Social Contract and Tom Paine's *Rights of Man* were far inferior as works
of the mind to the best thought of the eighteenth century, but they exerted
an incalculably great influence because they altered men's prejudices. Mr.
Mencken's book is of the same sort. The democratic phase which began in
the eighteenth century has about run its course. Its assumptions no longer
explain the facts of the modern world and its ideals are no longer congenial
to modern men. There is now taking place a radical change of attitude not
merely towards parliamentary government but towards the whole conception of popular sovereignty and majority rule. This change is as radical in
its way as that which took place, say between 1776 and 1848.

In the United States Mr. Mencken is the most powerful voice announcing the change. The effect of his tremendous polemic is to destroy,
by rendering it ridiculous and unfashionable, the democratic tradition of
the American pioneers. This attack on the divine right of demos is an almost exact equivalent of the earlier attacks on the kings, the nobles, and
the priests. He strikes at the sovereign power, which in America today consists of the evangelical churches in the small communities, the proletarian
masses in the cities, and the organized smaller business men everywhere.
The Baptist and Methodist sects, the city mobs, and the Chamber of Commerce are in power. They are the villains of the piece. Mr. Mencken does
not argue with them. He lays violent hands upon them in the conviction,
probably correct, that you accomplish results quicker by making your oppo-

*From the *Saturday Review of Literature* 3 (11 December 1926): 413–14. Copyright 1926
Saturday Review magazine. Reprinted by permission.

nent's back teeth rattle than by laboriously addressing his reason. Mr. Mencken, moreover, being an old newspaper man, has rather strong notions about the capacity of mankind to reason. He knows that the established scheme is not supported by reason but by prejudice, prestige, and reverence, and that a good joke is more devastating than a sound argument. He is an eminently practical journalist, and so he devotes himself to dogmatic and explosive vituperation. The effect is a massacre of sacred cows, a holocaust of idols, and the poor boobs are no longer on their knees.

Mr. Mencken is so effective just because his appeal is not from mind to mind but from viscera to viscera. If you analyze his arguments you destroy their effect. You cannot take them in detail and examine their implications. You have to judge him totally, roughly, approximately, without definition, as you would a barrage of artillery, for the general destruction rather than for the accuracy of the individual shots. He presents an experience, and if he gets you, he gets you not by reasoned conviction, but by a conversion which you may or may not be able to dress up later as a philosophy. If he succeeds with you, he implants in you a sense of sin, and then he revives you with grace, and disposes you to a new pride in excellence and in a non-gregarious excellence.

One example will show what happens if you pause to analyze his ideas. The thesis of this whole book is that we must cease to be governed by "the inferior four-fifths of mankind." Here surely is a concept which a thinker would have paused to define. Mr. Mencken never does define it, and what is more, he quite evidently has no clear idea of what he means. Sometimes he seems to think that the difference between the inferior four-fifths and the superior one-fifth is the difference between the "haves" and the "have nots." At other times he seems to think it is the difference between the swells and the nobodies, between the wellborn and those who come "out of the gutter." At other times he abandons these worldly distinctions and talks and thinks about "free spirits," a spiritual elite, who have no relation either to income or to a family tree. This vagueness as to whether the superior one-fifth are the Prussian Junkers or the Pittsburgh millionaires, or the people who can appreciate Bach and Beethoven, persists throughout the book.

This confusion is due, I think, to the fact that he is an outraged sentimentalist. Fate and his own curiosity have made him a connoisseur of human ignorance. Most educated men are so preoccupied with what they conceive to be the best thought in the field of their interest, that they ignore the follies of uneducated men. A Jacques Loeb would spend very little of his time on biology as taught in an Oklahoma High School. Even William James, who was more interested in the common man than any great philosopher of our time, was looking always for grains of wisdom in the heaps of folly. But Mr. Mencken is overwhelmingly preoccupied with popular culture. He collects examples of it. He goes into a rage about it. He cares so much about it that he cannot detach himself from it. And he measures it not by relative standards, but by the standards which most educated men reserve for a culture of the first order. He succeeds, of course, in establishing a *reductio ad absurdum* of the shibboleths of liberals. That is worth doing. But it is well to know what you are doing, and when Mr. Mencken measures the culture of the mass by the cultural standards of the elite, he is not throwing any real light on the modern problem. He is merely smashing a delusion by means of an effective rhetorical device.

I doubt, however, if he is aware that he is using a rhetorical device. When he measures the popular culture by the standards of the elite, the humor is all on the surface. The undertone is earnest and intensely sincere. One feels that Mr. Mencken is deeply outraged because he does not live in a world where all men love truth and excellence and honor. I feel it because I detect in this book many signs of yearning for the good old days. When Mr. Mencken refers to feudalism, to kings, to the Prussian aristocracy, to any ordered society of the ancient régime, he adopts a different tone of voice. I don't mean to say that he talks like an *emigré* or like a writer for the *Action Française,* but it is evident to me that his revolt against modern democratic society exhausts his realism, and that the historic alternatives are touched for him with a romantic glamour. The older aristocratic societies exist only in his imagination; they are idealized sufficiently to inhibit that drastic plainness of perception which he applies to the democratic society all about him.

The chief weakness of the book, as a book of ideas, arises out of this naive contrast in Mr. Mencken's mind between the sordid reality he knows and the splendid society he imagines. He never seems to have grasped the truth that the thing he hates is the direct result of the thing he most admires. This modern democracy meddling in great affairs could not be what it is but for that freedom of thought which Mr. Mencken to his everlasting credit cares more about than about anything else. It is freedom of speech and freedom of thought which have made all questions popular questions. What sense is there then in shouting on one page for a party of "liberty," and on another bewailing the hideous consequences? The old aristocracies which Mr. Mencken admires did not delude themselves with any nonsense about liberty. They reserved what liberty there was for a privileged elite, knowing perfectly well that if you granted liberty to everyone you would have sooner or later everything that Mr. Mencken deplores. But he seems to think that you can have a privileged, ordered, aristocratic society with complete liberty of speech. That is as thorough-going a piece of Utopian sentimentalism as anything could be. You might as well proclaim yourself a Roman Catholic and then ask that excerpts from the *American Mercury* and the works of Charles Darwin be read from the altar on the first Sunday of each month. If Mr. Mencken really wishes an aristocracy he will have to give up liberty as he understands it; and if he wishes liberty he will have to resign himself to hearing *homo boobiens* speak his mind.

What Mr. Mencken desires is in substance the distinction, the sense of honor, the chivalry, and the competence of an ideal aristocracy combined with the liberty of an ideal democracy. This is an excellent wish, but like most attempts to make the best of both worlds, it results in an evasion of the problem. The main difficulty in democratic society arises out of the increasing practice of liberty. The destruction of authority, of moral values, of cultural standards is the result of using the liberty which has been won during the last three or four centuries. Mr. Mencken is foremost among those who cry for more liberty, and who use that liberty to destroy what is left of the older tradition. I do not quarrel with him for that. But I am amazed that he does not see how fundamentally the spiritual disorder he fights against is the effect of that régime of liberty he fights for. Because he fails to see that, I think he claims too much when he says that he is engaged in a diagnosis of the democratic disease. He has merely described with great emphasis the awful pain it gives him.

In the net result these confusions of thought are a small matter. It is no crime not to be a philosopher. What Mr. Mencken has created is a personal force in American life which has an extraordinarily cleansing and vitalizing effect. How else can you explain the paradox of his popularity, and the certainty that before he dies he will find himself, like Bernard Shaw today, one of the grand old men, one of the beloved patriarchs of his time? How in this land where all politicians, pedagogues, peasants, etc. etc. are preposterous, has Henry L. Mencken, not yet aged fifty, become the pope of popes? The answer is that he has the gift of life. His humor is so full of animal well-being that he acts upon his public like an elixir. The wounds he inflicts heal quickly. His blows have the clean brutality of a natural phenomenon. They are directed by a warm and violent but an unusually healthy mind which is not divided, as most minds are, by envy and fear and ambition and anxiety. When you can explain the heightening effect of a spirited horse, of a swift athlete, of a dancer really in control of his own body, when you can explain why watching them you feel more alive yourself, you can explain the quality of his influence.

For this reason the Mencken manner can be parodied, but the effect is ludicrous when it is imitated. The same prejudices and the same tricks of phrase employed by others are usually cheap and often nasty. I never feel that in Mr. Mencken himself even when he calls quite harmless people cockroaches and lice. I do not care greatly for phrases like that. They seem to me like spitting on the carpet to emphasize an argument. They are signs that Mr. Mencken writes too much and has occasionally to reach for the effect without working for it. I think he is sometimes lazy, and when he is lazy he is often unfair, not in the grand manner but in the small manner. And yet his wounds are clean wounds and they do not fester. I know, beause I have fragments of his shellfire in my own skin. The man is admirable. He writes terribly unjust tirades, and yet I know of nobody who writes for his living who will stay up so late or get up so early to untangle an injustice. He often violates not merely good taste according to the genteel tradition, but that superior kind of good taste according to which a man refuses to hurt those who cannot defend themselves.

Nevertheless I feel certain that insofar as he has influenced the tone of public controversy he has elevated it. The Mencken attack is always a frontal attack. It is always explicit. The charge is all there. He does not leave the worst unsaid. He says it. And when you have encountered him, you do not have to wonder whether you are going to be stabbed in the back when you start to leave and are thinking of something else.

I have not written this as a eulogy, but as an explanation which to me at least answers the question why Henry L. Mencken is as popular as he is in a country in which he professes to dislike most of the population. I lay it to the subtle but none the less sure sense of those who read him that here is nothing sinister that smells of decay, but that on the contrary this Holy Terror from Baltimore is splendidly and exultantly and contagiously alive. He calls you a swine, and an imbecile, and he increases your will to live.

Views and Reviews
George S. Schuyler*

The other day a Senegambian damsel rushed into my office and breathlessly inquired whether or not I was going to "answer" H. L. Mencken's recent article in the *New York World*, in which he dwelt at length on the black liberals and intelligentsia around Gotham. Why, I inquired, is it necessary to answer Brother Henry? In the main, I think what he said is true. Indeed, I have said much the same thing myself. That a number of the so-called Negro literati are mere hacks is quite apparent to the most casual reader. When Prof. Mencken says that the literary and artistic accomplishments of the Sons of Ham in these United States "have been very modest," he is telling what God loves. It is true that in the field of music where they are supposed to be unusually gifted, they have been far surpassed by the whites, and that, even in the field of ragtime and jazz. Nor, as Mencken says, are our composers, such as we have, doing anything much with the spirituals.

Even in his criticism of the poetical output of the sable bards, I think the editor of *The American Mercury* is on pretty sound ground. I do not think he has given them sufficient credit, yet, judged by world standards, they haven't made such a big noise. If you doubt this, pick up a volume of

*From the *Pittsburgh Courier*, 30 July 1927. Reprinted by permission of the *Pittsburgh Courier*.

Tennyson, Swinburne, Shelley, Keats, Whitman or even Longfellow, and your doubts will be removed. Even judged by the standard of Amy Lowell, Robinson, Sandburg, Frost or even Robert Service, they are second-rate. And I agree with Mencken that in prose their record is worse, and that even in writing on the problems of the race they have fallen short of the whites.

Well, what does this mean? Does it mean that the Negro is inferior to the white. Yes; inferior in opportunity and inferior in technique. Art is parasitic. It must have a monied class to which to adhere for its sustenance, for great art must always have a limited audience and is seldom popular. Almost all great artists whether with pen or brush have been subsidized or have had great personal wealth, and thus free from the struggle to make a living. There are few examples in the history of art and literature to which one can point where, money and leisure being absent, great work has been done. Negro composers in order to get along and make a living have had to take up most of their time writing coarse popular songs about "Mah Baby" and "Mah Man," while Negro writers have been largely engaged in writing racial propaganda and trying to voice the aspirations of what Dr. Du Bois once called "the mired mass."

On the other hand, it seems to me that Br'er Mencken's attitude is a little pontifical. He forgets, it seems to me, that American writers generally haven't contributed much timeless literature, nor have any American composers, white or black, rivalled Beethoven, Wagner or Liszt. Our American poets, too, with the possible exception of Whitman and Poe, are decidedly not of the first water. The fact is that this is a young country just emerging from the pioneering stage. Heretofore, it has been absorbed with building a civilization and has just begun to criticize and interpret it. In the future it is quite probable that our American artists and writers will create just as lovely poems, books, sculptures and paintings as any of the European masters, but up to the present time, with the exception of Sargent, Whistler, Pennell, Borglum, Whitman and a handful of others, we have not done so.

I cannot help but agree with Br'er Henry when he opines that "the Negro has ventured into the arts too soon" and that the arts "can flourish only in a house more solid and stable than the one he is just moving into." Art and literature are the twin crowns of a civilization, and there must be something pretty solid under them. Mencken says that the Negro's greatest achievement in the next two generations will be in business, and I quite agree with him. Wealth and leisure must come first before we can properly subsidize art—unless wealthy white folks are to do the subsidizing, as they now support our schools, our colleges, our Y. M. C. A., our Y. W. C. A. and our social service organizations. I am not particularly adverse to a talented Negro getting a handout from a white plutocrat. Why shouldn't he? After all he is an American, and whatever art or literature he creates he will be American and not Negro, as some of our mystics are wont to think.

The Critic and American Life   Irving Babbitt*

A frequent remark of the French about Americans is: "They're children"; which, interpreted, means that from the French point of view Americans are childishly uncritical. The remark is relevant only in so far as it refers to general critical intelligence. In dealing with the special problems of a commercial and industrial society Americans have shown that they can be abundantly critical. Certain Americans, for example, have developed a critical keenness in estimating the value of stocks and bonds that is nothing short of uncanny. The very persons, however, who are thus keen in some particular field are, when confronted with questions that call for general critical intelligence, often puerile. Yet in an age like the present, which is being subjected to a constant stream of propaganda in everything from the choice of its religion to its cigarettes, general critical intelligence would seem desirable.

As a matter of fact, most persons nowadays aspire to be not critical but creative. We have not merely creative poets and novelists, but creative readers and listeners and dancers. Lately a form of creativeness has appeared that may in time swallow up all the others—creative salesmanship. The critic himself has caught the contagion and also aspires to be creative. He is supposed to become so when he receives from the creation of another, conceived as pure temperamental overflow, so vivid an impression that, when passed through his temperament, it issues forth as a fresh creation. What is eliminated in both critic and creator is any standard that is set above temperament and that therefore might interfere with their eagerness to get themselves expressed.

This notion of criticism as self-expression is important for our present subject, for it has been adopted by the writer who is, according to the last edition of the *Encyclopedia Britannica,* "the greatest critical force in America"—Mr. H. L. Mencken. "The critic is first and last," says Mr. Mencken, "simply trying to express himself; he is trying to achieve thereby for his own inner ego the grateful feeling of a function performed, a tension relieved, a katharsis attained which Wagner achieved when he wrote *Die Walküre,* and a hen achieves every time she lays an egg." This creative self-expression, as practiced by himself and others, has, according to Mr. Mencken, led to a salutary stirring up of the stagnant pool of American letters: "To-day for the first time in years there is strife in American criticism. . . . Heretics lay on boldly and the professors are forced to make some defence. Often going further they attempt counter-attacks. Ears are bitten off, noses are bloodied. There are wallops both above and below the belt."

But it may be that criticism is something more than Mr. Mencken would have us believe, more in short than a squabble between Bohemians, each eager to capture the attention of the public for his brand of self-

*From the *Forum* 79 (February 1928): 161–68. Reprinted by permission of *Current History.*

expression. To reduce criticism indeed to the satisfaction of a temperamental urge, to the uttering of one's gustos and disgustos (in Mr. Mencken's case chiefly the latter) is to run counter to the very etymology of the word which implies discrimination and judgment. The best one would anticipate from a writer like Mr. Mencken, possessing an unusual verbal virtuosity and at the same time temperamentally irresponsible, is superior intellectual vaudeville. One must grant him, however, certain genuine critical virtues—for example, a power of shrewd observation within rather narrow limits. Yet the total effect of his writing is nearer to intellectual vaudeville than to serious criticism.

The serious critic is more concerned with achieving a correct scale of values and so seeing things proportionately than with self-expression. His essential virtue is poise. The specific benefit he confers is to act as a moderating influence on the opposite insanities between which mankind in the lump is constantly tending to oscillate—oscillations that Luther compares to the reelings of a drunken peasant on horseback. The critic's survey of any particular situation may very well seem satirical. The complaint that Mr. Mencken is too uniformly disgruntled in his survey of the American situation rather misses the point. Behind the pleas for more constructiveness it is usually easy to detect the voice of the booster. A critic who did not get beyond a correct diagnosis of existing evils might be very helpful. If Mr. Mencken has fallen short of being such a diagnostician, the failure is due not to his excess of severity but to his lack of discrimination.

The standards with reference to which men have discriminated in the past have been largely traditional. The outstanding fact of the present period, on the other hand, has been the weakening of traditional standards. An emergency has arisen not unlike that with which Socrates sought to cope in ancient Athens. Anyone who is untraditional and seeks at the same time to be discriminating must almost necessarily own Socrates as his master. As is well known, Socrates sought above all to be discriminating in his use of general terms. The importance of the art of inductive defining that he devised may perhaps best be made clear by bringing together two sayings, one of Napoleon—"Imagination governs mankind"—and one of John Selden—"Syllables govern mankind." Before allowing one's imagination and finally one's conduct to be controlled by a general term, it would seem wise to submit it to a Socratic scrutiny.

It is, therefore, unfortunate that at a time like the present, which plainly calls for a Socrates, we should instead have got a Mencken. One may take as an example of Mr. Mencken's failure to discriminate adequately, his attitude toward the term that for several generations past has been governing the imagination of multitudes—democracy. His view of democracy is simply that of Rousseau turned upside down, and nothing, as has been remarked, resembles a hollow so much as a swelling. A distinction of which he has failed to recognize the importance is that between a direct or unlimited and a constitutional democracy. In the latter we probably have the best thing in the world. The former, on the other hand, as all thinkers of any penetration from Plato and Aristotle down have perceived, leads to the loss of liberty and finally to the rise of some form of despotism. The two conceptions of democracy involve not merely incompatible views of government but ultimately of human nature. The desire of the constitutional democrat for institutions that act as checks on the immediate will of the people implies a similar dualism in the individual—a higher self that acts restrictively on his ordinary and impulsive self. The partisan of unlimited democracy on the other hand is an idealist in the sense of that the term assumed in connection with the so-called romantic movement. His faith in the people is closely related to the doctrine of natural goodness proclaimed by the sentimentalists of the eighteenth century and itself marking an extreme recoil from the dogma of total depravity. The doctrine of natural goodness favors the free temperamental expansion that I have already noticed in speaking of the creative critic.

It is of the utmost importance, however, if one is to understand Mr. Mencken, to discriminate between two types of temperamentalist—the soft and sentimental type, who cherishes various "ideals," and the hard, or Nietzschean type, who piques himself on being realistic. As a matter of fact, if one sees in the escape from traditional controls merely an opportunity to live temperamentally, it would seem advantageous to pass promptly from the idealistic to the Nietzschean phase, sparing oneself as many as possible of the intermediary disillusions. It is at all events undeniable that the rise of Menckenism has been marked by a certain collapse of romantic idealism in the political field and elsewhere. The numerous disillusions that have supervened upon the War have provided a favoring atmosphere.

The symptoms of Menckenism are familiar: a certain hardness and smartness and disposition to rail at everything that, rightly or wrongly, is established and respected; a tendency to identify the real with what Mr. Mencken terms "the cold and clammy facts" and to assume that the only alternative to facing these facts is to fade away into sheer romantic unreality. These and similar traits are becoming so widely diffused that, whatever one's opinion of Mr. Mencken as a writer and thinker, one must grant him representativeness. He is a chief prophet at present of those who deem themselves emancipated but who are, according to Mr. Brownell, merely unbuttoned.

The crucial point in any case is one's attitude toward the principle of control. Those who stand for this principle in any form or degree are dismissed by the emancipated as reactionaries or, still graver reproach, as Puritans. Mr. Mencken would have us believe that the historical Puritan was not even sincere in his moral rigorism, but was given to "lamentable transactions with loose women and fiery jugs." This may serve as a sample of the assertions, picturesquely indiscriminate, by which a writer wins immediate notoriety at the expense of his permanent reputation. The facts about the Puritan happen to be complex and need to be dealt with very Socratically.

It has been affirmed that the point of view of the Puritan was Stoical rather than truly Christian, and the affirmation is not wholly false. The present discussion of the relationship between Puritanism and the rise of capitalism with its glorification of the acquisitive life also has its justification. It is likewise a fact that the Puritan was from the outset unduly concerned with reforming others as well as himself, and this trait relates him to the humanitarian meddler or "wowser" of the present day, who is Mr. Mencken's pet aversion.

Yet it remains true that awe and reverence and humility are Christian virtues and that there was some survival of these virtues in the Puritan. For a representative Puritan like Jonathan Edwards they were inseparable from the illumination of grace from what he terms "a divine and supernatural light." In the passage from the love and fear of God of an Edwards to the love and service of man professed by the humanitarian, something has plainly dropped out, something that is very near the centre. What has tended to disappear is the inner life with the special type of control it imposes. With the decline of this inner control there has been an increasing resort to outer control. Instead of the genuine Puritan we then have the humanitarian legalist who passes innumerable laws for the control of people who refuse to control themselves. The activity of our uplifters is scarcely suggestive of any "divine and supernatural light." Here is a discrimination of the first importance that has been obscured by the muddy thinking of our half-baked intelligentsia. One is thus kept from perceiving the real problem, which is to retain the inner life even though one refuses to accept the theological nightmare with which the Puritan associated it. More is involved in the failure to solve this problem than the Puritan tradition. It is the failure of our contemporary life in general. Yet, unless some solution is reached by a full and free exercise of the critical spirit, one remains a mere modernist and not a thoroughgoing and complete modern; for the modern spirit and the critical spirit are in their essence one.

What happens, when one sets out to deal with questions of this order without sufficient depth of reflection and critical maturity, may be seen in Mr. Sinclair Lewis's last novel. He has been lured from art into the writing of a wild diatribe which, considered even as such, is largely beside the mark. If the Protestant Church is at present threatened with bankruptcy, it is not because it has produced an occasional Elmer Gantry. The true reproach it has incurred is that, in its drift toward modernism, it has lost its grip not merely on certain dogmas but, simultaneously, on the facts of human nature. It has failed above all to carry over in some modern and critical form the truth of a dogma that unfortunately receives much support from these facts—the dogma of original sin. At first sight Mr. Mencken would appear to have a conviction of evil—when, for example, he reduces democracy in its essential aspect to a "combat between jackals and jackasses"—that establishes at least one bond between him and the austere Christian.

The appearance, however, is deceptive. The Christian is conscious above all of the "old Adam" in himself: hence his humility. The effect of Mr. Mencken's writing, on the other hand, is to produce pride rather than humility, a pride ultimately based on flattery. The reader, especially the young and callow reader, identifies himself imaginatively with Mr. Mencken and conceives of himself as a sort of morose and sardonic divinity surveying from some superior altitude an immeasurable expanse of "boobs." This attitude will not seem especially novel to anyone who has traced the modern movement. One is reminded in particular of Flaubert, who showed a diligence in collecting bourgeois imbecilities comparable to that displayed by Mr. Mencken in his *Americana*. Flaubert's discovery that one does not add to one's happiness in this way would no doubt be dismissed by Mr. Mencken as irrelevant, for he has told us that he does not believe in happiness. Another discovery of Flaubert's may seem to him more worthy of consideration. "By dint of railing at idiots," Flaubert reports, "one runs the risk of becoming idiotic oneself."

It may be that the only way to escape from the unduly complacent cynicism of Mr. Mencken and his school is to reaffirm once more the truths of the inner life. In that case it would seem desirable to disengage, so far as possible, the principle of control on which the inner life finally depends from mere creeds and traditions and assert it as a psychological fact; a fact, moreover, that is neither "cold" nor "clammy." The coldness and clamminess of much so called realism arises from its failure to give this fact due recognition. A chief task, indeed, of the Socratic critic would be to rescue the noble term "realist" from its present degradation. A view of reality that overlooks the element in man that moves in an opposite direction from mere temperament, the specifically human factor in short, may prove to be singularly one-sided. Is the Puritan, John Milton, when he declares that "he who reigns within himself and rules passions, desires, and fears is more than a king," less real than Mr. Theodore Dreiser when he discourses in his peculiar dialect of "those rearranging chemisms upon which all the morality or immorality of the world is based"?

As a matter of fact, according to the degree and nature of the exercise of the principle of control, one may distinguish two main types of realism which may be denominated respectively religious and humanistic: as the principle of control falls into abeyance, a third type tends to emerge, which may be termed naturalistic realism. That the decline of the traditional controls has been followed by a lapse to the naturalistic level is indubitable. The characteristic evils of the present age arise from unrestraint and violation of the law of measure and not, as our modernists would have us believe, from the tyranny of taboos and traditional inhibitions. The facts cry to heaven. The delicate adjustment that is required between the craving for emancipation and the need of control has been pointed out once for all by Goethe, speaking not as a Puritan but as a clear-eyed man of the world. Everything, he says, that liberates the spirit without a corresponding growth in self-mastery is pernicious. This one sentence would seem to cover the case of our "flaming youth" rather completely.

The movement in the midst of which we are still living was from its inception unsound in its dealing with the principle of control. It is vain to expect from the dregs of this movement what its "first sprightly running failed to give." Mr. Carl Sandburg speaks of the "marvelous rebellion of man at all signs reading 'Keep off.' " An objection to this purely insurrectional attitude is that, as a result of its endless iteration during the past century and more, it has come to savor too strongly of what has been called "the humdrum of revolt." A more serious objection to the attitude is that it encourages an unrestricted and merely temperamental liberty which, paradoxically enough at first sight, affords the modern man no avenue of escape from the web that is being woven about him by the scientific determinist.

Realists of the current type are in point of fact intimately allied with the psychologists,—glandular, behavioristic, and psychoanalytical,—who, whatever their divergences among themselves, unite in their deterministic trend and therefore clash fundamentally with both religious and humanistic realists. The proper method of procedure in defending the freedom of the will would seem to be to insist upon it as a fact of experience, a fact so primary that the position of the determinist involves an evasion of one of the immediate data of consciousness in favor of a metaphysical dream. What is genuinely experimental in naturalistic psychology should of course be received with respect; but the facts of which it takes account in its experiments are unimportant compared with the facts it either neglects or denies. Practically it is running into grotesque extremes of pseudo-science that make of it a shining mark for the Socratic critic.

Here at all events is the issue on which all other issues finally hinge; for until the question of moral freedom—the question whether man is a responsible agent or only the plaything of his impulses and impressions —is decided, nothing is decided; and to decide the question under existing circumstances calls for the keenest critical discrimination. Creation that is not sufficiently supported by such discrimination is likely to prove premature. . . .

H. L. Mencken: Doctor Rhetoricus   I. J. Semper*

For the past two decades H. L. Mencken has been the bane of American educators—a "hardboiled heretic," full of sound and fury, as destruc-

*From the *Catholic World* 130 (October 1929): 30–39. Reprinted by permission of the *Catholic World*.

tive as an earthquake, as ruthless as a Hun, and about as welcome as the Black Death. Consult his *magnum opus* on education (*Prejudices: Third Series*) and his various syndicated syllabi of pedagogical errors, and you will find that, metaphorically speaking, he plunges college presidents into caldrons of boiling oil, shoots professors at sight, poisons superintendents, ravishes schoolmarms, slaughters students *en masse*, bombs parent-teachers associations, and burns down the little red schoolhouse to roast the educational pig. And yet in spite of all this *Schrecklichkeit*, it would seem that his bark is far worse than his bite. Nothing could be more significant as indicating not only a change of heart in Mr. Mencken but even a subconscious pedagogical bias than the publication in 1926 of a college textbook entitled *Readings from the American Mercury*, edited by a professor of English with the *imprimatur* and *nihil obstat* of Mr. Mencken himself. This book, which is frankly intended for the satchels of sophomores, and which no doubt has garnered its quota of "adoptions," is a practical text on the art of growing the hardy and perennial "flowers of rhetoric" which bloom in the garden of the *American Mercury*. It is unnecessary to state that its chief interest lies in the four chaste little essays contributed by Mr. Mencken himself. There is, of course, grim irony in the thought that the future Babbitts of this country should be required to take Mr. Mencken as a rhetorical model, but there can be no question about his ability to teach them. He is easily the master rhetorician of our age, a magician who works wonders with words, a veritable *Doctor Rhetoricus* who has taken his degree *Maxima cum laude*, not in any anaemic institution of higher learning, but in the wide open spaces of journalistic encounter and public debate.

Mr. Mencken's admirers laud him as an artist whose rhetorical devices, far from being the marks of trick or artifice, have the single aim of persuading others of the truth of what he thinks and feels. It has been suggested, however, that he is the rhetorician *in vacuo*, a mere dealer in words with a flair for persuasion who, caring little or nothing for his subject, is content to achieve what Professor Irving Babbitt styles "superior intellectual vaudeville." Whichever view we adopt (and most of his readers incline strongly one way or the other), the fact remains that he is a rhetorician for better or for worse. Indeeed such is the implication of his oft-quoted remark: "I think it is craftsmanship that I admire most in the world."

II

Like every first-class rhetorician, Mr. Mencken possesses an eight-cylinder vocabulary which is at once the wonder and the despair of his critics. For the past quarter of a century he has scanned and used words as no other writer of our generation. His bulky tome, *The American Language*, is an enduring monument to his close study of the current idiom; and, according to his own computation, he has written over 7,500,000 words. If words were soldiers, he would rank as a field marshal. His amazing vocabulary is compounded of many simples, native and foreign, but its basic elements are the common and homely words of the dictionary of life, as he himself once declared in a moment of proud humility: "Well, the complaint that I hear most often is that my English is unintelligible—that it is too full of 'hard' words. I can imagine nothing more astounding. My English is actually almost as bald and simple as the English of a college yell. My sentences are short and plainly constructed. I resolutely cultivate the most direct manner of statement; my vocabulary is deliberately composed of the words of everyday" (*Prejudices: Third Series*). That statement is literally true as far as the great bulk of his writing is concerned. He writes as other men talk—in the racy, fluent, tuneful idiom of everyday. His vigor and his power of suggestion spring from the concreteness of his diction—the specific word, the homely phrase, the striking epithet, the verb full of life and movement. Open any of the *Prejudices* at random and you will unquestionably run across "hard" words, but on examination you will also find that his diction in the main is the "language such as men do use."

But Mr. Mencken would not be a genuine virtuoso of words if he did not splash around in his vocabulary. Like the strong man in the circus, he overthrows with abounding vigor, and he likes to give his customers a few extra thrills for their money. While the bulk and staple of his vocabulary is homespun, he does not hesitate to use technical terms and foreign importations when they will display his verbal virtuosity. He is well versed in the literature of medicine, of music, and of many sciences, sacred and profane, and out of sheer gusto he bombards his readers with the barbaric names of horrible diseases, musical marginalia, and the Latin and Greek nomenclature of the sciences. On occasion he turns a triple somersault to the tune of "harsh, cacophonous chords for bombardons and ophicleides in the bass clef." When he cannot find a technical term to suit his purpose, he coins one with mocking pseudo-scholarship out of a dog-Latin all his own. In his pages not infrequently *homo neanderthalensis* stalks *bos taurus; pithecanthropus erectus* invites his soul with *nicotiana tabacum;* and *homo sapiens*, when he is not dodging streptococci or dosing himself with Bulgarian bacilli, cocks a scornful eye at *homo boobiens*. Mr. Mencken has also resolutely refused to lower the bars on the languages of Continental Europe. He believes that a living language is like a man suffering from small internal hemorrhages, and hence that it stands in absolute need of "constant transfusions of new blood from other tongues." In many cases he draws upon foreign sources in the interest of precision. The English language has no exact and handy equivalents for a number of his beloved alienisms; for example, *agent provocateur, amour propre, beau ideal, cliché, con amore, demi-monde, haut monde, in petto, intelligentsia, Kultur, Weltpolitik, Weltschmerz*. But when he sprinkles his pages with foreign locutions like *aluminados, banderillas, Frauenzimmer, Gelehrten, gendarmerie, Katzenjammer, Kartoffelsuppe, plaza de toros, Polizei, Privat-Dozenten*, which suggests an educational holiday tour of Europe, it is obvious that he is prompted partly by the desire to stage a good show and partly by the spirit of pure deviltry.

Perhaps the most spectacular aspect of Mr. Mencken's vocabulary is its range, particularly in words which sneer and deride and shrivel. If Paul Elmer More classifies him among "brawling vulgarians," if Fred Lewis Pattee styles him "a vulgar and furiously erupting Stromboli," and if he is often described in the public prints as "a critic with whips and scorpions," it is mainly because he possesses in an eminent degree a vocabulary of vituperation. He is primarily a satirist who points his finger of scorn at gulls and knaves, and their imbecilities. An honor roll of verbal shock troops in his army of words which spell contempt and derision would read as follows: For gulls—blanks, boobs, clod-hoppers, dolts, dunderheads, goose-steppers, half-wits, hinds, idiots, imbeciles, morons, numskulls, peasants, poltroons, serfs, vacuums, yahoos and yokels. For knaves—back-slappers, bigwigs, boob-bumpers, bosh-mongers, charlatans, cheapjacks, cheer leaders, clowns, frauds, go-getters, ignoramuses, magnificoes, medicine men, mountebanks, pedants, platitudinarians, pollyannas, pundits, puppets, quacks, rabble-rousers, shams, smellers, snoopers, snouters, witch-doctors, wowsers and zanies. For imbecilities—balderdash, banalities, bilge, blather, bosh, bugaboos, buncombe, bunk, cavortings, claptrap, comstockery, drivel, donkeyisms, fudge, gush, hokum, hocus-pocus, idiocies, piffle, pishposh, puerilities, rumble-bumble, taboos, tosh and twaddle.

It is plain that Mr. Mencken believes in calling a spade by its proper name. If, as he holds, the essence of good style is fitness, he is not to be blamed "for using vulgar words for vulgar things." When he manhandles a charlatan he employs words which fit the subject and the occasion; and here he has the support of Macaulay: "The first rule of all writing—that rule to which every other is subordinate—is that the words used by the writer shall be such as most fully and precisely convey his meaning to the great body of his readers. All considerations about dignity and purity of style ought to bend to this consideration." It cannot be questioned that the strong words used by Mr. Mencken, both in denotation and connotation, convey his ideas fully and precisely. We may not agree with him, but we can never mistake his meaning. Macaulay's dictum would even justify some of the slang with which Mr. Mencken peppers his philippics. Indeed he himself distinguishes between slang which acquires "a special and limited meaning, not served by any existing locution," and slang which "is adopted by the populace as a counter-word" of doubtful significance. In practice, however, he does not always observe this fine distinction. The term "wowser," for instance, to which he is so partial, may have "a special and limited meaning, not served by any existing locution," but the same can hardly be predicated of such shopworn counters as "boozehound," "cutie," "gal," "souse," and "stewed."

No less astounding than his range in the use of words is his fertility of invention. George Jean Nathan, if we credit Mr. Mencken, "carries the avoidance of the *cliché* to the length of an *idée fixe*." Mr. Mencken himself is no less dominated by a lively horror of rubber-stamps. He coins new words like "booboisie," "grammatomaniacs," "moronia," "yokelry," and he weaves old words into new and startling patterns. We subjoin some typical Menckenisms selected at random: anaesthetic to ideas, brummagem emotion-squeezers, by the chautauqua out of *The Atlantic Monthly*, coroner's inquest criticism, intellectual Bad Lands, making botany obscene, romance in baggy breeches, a slaughter-house of ideas, swami séances in dark, smelly rooms, swathing the bitter facts of life in bandages of soft illusion. Like Matthew Arnold he knows how to invent telling nicknames, which he uses over and over again. Prof., Dr., the rev. clergy, *Boobus Americanus*, the Bible Belt, are familiar examples. Some of his most felicitous labels are to be found in the titles of articles, as witness "A Merchant of Mush" (Henry Sydnor Harrison), "Star-Spangled Men" (United States army officers), "The Ulster Polonius" (George Bernard Shaw).

Mr. Mencken's pages show an unusually large sprinkling of proper names, although he rarely quotes from any author, a feat on which he prides himself. "My stuff," he once said to a friend, "is not allusive. That is, I do not adorn it with the customary trite quotations from Emerson, Goethe, Shakespeare and the Bible. I seldom quote even the men I admire most, Nietzsche, Huxley, Beethoven and Carlyle." He does not quote, it is true; but he achieves an equivalent in rhetorical effect by the frequent use of proper names. And like most rhetoricians he loves the ringing roll call of resounding proper names. Again we take our specimens at random: Americans: "Jefferson, Hamilton, Sam Adams, Aaron Burr, Henry Clay, Calhoun, Webster, Sumner, Grant, Sherman, Lee." Musicians: "Beethoven, Schubert, Schumann, Brahms, Bach, Haydn, Handel." *Femmes de France:* "Thérèse! Sophie! Olympe! Marie! Suzette! Odette! Denise! Julie!"

Mr. Mencken deserves the title of rhetorical doctor on the score of his vocabulary alone. In his choice and use of words he has range, idiomatic flavor and pungency of phrasing—surely an ideal equipment for a satirist. But he is curiously lacking in words of color. One looks in vain for a single splash of scarlet. His vocabulary is full of clang, but no tint; the hurly-burly of the storm is in it, but no rainbow. Perhaps the explanation is to be sought in the fact that his personal tastes are all in favor of music and against painting, an art which, with its lack of movement, is for him a one-legged affair. At any rate he uses words for their sound-value and movement, with a pronounced liking for the stentorian and the tempestuous. He can roar like a lion; he seldom coos like a dove. He is a Wagner with a touch of jazz; his orchestration is almost always scored *fortissimo* and *sforzando*, with saxophones, trumpets and kettledrums lording it over the flutes and harps.

III

It is not uncommon to-day to find an impressive vocabulary, especially in words of a scholarly character, wedded to awkwardness of expression as revealed in long, involved, cacophonous sentences weighted down with excess baggage. Many a savant who knows words is utterly unable to set them to a tune and make them dance. In the extract which we have already quoted, Mr. Mencken describes the sentence-structure which he favors on principle: "My sentences are short and plainly constructed. I resolutely cultivate the most direct manner of statement." He is indeed our greatest living master of the short sentence; and here we have the rhetorical key to his lucidity, his forcefulness and his animation. The following paragraph on the Roosevelt of the square deal is typical of a sentence-structure which is stripped for action:

> But Roosevelt was never polite to an opponent; perhaps a gentleman, by American standards, he was surely never a gentle man. In a political career of nearly forty years he was never even fair to an opponent. All of his gabble about the square deal was merely so much protective coloration, easily explicable on elementary Freudian grounds. No man, facing Roosevelt in the heat of controversy, ever actually got a square deal. He took extravagant advantages; he played to the worse idiocies of the mob; he hit below the belt almost habitually. One never thinks of him as a duelist, say of the school of Disraeli, Palmerston and, to drop a bit, Blaine. One always thinks of him as a glorified longshoreman engaged eternally in cleaning out bar-rooms—and not too proud to gouge when the inspiration came to him, or to bite in the clinches, or to oppose the relatively fragile brass knuckles of the code with chairlegs, bung-starters, cuspidors, demijohns, and ice-picks (*Prejudices: Second Series*).

Mr. Mencken writes with gigantic gusto, almost with fury, and even his bitterest enemies admit that he writes well. His sentences are epigrammatic in point and vigor and they follow one another like bullets from a machine gun. In the above quotation he gives us a characteristic series of short, staccato sentences, which mount to a swift climax on the argot of the defunct saloon. His meaning is clear and his movement is rapid. He does not wabble; he does not qualify; he does not hem or haw; he does not lose himself in bypaths or blind alleys. The quick succession of his ideas and the brevity of phrase, clause and sentence, impart to his style a tempestuous tempo which sweeps the reader along in spite of himself. Mr. Mencken maintains that the critic should use whatever tools will work. "If pills fail, he gets out his saw. If the saw won't cut, he seizes a club." In the short sentence he has found an admirable tool for his destructive criticism. Indeed he wields it like a club to brain his victims by powerful blows delivered in rapid succession.

If the virtues of Mr. Mencken's foreshortened style are clarity, energy and animation, its chief defect is a journalistic cocksureness. According to his biographer, Isaac Goldberg, Mr. Mencken's newspaper training accounts for his "eagerness to reach at once for the heart of the matter and to spread it forth clearly to the view." But in his effort to clarify, he simplifies too much. His statements have no qualifications, for he consistently refuses to dilute his thought "with various discreet whereases." In the brief paragraph on Roosevelt, it is either "always" or "never." "Roosevelt was *never* polite to an opponent."—"He was surely *never* a gentle man."—"He was *never* even fair to an opponent."—"One *never* thinks of him."—"One *always* thinks of him." All is clear; everything is easy to explain; nothing is hidden or doubtful. An objection is dismissed with a wave of the hand as furnishing no difficulty even for an idiot. If Roosevelt, for instance, was sincere in preaching the doctrine of the square deal, then "all his gabble about the square deal was merely so much protective coloration *easily* explicable on *elementary* Freudian grounds." At times Mr. Mencken gives the impression that he is omniscient, and one is tempted to say of him what Lord Melbourne said of Macaulay: "I wish I were as cocksure of any one thing as Macaulay is of everything."

Mr. Mencken uses a triple combination of phrases, of clauses, and even of sentences, to give variety and rhythm to his sentence-structure. He often follows up a succession of short sentences, which, if continued, would become monotonous, with longer sentences in triple formation. The last three sentences in the extract on Roosevelt illustrate this practice. Likewise, when the mood of lyricism is upon him, his thoughts frequently march to the music of the mystic numeral three. A passage in his article on William Jennings Bryan is to the point. Having described Bryan's hold over the people of the West and the South, he continues in the following strain:

> But out where the grass grows high, and the horned cattle dream away the lazy afternoons, and men still fear the powers and principalities of the air—out there between the corn-rows he held his old puissance to the end. There was no need of beaters to drive in his game. The news that he was coming was enough. For miles the flivver dust would choke the roads. And when he rose at the end of the day to discharge his Message there would be such breathless attention, such a rapt and enchanted ecstasy, such a sweet rustle of amens as the world had not known since Johann fell to Herod's ax (*Prejudices: Fifth Series*).

Here we have the triple combination thrice repeated—in the three parallel clauses of the first sentence, in the three short sentences that follow, and in the three parallel clauses of the last sentence. Moreover, the entire passage is keyed to the drum-beat of blank verse, and actually scans after the best manner of such eminent and facile rhetoricians as Charles Dickens and Robert Ingersoll.

IV

Mr. Mencken is candid enough to admit that on occasion he employs "all the ancient and horrifying devices of the art of rhetoric." Among these devices none bulks larger in his writing than alliteration. He is continually invoking "apt alliteration's artful aid" to give epigrammatic point to his words. If all his alliterative combinations could be lifted from his pages and set end to end, they would constitute a line of solid type reaching from his office in New York to his home in Baltimore. We have culled a few choice specimens: boomers and boosters, campus critics, cow country, gigantic grotesquerie, hamstringing and horn-swoggling, immemorial mumbo-jumbo, Methodist millennium, Signorina Montessori of the Magical method, official optimists, *pianissimo* pronunciamentoes, pedagogical Prussianism of the professors, preposterous popinjays, pulpit pornographers, to purr in peace, to sob for Service, Sganarelles and Scaramouches. Sometimes he spouts alliteration like a geyser, as witness the following sentence: "He [James Huneker] ranks Beethoven miles above the native gods, and not only Beethoven, but also Bach and Brahms, and not only Bach and Brahms, but also Berlioz, Bizet, Bruch and Bülow and perhaps even Balakirew, Bellini, Balfe, Borodin and Boieldieu" (*A Book of Prefaces*).

Mr. Mencken has also mastered the trick of using high-powered epithets as stylistic stimulants. Some of his epithet-noun combinations are as piquant as they are original; for example, anthropoid majority, brummagem Grails, diabetic East, jitney geniuses, paralyzed cerebrums, shoddy souls. In his use of vehement epithets he is forever piling Ossa on Pelion. Just as he knows only two types of men—*homo sapiens* and *homo boobiens,* so he knows only the two extremes of comparison—the superlatively great and the insignificantly small. He hymns James Gibbons Huneker as "the solitary Iokanaan in this tragic aesthetic wilderness," and he incontinently damns Rudyard Kipling as "a tin-pot evangelist." Apotheosis or annihilation! It is more often the latter when he is engaged in his favorite pastime of smashing the idols of the tribe to the tune of astounding imbecilities, childish gush, hysterical sputterings, infantile poppycock, meaningless gibberish, preposterous tosh, and super-imbecile boob-traps. An entire page could be filled with words to which he has prefixed the intensifier "preposterous." His fondness for this adjective suggests that he missed a golden opportunity for an alliterative effect when he did not entitle his books *Preposterous Prejudices*.

His violently contrasted literary prejudices make it plain that he knows how to use Macaulay's chief rhetorical device—antithesis. He builds up sentences, paragraphs, entire essays on ideas which heighten each other by being placed in juxtaposition—Conrad versus Kipling, Dreiser versus Comstock, the Puritans versus the *intelligentsia*, New York versus Baltimore, prose versus poetry, the genuine aristocracy of England versus the bogus aristocracy of America. The following passage from his essay on George Bernard Shaw displays him at his best:

> In the theory that he is Irish I take little stock. His very name is as Scotch as haggis, and the part of Ireland from which he springs is peopled almost exclusively by Scots. The true Irishman is romantic. He senses life as a mystery, a thing of wonder, an experience of passion and beauty. In politics he is not logical, but emotional. In religion his interest centers, not in the commandments, but in the sacraments. The Scot, on the contrary, is almost devoid of romanticism. He is a materialist, a logician, a utilitarian. Life to him is not a poem, but a series of police regulations. God is not an indulgent father, but a hanging judge. There are no saints, but only devils. Beauty is lewdness, redeemable only in the service of morality. It is more important to get on in the world than to be brushed by angels' wings. Here Shaw runs exactly true to type (*Prejudices: First Series*).

The Menckenian similitudes deserve a chapter by themselves. He has at his service whole troops of daring and highly flavored metaphors and similes, which are doubly dramatic, because the reader often whoops with recognition and startles with surprise. His command of odd and striking details and his uncanny gift of pouncing upon a revealing likeness between the most incongruous things, are conducive to light and laughter, if seldom to sweetness. If, for instance, the subject under discussion be suppressed desires, we read: "No doubt the real man lies in the depths of the subconscious, like a carp lurking in the mud." If it be Huneker's habit of losing himself in musical bypaths, we are told that he "was apt to go chasing after strange birds and so miss seeing the elephants go by." Mr. Mencken's skill in the use of homely figures never found happier expression than in the simile with which he brings his famous passage on the function of the critic to a brilliant close:

> He is, first and last, simply trying to express himself. He is trying to arrest and challenge a sufficient body of readers, to make them pay attention to him, to impress them with the charm and novelty of his ideas, to provoke them into an agreeable (or shocked) awareness of him, and he is trying to achieve thereby for his own inner ego the grateful feeling of a function performed, a tension relieved, a *katharsis* attained which Wagner achieved when he wrote '*Die Walküre*,' and a hen achieves every time she lays an egg (*Prejudices: Third Series*).

Even when his similitudes are "jazzy," their aptness and verve often redeem them. Recall the disquisitions of rhetorical handbooks on the theme, "the style is the man," and then listen to Mencken as he plays it on his saxophone:

> For the essence of a sound style is that it cannot be reduced to rules— that it is a living and breathing thing with something of the devilish in

it—that it fits its proprietor tightly and yet ever so loosely, as his skin fits him. It is, in fact, quite as securely an integral part of him as that skin is. It hardens as his arteries harden. It has *Katzenjammer* on the days succeeding his indiscretions. It is gaudy when he is young and gathers decorum when he grows old. On the day after he makes a mash on a new girl it glows and glitters. If he has fed well, it is mellow. If he has gastritis it is bitter. In brief, a style is always the outward and visible symbol of a man, and it cannot be anything else (*Prejudices: Fifth Series*).

But it must be confessed that one encounters in his pages any number of extravagant, and even impudent, comparisons. He cannot resist the temptation to tie a can to the tail of his sentence in the form of a simile or metaphor of belittling significance. He will have it, for example, that there are love affairs "in the manner of Dubuque, Iowa"; that teaching Sanskrit at Bryn Mawr is about as intelligible as "setting off fire-works in a blind asylum"; and that "a professor must have a theory, as a dog must have fleas." The plain truth is that Mr. Mencken has a bias for buffoonery which finds a convenient outlet in the typically American habit of gross and unabashed overstatement. Only the native heath of the chautauqua and the chamber of commerce, of Hollywood and Lucky Strike cigarettes, of Phineas T. Barnum and William Randolph Hearst, could have inspired his rip-roaring tropes. What could be more American in spirit than his word-picture of Roosevelt, "with red-fire raging within him and sky-rockets bursting his veins," emitting a "whoop," leaping upon "his cayuse," and "screaming for war"? In fact, the sky is the limit when Mr. Mencken is in the mood of hilarious hyperbole. Lest we do him grave injustice, we hasten to quote his description of the palmy days of the late Judge Gary: "As I say, Judge Gary ought to be a happy man. The sun shines upon him from all four parts of the compass. Congress, well rehearsed, plays soft jazz for him; bishops bring him his toddy; a straw issues from the White House and tickles him behind the ear" (*Prejudices: Fifth Series*).

Any treatment of Mr. Mencken's rhetorical devices would be utterly inadequate without some reference to his use of what may be styled anti-rhetorical rhetoric. If his "bag of tricks" did not include this hoary but handy device it would be as empty as a golf bag which was minus a putter. Every rhetorician worthy the name issues bulls anathematizing rhetoric with all its works and pomps. Al Smith knew what he was doing when time and time again during the campaign he repudiated with holy horror what he called "language." "No orator," my masters, but "a plain blunt man," accustomed to speak from the heart, and full of righteous indignation for the windy periods of his political opponents! This anti-rhetorical rhetoric is far more subtle and persuasive than the standard article, because it alone is able to reach the man who thinks that he is immune to "rhetoric." Accordingly, Mr. Mencken, like Al Smith, frequently invites comparison between his own rugged plainness of speech and the "fossilized and hollow rhetoric" of other writers. On one occasion he prints a passage from Clayton Hamilton, which he styles "a fragile dahlia from the rhetorical garden of Clayton Hamilton, M.A."; and on another, he engenders a faint suspicion that even he, the mighty Mencken, sometimes falls from grace: "A certain sough of rhetoric may be here. Perhaps I yield to words as a chautauqua lecturer yields to them belaboring and fermenting the hinds with his Message from New Jerusalem" (*Prejudices: Third Series*). And then one encounters in his pages little personal asides generally in a vein of jocular self-depreciation, from which Mr. Mencken emerges as the plain blunt man, claiming brotherhood with emancipated and sophisticated souls. "Consider my own case," he begins, slapping his reader on the back; and there follows a sort of when-good-fellows-get-together appeal. Of course the reader is flattered to learn that Mencken, whom the *Encyclopedia Britannica* hails as "the greatest critical force in America," is no obscene rhetorical highbrow, but an ingratiating fellow, weighing one hundred and eighty pounds, able to toss off a stiff dram "of ethyl alcohol in dilute aqueous solution" with "a liver far beyond pills and prayer," and the author of *The American Language*, "a very modest work." In sooth Shakespeare's Marc Antony come to life!

V

That Mr. Mencken is a brillant and provocative rhetorician of the bellicose type is beyond cavil. The accusation most often brought against him is that he lacks the greatest of all persuasives which buttress the art of the rhetorician—character and conscience. His fondness for buffoonery, for instance, leads him into excesses which are in bad taste and which create the impression that he is a playboy. And yet there is method in his madness. He is no fastidious recluse with a select clientele like Paul Elmer More but a popular debater who peddles his wares in the public marts, "where merchants most do congregate." In order to get a hearing at all he must stage a good show, which he does "sometimes with a bladder on a string, usually with a meat-ax." We may not approve his methods but we must admire his zeal and frankness. He confesses that he tries to force people to read him "by mountebankish devices," and he complains that frequently his readers take his "idle jocosities with complete seriousness."

His destructive fury which at times suggests the bull in the china shop is another reason why he repels many readers who, even when they do not question his sincerity, are convinced that he is irresponsible and unreliable. It is a mistake, however, to take his Prussian "frightfulness" at face value. He is like a marksman who, in order to hit his target, overshoots it. At any rate he functions on the principle that in America, the land of extravagance, it is only by extravagant satire that a social critic of his type can make any impression at all. And then it cannot be forgotten that the bulk of his destructive criticism is directed against stupidity and hypocrisy. Is his healthy hatred of twaddle and buncombe to count for naught? Does he accomplish nothing when he attacks impostures in high places and in low? Is he an enemy of the people when he drags ugly things into the open? The plain truth is that he strikes a responsive chord when he writes: "Every normal man must be tempted, at times, to spit on his hands, hoist the black flag, and begin slitting throats." His following, which grows more formidable every day, is explicable only on the supposition that a large number of his readers who do not swallow him whole agree with him on many points. In fact he is so often on the side of the angels that it is simply impossible to dismiss him with the contemptuous label of destructive critic. . . .

4: *Reputation in Decline, Reputation Recovered, 1930–1956*

[Review of *Treatise on the Gods*] Reinhold Niebuhr*

A book on religion by Mr. Mencken was inevitable. It is difficult to hold a variety of prejudices and opinions upon a subject without finally classifying and arranging them and bringing to their support such scholarship as seems necessary to give them dignity and prestige. Mr. Mencken has long had his opinions about religion. It now appears that he has also engaged in considerable research in the history of religions, though it may be questioned whether his diligence or insight justifies his not too modest judgment upon himself: "I am myself a theologian of considerable gifts."

It goes without saying that this treatise on the gods is interesting reading. The description of the fortuitous emergence of the first priest, an adventurous soul in some primitive tribe, who stopped a flood by spanking the waters in anger, and by his accidental success achieved the prestige of a magic worker among his fellows, is real literature. So also is the final chapter in which the author forgets his sneers to praise the "lush poetry" of the Bible. In between there is a great deal of vigorous writing, but it hardly deserves the extravagant praise which eager devotees have given it, except one regards the use of the bludgeon as the mark of great literature. It is vigorous writing, of course, in the same sense that Martin Luther's fulminations against the Pope were vigorous. The gleam of fanaticism is in Mr. Mencken's eye while he inveighs against the bigotry of the priests and the stupidity of their followers. It is only when dealing with moral and social issues that he achieves the heights of complete detachment, and in this case the detachment is that of the cynic rather than that of the scientist.

The main thesis of the treatise is that religion is magic. Religion is interested in bending the mysteries of the world to human ends. Whatever of ethical or aesthetic characteristics have developed in the life of religion are merely accretions and are not to be treated too seriously. Such a thesis covers a very considerable portion of primitive religion and an only slightly less considerable portion of the religion of the average religious person of this era. But it does not cover all of the facts of either this or the primitive

*From the *Atlantic Monthly* 145 (June 1930): 18. Reprinted by permission of Mrs. Ursula Niebuhr.

day. In his study of primitive religions Professor Bronislaw Malinowski makes an interesting distinction between the early religious magic and the religious rite, which Mr. Mencken would have done well to consider. The appreciative attitude toward the beneficent mysteries of the world and of life revealed in the primitive religious rite is the seed out of which has flowered the whole side of religion which concerns itself, not with bending physical circumstances to the human will, but with the contemplation and appropriation of all the inner and outer beneficences of life as the grace of God. Mr. Mencken knows nothing about the mystics who were engaged in the business of transcending physical circumstances rather than in coercing them to conform to human purposes and whose cry of victory was that they knew "how to be abased and how to abound." Nor does he know anything about the long line of prophets whose ethical insights were nurtured in the religious experience and contributed mightily to the advancement of the race. To him all this is a closed book. The only qualification he makes on the rigor of his thesis is to regard the priest as something of a poet as well as magician on occasions.

All this does not help us much to analyze the complexities of religion and to "separate the precious from the vile," the ethical and spiritual from the magical in the religion of our day. It really tells us little more than how one fanatic feels about other fanatics of a different stripe.

Mr. Mencken Leaves the *Mercury*   Anonymous*

The retirement of Mr. Mencken from the editorship of the *American Mercury* may not mark an epoch in American literature but it has significance as one of the signs of the passing of a type of criticism which during the past decade has had a vogue disproportionate to its value. Mr. Mencken's scorn of the "booboisie" and his Rabelaisian laughter at the queer antics of the "Bible belt" have been his conspicuous contributions to the interpretation of American culture. His monthly exhibits of "Americana," for the most part culled from the provincial press, have constituted a continuing satire on the manners and customs of what he considered the benighted elements of the country—a satire unique in that it made the unlucky dogs tie the cans to their own tails. It was clever stuff, without a doubt. No one can do the sort of thing that Mr. Mencken does any better than he. But it is not the thing that most needs to be done at present. One had already begun to sense a disquieting untimeliness in these keen cynicisms which professed to be so absolutely timely. Their subject-matter was of today, but

*Reprinted by permission from the 18 October 1933 issue of the *Christian Century*.
© 1984 Christian Century Foundation.

their spirit was of yesterday. We are fed up with cynicism. "Oh yeah" has lost its charm. Criticism must pass into a somewhat more sober and disciplined mood to get a favorable hearing. We no longer relish being told that we are fools. We have heard it often enough, and have admitted it. To continue rubbing it in seems scarcely good sportsmanship; in any case it is not good journalism. Perhaps the *American Mercury* will lead in a new direction, as it has so competently though often exasperatingly led in the old, or perhaps it will just cease to lead. Whichever happens, Mencken's abandonment of his post as the mentor of American mores is symptomatic of a change in the American mood.

A Philological Romance [Review of *The American Language,* 4th edition]
J. B. Dudek*

This new edition of Mr. Mencken's magnum opus is a phenomenal achievement. To call it an "edition" is misleading. Not only has the book been thoroughly revised, rearranged, corrected, and brought up to date, but, saving a few passages, it has been so completely rewritten and so much new material has been added—the present volume is double the size of its immediate predecessor—that, excepting the title and the author's name, it is an entirely new work. Here we have a scholarly discussion, in 325,000 words, of the development of English in the United States, but so diverting a piece of writing withal that, from preface to index (of course there is an index!), one is scarcely aware that it is a scientific treatise of the first order. A bulky volume of 800 pages plus, which no one perhaps will set out to read seriatim, it nevertheless tempts the reader who opens it timorously to skip joyfully from one charming page to another. He encounters adventure, romance, mystery. Finally he is spellbound, and sitting up, away into the small hours of the night, reluctant to lay down this philological *Anthony Adverse* without seeing it through to the finish. The publisher's advance announcement recommended the book for the bedside. Prudently, nothing was said of it as a cure for insomnia, for in that capacity it would assuredly fail. Mr. Mencken is not a writer to be read half asleep. Lest any one be discouraged by a book obviously impossible to dispatch at one sitting, let it be observed here that each chapter is so complete in itself that it may be read independently. Thus, the book may be divided into convenient slices, which need not be taken in order.

The first edition of Mr. Mencken's *American Language* came out in

*From the *Saturday Review of Literature* 14 (16 May 1936): 10–11. Copyright 1936 *Saturday Review* magazine. Reprinted by permission.

March, 1919. Limited to 1,500 copies, it was almost immediately exhausted. A second edition, revised and enlarged, appeared in December
1921, and a third, again revised and enlarged, in February 1923. This last
has, heretofore, been the most familiar and popular. Although a relatively
expensive book, sales were steady and comparatively large, five reprintings
having been necessary. The work was published also in England, the first
British edition being, with a few minor changes, the same as the American
third; there is also a German translation, *Die Amerikanische Sprache*, by
Heinrich Spies (Berlin, 1927), much abbreviated, however, condensing in
less than 200 pages (including index) the American third which contained
over 400 pages of text, exclusive of a long bibliography and the index.

The formal bibliography is wisely omitted in the Fourth Edition, but
bibliographical references are given in abundant footnotes, frequently as interesting and witty as the text. Those who enjoy a hearty guffaw should by
no means miss the third footnote on page 498, or the one on page 501. The
latter has a Rabelaisian piquancy which, though never obtrusive, is not absent elsewhere throughout the book. The List of Words and Phrases, expanded to seventy three-column pages, is a veritable dictionary of 12,000
Americanisms, including the earliest Colonial loan words as well as juicy
examples of modern slang. Non-English words discussed in the text, especially in the Appendix, are not repeated in the word list, but the proper
names occurring in Chapter X are.

To quote from the author's preface, the reader familiar with former
editions will find that this one "not only presents a large amount of material
that was not available when they were written, but also modifies the thesis
that they set forth." When Mr. Mencken first started writing on the subject
in the Baltimore *Evening Sun* (1910),

> the American form of the English language was plainly departing from
> the parent stem and it seemed at least likely that the differences between
> American and English would go on increasing. But since 1923 the pull of
> American has become so powerful that it has begun to drag English with
> it, and in consequence some of the differences once visible have tended
> to disappear. The two forms of the language, of course, are still distinct
> . . . and when an Englishman and an American meet they continue to be
> conscious that each speaks a tongue that is far from identical with the
> tongue spoken by the other. But the Englishman, of late, has yielded so
> much to American example . . . that what he speaks promises to become,
> on some not too remote tomorrow, a kind of dialect of American, just as
> the language spoken by the American was once a dialect of English. The
> English writers who note this change lay it to the influence of the Ameri-
> can movies and talkies, but it seems to me there is also something more,
> and something deeper. The American people now constitute by far the
> largest fraction of the English-speaking race, and since the World War
> they have shown an increasing inclination to throw off their old subservi-
> ence to English precept and example. If only by force of numbers, they

are bound to exert a dominant influence upon the course of the common language hereafter.

This argument, supported by conclusive evidence, is elaborated in Chapter I, "The Two Streams of English." Here is a delightful serio-comic essay on the discussions provoked by early Americanisms, the fury with which English reviewers and American pedagogues attacked them, the American writers' sympathetic attitude toward the "barbarisms," and their encounters with the English critics, in which the Americans patently scored. Not the least amusing is a discussion of sporadic efforts made in this country to impose the "United States" language by law.

The second, a very brief chapter, entitled "The Materials of Inquiry," setting forth the essential characteristics of the new language and enumerating the categories of Americanisms established by past observers, is partly reprinted from the previous edition but still considerably revamped. The third and fourth chapters are a history of the development of American-English from the arrival of the first settlers up to and including the Civil War, but words borrowed from Indian tongues, from the Dutch, French and Spanish, are amply discussed, as also the fashioning of neologisms from English material. The period covered by Chapter IV was enormously fertile, and during it the language acquired most of its present distinguishing marks. The fifth chapter treats at length of word-formation processes now active. The sixth demonstrates the vast influence of American on parent English. It is here that Mr. Mencken most plausibly contends that the two languages remain definitely unlike, even in honorifics, euphemisms, *verboten* words, and expletives. Chapters VII and VIII deal admirably with American pronunciation and spelling, respectively, and in Chapter IX is the first formal grammar of the American vulgate ever essayed. Perhaps the finest chapter in the book is the tenth, "Proper Names in America." Surnames, given and place names receive hospitable attention, and there are startling revelations.

A book the size of Mr. Mencken's already formidable tome would not suffice for an adequate survey of American slang; but, within Chapter XI, he has compacted practically everything of permanent value to be extracted from the overwhelming, unstable mass of raw material that must be available. There is a section on the cant and argot of circus men, hoboes and other groups, including, *mirabile dictu,* pedagogues!

Chapter XII, "The Future of the Language," complements the opening chapter, and here Mr. Mencken becomes prophetic. The English language, he points out, is practically a world language; it still has sizeable competitors only in French and German. But, he says:

My own experience may be added for whatever it is worth. I have visited, since the World War, sixteen countries in Europe, five in Africa, three in Asia, and three in Latin-America, beside a large miscellany of islands, but I don't remember ever encountering a situation that English could not resolve.

He doubts that, as English spreads, it will be able to maintain its present (British) form; the foreigner must eventually make his choice between that and the American; but, despite differences, defects, and drawbacks, "English goes on conquering the world," and it is not difficult to predict which form is more apt to win.

The Appendix, on non-English dialects, is a book in itself. Not only is the speech of the larger foreign groups in America—Germans, Swedes, Jews, Greeks, Italians, Slavs—considered in detail, but that of Icelanders, Arabs, Chinamen, Japs, Armenians, and Hawaiians. Mr. Mencken has expanded to eighty-six pages a section which, in his third edition, filled but twenty-eight. Some knowledge of the various languages would be advantageous for an appreciation of this Appendix, but even the reader knowing only English (excuse me, American!) will chuckle over the disaster that has overtaken foreign tongues in the land of the free. Evidently, in linguistic matters there has been not only liberty but unbounded license. The setting up and proof-reading of this section must have driven more than one person insane, yet misprints are surprisingly few. Those discoverable will doubtless be corrected before the book is electrotyped. All in all, the volume is a magnificent piece of typography from the Plimpton Press.

It is hard to charge the learned author with mortal sins of commission, though Anglophiles, prudes, pedagogues, and purists will be prompt to tear him limb from limb. His main thesis will probably be denied *in toto*, but disproving it is quite another matter. As for sins of omission, every reader will think instantly of some pet word or phrase which Mr. Mencken should have included. This reviewer, for instance, searched vainly for the abomination "kiddie," which, for over fifteen years to his personal knowledge, has designated a child from the toddling age up to approaching puberty and has not yet died a richly deserved and horrible death. Even the noun "kid" is missing, though "kidding" is mentioned. "Kido," in the third edition, is omitted in this, probably as now obsolete. Among words overworked by the newspapers and at business men's luncheons, some of the "most outstanding," like "virtually," "group" (meaning anything from an insignificant sewing circle to the whole *corpus* of the R. C. Church), "visualize," and "alleged," are absent. After an "alleged" criminal has been sentenced to the electric chair, it seems the height of precaution and idiocy to keep on rehashing that he "allegedly" murdered the woman, an "alleged" underworld character, by strangulation after an "alleged" assault, etc., etc., when the possiblity of legal action against the publisher by the *dramatis personae* is exceedingly remote. Incidentally, there is no discussion of a hypothetical ukase compelling newspaper men to write, say, "Her head *virtually was* severed from her body," "U.S. *still is* neutral," "He *soon* is expected," or "*Almost it* is impossible," instead of constructions a normal person would use. There is the well known pedantry about the split infinitive, but what commandment forbids splitting a periphrastic tense?

But it is manifestly unfair to expect that Mr. Mencken should have included everything or that he should have made his book a mere lexicon. He sagely leaves that function to the compilers of "The Dictionary of American English on Historical Principles" now under way at the University of Chicago. Privately, I am informed that, for fear of scaring off readers, he rejected at least three times as much material, submitted to him by voluntary contributors, as he used. The job of judicious selection alone must have been a formidable one. Apparently, however, this penetrating observer, not only of the American but of the international scene, enjoyed his task hugely and his delight is infectious.

H. L. Mencken   Louis Kronenberger*

Mencken came in like a lion. Like a revolutionary, overthrowing half the props that supported America's conception of itself—and not merely its beliefs and moralities, but its peace of mind. His scathing mockery of those who made our laws, our culture and our social sanctions electrified an age that had few pioneers, and no pioneer save Mencken with a loud voice. College professors, shocked at his view of life in general and insulted by his view of themselves, virtually regarded him as Antichrist. Women's clubs put off discussing him from year to year. Right-thinking business men disposed of him as a Bolshevik. But the War had produced a whole new generation, out of joint with the old traditions and hostile toward them, who were stirred by Mencken's rhetoric and ideas, and who were eager to be infected with his laughter. It suited their temper to learn from him that all our sacred cows were incredibly stupid and clumsy field beasts; to learn, for that matter, that despite what they had been taught in the past, nothing was sacred.

For a few years after 1918, when Mencken's influence was waxing or at its height, America was intellectually in a disobedient mood. Cheated in the War of actual scars, she managed to acquire a very convincing case of shell-shock and St. Vitus' dance, to want new and quick sensations, to practise exhibitionism under the name of defiance, and to visit death upon the timid, genteel and sanctimonious values that so long had kept her dead. Truth might be hard to reveal, but cant was easy to expose; adjustment might be hard to come by, but repressions were easy to throw off. There was much talk and some show of liberalism, but certainly the commoner phrase and the commoner aspiration was to be "emancipated." The fraudu-

*From the *New Republic* 88 (7 October 1936): 243–45.

lent nature of the War, the sharp decline in religious faith, the advancement of science, the birth of psychoanalysis, the new experimentalism in
the arts, were at once the causes and the symptoms of this aspiration.
There was a small group, well informed, social-minded, political-minded,
who rationally absorbed these other ideas into an attitude that had its feet
on the ground and an eye to the future. But for many others, most of them
immature, these ideas were chiefly a pretext for escape, for asserting one's
independence and skepticism. For them the great problem was to be delivered at any cost from outworn dogmas.

Mencken lay to their hand, and they to Mencken's. He was not of the
liberal camp—a pooled enterprise resting on more or less common ideas
about life—but an "advanced" individualist, stemming loosely from individ-
ualists of a previous age. Among his forebears, Nietzsche was that kind of
philosopher, Wagner that kind of composer, Shaw that kind of pamphleteer, Huneker that kind of critic. These men were not so much rebellious
of the thinking of their day as subversive of it. They simply pushed out on
the offensive. In time each exerted much influence, for a personal idiom is
always more likely to exert influence than an impersonal ideology. Clearly
Mencken followed in their footsteps. He had a personal idiom unmatched
in his generation; it could be instantly felt; and coming at a moment when
individualism on its lower levels was the gospel of American life, it was
bound to command a hearing.

Mencken like the others took the offensive. For years culture in America had been standing still, corruption had been growing and criticism on
all fronts had been paralyzed by timidity and ignorance. But the War had
torn off a few masks, dislodged a few certainties, given doubt and skepticism an opening. Mencken proceeded to widen and enlarge that opening
enormously. Wilson's last days and Harding's brief ones, the fight over censorship, the advent of prohibition—any number of things strengthened his
cause. He launched a massive attack on everything this country held invio-
late, on most of what it held self-evident. He showed how our politics was
dominated by time-servers and demagogues, our religion by bigots, our
culture by puritans. He showed how the average citizen, both in himself
and in the way he let himself be pulled round by the nose, was a boob. He
burst out that the country was a desert of philistine vulgarity, and could
only be looked upon at all because it was so endlessly comic. Any progress
that might be attempted in the cities was blocked by envious blue-nosed
"peasants" on the farm. The high priests of culture—professors and academicians—were enemies of culture. Sex was defiled by the filthy-minded-
ness of prudes. It was impossible, Mencken insisted, for any sensitive or
civilized person to be a party to conditions so revolting; he could only laugh
at them and turn away.

The upshot of this unsparing diagnosis—which in theory constituted a
kind of wholesale muckraking—was not a general movement toward re-

form, but a special movement toward withdrawal. It fostered the cult of the civilized minority. In the thick of his blistering charges against American life in general, Mencken somehow contrived to make the individual reader feel exempt from the indictment, an *âme bien née* who belonged on the side of Mencken and the angels. Thus the situation, from the outset, was ironical. Mencken, exposing the ghastly inadequacies of all matters of public interest, encouraged his readers to be too snobbish to give a damn about them. He insisted he could offer no remedy and was amused that he should be expected to. Those whom he influenced at once accepted his conclusions, turned their backs on the national plight and set up as a civilized minority.

Most of the literature of the day moved in the same direction. It came in two forms, each of them congenial to Mencken's teachings: satire at the expense of a stunted America, and a tony skepticism that considered life in the raw intolerable, and life in general comic. This second style of writing, as refined by the watered esthetics of Cabell, Hergesheimer, Van Vechten, Frances Newman and others, soon became mere snobbism. The first, though often in the Mencken spirit, yet had a more serious effect upon our cultural life because it was sometimes launched with more sense of protest than Mencken would have approved of. Sinclair Lewis, for example, fought now and then where Mencken never did more than egg on. But in general the satire was something to smile over to the same extent that the skepticism was something to feel uppish about. In short, if most men will act like fools, let wise men be amused by their antics.

This concept, which is really the cornerstone of Mencken's thinking, is equally the index—for I shall no longer attempt to hide my bias—to his utter inadequacy. He approached his job with keen intelligence, a wealth of facts and a superb gift for communication. But he approached it without the seriousness of a true satirist, and was content that his findings should arouse an unreflective mirth. What he liked was the noise and fun of battle. That is all right in its place, gusto and audacity are great weapons; but a real satirist will of course go farther. Even if he cannot in honesty seek to convert people to a program, at least he will seek to convert them to the necessity of finding one: to make them feel responsible, to make them care. Mencken did just the other thing. He sought to make them laugh, he labored to *épater le bourgeois*, he kidded the good along with the bad, he tried to find a common denominator of absurdity in virtually everything: finally his craving to say the unexpected wore down his integrity against saying the untrue. Charity relief, free education, the liberalism of younger college professors came in for the same pummeling as the worst antics of the vice-snoopers.

The tone, at length, became that of an unredeemed cynicism: the tone, not of a man who did not believe, but of a man who did not want to believe. "I have no remedy to offer," was uttered, not humbly, but smugly.

Now any man worth his salt who is bitten by skeptical pessimism must feel the double responsibility of his position—must see that the more life darkens, the more imperative becomes the search for light. So a Matthew Arnold, seeking to combat in his generation many of the abuses that Mencken railed against half a century later, sweated after a solution and, forlornly pinning his hopes on Culture, drove furiously. He may have seemed a little ridiculous at times, but he never seemed cheap. Mencken, on the other hand, was no more an honest skeptic than he was an honest satirist. *Que sçais-je?* stands at the very opposite pole to the gaudy knowingness that has crept more and more into Mencken's manner. He has taken the Easiest Way of the philosopher, the least responsible way of the citizen. "If I am convinced of anything," he said in 1927, "it is that Doing Good is in bad taste." Just so Hergesheimer held that giving money to starving children in Europe was "one of the least engaging ways in which money could be spent" (if we can trust a story repeated in Emily Clark's *Innocence Abroad*); just so Cabell said, "I burn with generous indignation over this world's pigheadedness and injustice at no time whatever."

Mencken, far from leading America out of the wilderness, merely bade the elect, from some secure elevation, watch their less enlightened brethren wriggle and squirm. Nor was their security rooted in laughter alone; it was the security of the good years, of mirth begotten by prosperity, when Mencken's verbal antics stood out boldly, and his toryism did not. For in these days of our democratic inflation, his un-American brand of reaction, his own version of Nietzsche, seemed just one more instance of his striving to be perverse, of his insistence upon being different. Indeed if he seemed then Tory at all, he seemed—in Max Beerbohm's phrase—like a Tory anarchist. But Mencken's toryism never really was, and now nowhere seems, playful. He was perhaps most in earnest when he went to work against three-fourths of the ideas that all progressive systems would deem self-evident and share in common; perhaps most in earnest when, snorting at ignorant Red-baiting, he indulged in a subtler Red-baiting of his own. In a dozen books you could hardly hope to achieve what Mencken achieved merely by reiterating the phrase "poor old Debs." Goebbels couldn't improve on his description of Marx as "a philosopher out of the gutter."

Consider briefly a few manifestations of Mencken as a reactionary—and not merely as a political reactionary. In the space of twenty pages of *Prejudices: Fifth Series* he comes out against birth control ("I believe that the ignorant should be permitted to spawn *ad libitum* that there may be a steady supply of slaves"); in defense of capital punishment; in favor of war. Elsewhere he opposes circulating the theory that crime is mostly pathology; endlessly he jeers at education; endlessly he extols the Junker system. Nor does a lifetime of ridiculing the stand-patters in art cancel out the fact that in practice Mencken much oftener ridicules novelty of expression than he endorses it. Plainly enough (and almost as plainly then as now), most of the artistic isms and movements of his day were showy frauds, and he reached the right verdict about them; but always in Mencken there was a predisposition to annihilate them on principle, and he saw no difference at all between the gifted early Stravinsky and somebody who composed a to-ne-poem for frigidaires. He simply hid a conservative's taste under a fire-brand's vocabulary.

It was in his popularizing of a few cardinal ideas—the farcical aspects of democracy, the loutish intolerance of the "peasantry," the folly of being contaminated by the mob, the vast quackery in American life—that Mencken exerted his strongest influence; for at length there was scarcely a literate man in America who was unaware of the bold top line of Mencken's oculist-chart. But it was more precisely in his comment on books and the intellectual scene that Mencken helped to govern the American mind. The literary essays in *A Book of Prefaces* and the earlier volumes of *Prejudices*, the editorials and book reviews in *The Smart Set* and the earlier issues of *The American Mercury*, proved formidable instruments—probably the most formidable of their day—in creating literary trends and reputations. If the lower-browed Phelps could help sell a quarter-million *If Winter Comes*, the tougher-minded Mencken could help sell as many *Babbitts*. Al-most unaided, Mencken first set the Middle Western school of fiction on its feet. Doubtless an Anderson or a Hecht would have found his market anyway, but except for Mencken I doubt whether a Ruth Suckow or a G. D. Eaton would ever have been heard of. He was of immense value also in promoting the careers of men like Hergesheimer and Cabell, writers who, using a different idiom from Mencken's, yet preached a similar view of life. Both schools that he espoused came in for a profitable run; both are bankrupt to-day; neither one produced any writer of first-rate talent. Sin-clair Lewis and the less classifiable Scott Fitzgerald were by far Mencken's best bets among the writers coming up in his prime—for his praise of Lard-ner came belatedly; and among Americans of an earlier day Dreiser is per-haps the only one whom Mencken was right about and whose career he helped to establish.

Mencken's most valuable single contribution to American criticism was his fight to purge our literature of its puritanism and gentility. By jumping on the bodies of timid critics and timid novelists alike, by discrediting their flabby values and bloodless evasions, he more than any other man opened up pioneer spaces, and enabled us, at least technically, to come of age. Sex ceased to be a bugaboo, squalor a tabu, decorum a virtue, iconoclasm a subversion of ethics. So far, so good. Where Mencken fell down, however, was in lacking an esthetic judgment to match his common sense. A very good pamphleteer, he turned out to be a very bad critic. Once he got into the temple of art, he seemed no better than an adventurer. He drummed up bad novelists and shouted good ones down. He called Robert Frost "a Whittier without the whiskers" and proceeded forthwith to exalt John Mc-

Clure and Lizette Woodworth Reese. For poetry, of course, he notoriously had no genuine feeling at all. He is a fairly good amateur critic of music, though when he makes such statements as that the "Egmont" Overture is an aphrodisiac, one can only look blank. Quite possibly his best criticism lies in scattered remarks about men's religious, philosophical and scientific beliefs, where he is often searching and alert. But in the end we are confronted by someone who, though he touched on almost all topics in a critical spirit, was of no real consequence as a critic.

His importance, on the serious side, lies—as I have hinted—in his ability as a pamphleteer. He shattered many weak-kneed idols; he crushed the drowsy venom out of many serpents still trying to hiss in the late afternoon; he railed against thou-shalt-nots that did not make sense; he gave us some idea of how often we could be duped and fooled. If he had no true sense of the profound, he had an unfailing sense of the absurd, and that had its serious value in the pamphleteer. To the role of comedian he brought great gifts. He had an eye not only for marking out stray instances of the fatuous, but also for playing one instance against another, for shaping them into patterns, for giving them true reach and breadth. He was one of the best phrase-makers, both journalistic and literary, of his generation; and he had at his command a preternaturally bold and vivid style. His prose reveals an absolutely personal idiom. Mencken had manner and will be read for his manner, at least in small draughts, a fair while after his content has gone into the rubbish heap. His style has drawbacks, of course— the greatest being that, as somebody said of Macaulay's, it is a style in which it is impossible to tell the truth.

For, like all men too fond of shocking, too intent on making a point, too desirous of seeming original, Mencken indulged in much disingenuous thinking, much cleverness; and these blemishes remain blemishes quite apart from the abuse he made of his cynicism, the sly weapon he made of his conservatism. To bring Mencken up to date is only to say that most of his virtues have declined and that all of his faults have increased. The critic in him touched the low of a lifetime when, a year and a half ago, he published his shabby and unscrupulous essay on the proletarian school of novelists; the Tory in him went farthest right when, very recently, he published his cheap word-juggling on Roosevelt and the New Deal. In each instance the attack was not levied on valid grounds in a critical spirit, but was hurled on extrinsic grounds with a demagogue's appeal to mob psychology. We can hardly hope to find Mencken turning over new soil of any kind in the future. He has come to a dead halt both in ideas and in curiosity. He will fall back, I think, with narrower and narrower gauge, upon the assumptions that have always fathered his thinking. These are assumptions that have long fathered the thinking, not of our best philosophers, but of the secure and the complacent, those who when Rome burns can escape to their villas at Baiae. But even the Baiaes of this world are not made of asbestos.

[Review of *Happy Days*]   Hamilton Owens*

Mr. Mencken was born on Defenders Day, 1880, so that his extremely personal story of the first twelve years of his life is, to a full half of us, very recent history indeed. If we consider his book as the story of an aspect of Baltimore city and its environs, which to a large extent it is, then it is a story very familiar and dear to many of us. The streets and alleys of the town in which we grew up, the cobble-stones and the grass which grew between them, the horse cars, the parks and squares, the policemen, the street games, the picnics, the corner grocers and their wares, the cooks and the candies—all these remembered details emerge with such vividness that they provoke at times an almost unendurable nostalgia.

But though Mr. Mencken professes to regard himself as a normal boy, in a normal family, indulging in normal pastimes and getting normal pleasures from these pastimes, it is very clear to the reader, after a few pages, that from the very beginning this product of a Baltimore family was seeing more clearly and judging more exactly even in those early days than most of us were able to do. It wasn't only that he had a good time,—he knew he was having a good time and he knew why he was having a good time. If this had not been true, if he had not at that early age seen life as a pattern, he could not have remembered so much of its detail nor have been able in after years to set that detail down in its proper perspective.

The plain truth is that the author of this book and of so much other writing which has by turns infuriated and delighted his fellow citizens has been, for all his pretense, a sensitive individual with a highly developed power of selection (i.e. an artist) from the very beginning. Reading these pages, superficially so artless and so casual, one reaches the conclusion that even in his infancy Mr. Mencken was not only living his normal life, but that already he was making mental notes on it as possible literary material; that indeed, he chose to live the sort of life which would make the sort of autobiography he intended to write. It is almost as if he had foreseen the later phenomenon which is called proletarian literature and had determined to prove, in his own existence, its falsity, or at least its lack of universality. His own childhood, he insists, had no psychological, sociological or politico-economic significance. It was placid, secure, uneventful and happy. "We were encapsulated in affection," he writes, "and kept fat, saucy and contented." So, I suspect, were most American children at that time, and before and since, even though in these later days at some occasional cost to the taxpayer.

Obviously, the man who doesn't blame his parents or his times or his environment for his shortcomings is either an unusual man or else a peculiarly honest one. Mr. Mencken seems to be both.

*From *Maryland Historical Magazine* 35 (March 1940): 81–82. Reprinted by permission of the *Maryland Historical Magazine*.

[Review of *Newspaper Days*]   Hamilton Owens*

Mr. Mencken's book has already been widely discussed. It is, as most bookish people know, the second volume of his reminiscences. The first, *Happy Days*, . . . took the author through his childhood. The present volume, as its title implies, describes the beginning of his professional career on the old Baltimore *Herald*.

The thing to remember in reading the recollections of a man like Mencken is that he is, by temperament as well as by conviction, both artist and honest man, an almost impossible combination. He is determined, to tell the truth and at the same time make his tale of the moment an artistic whole. Occasionally, the artistic urge gets the better of him and he is guilty of what he calls "stretchers." The book does not suffer thereby.

This *caveat* entered, *Newspaper Days* can be considered for what it is: a remarkable man's delight in his exploits and escapades in the period in which the sap of man runs fastest. It is Baltimoreana, of course. But it is Baltimore as seen through the eyes of a youth who had every day more energy, physical and mental, than most of us can command on our best days. Also, and especially, it is Baltimore uncorseted, as young reporters mostly see it. Here are the police courts, the politics, the saloons; the murderers and their hangings; the prostitutes in their leisure hours and the judges in their cups; the petty rivalries of newspapers; the appalling ignorance of the principles of their own profession on the part of some of the practitioners of the journalist's art.

All these things are in it and many more. But none is more important than the occasional glimpses the author gives into the workings of his own mind at this impressionable period. For it was precisely at this juncture, when the raucous youth was, by his own account, giving most of his attention and no little of his adoration to men whose claim to fame was that they could drink more beer than other men, that the same young man was establishing his taste for what he calls "beautiful letters" and formulating those esthetic criteria which made him, fifteen years later, the acknowledged dictator of American fiction. The relationship here is so subtle that analysis of it is beyond me. But I suspect it is precisely because Mencken did see the seamy side of American urban life and was entertained by it instead of being shocked by it that he was able to evoke and direct the literature describing it.

. . . . Mencken always had an appreciation, of a sort, for the countryside, as a number of charming passages in *Happy Days* testified. But the man is essentially urban. His need to see things growing and help them grow can be satisfied within the limits of a Baltimore back yard. His solace is not nature but the company of his fellows. His best moments, as all his

*From *Maryland Historical Magazine* 36 (December 1941): 444–45. Reprinted by permission of the *Maryland Historical Magazine*.

writings attest, are those spent in a *bierstube* with a companion on the other side of the table as immune to illusion as himself. . . .

Linguistic Patriot [Review of *The American Language: Supplement I*]   Harold Whitehall*

The last few months have given us several works of popular linguistic importance. First came the Hogben-Bodmer *Loom of Language;* then, Joseph Shipley's *Dictionary of Word Origins* cheek by jowl with G. [R.] Stewart's *[Names] on the Land*. Now comes the long-expected Mencken volume—by intention, the first of two supplements to *The American Language* (4th edition), but actually a book to be read in its own right and on its own merits. Such is the intrinsic interest of the subject that even the dullest philological drudge cannot make words uninteresting. But Mencken is the first American writer since Sapir to make them dramatic.

Mencken's general position on language has been clear ever since the first edition of *The American Language* in 1919. He was (and in a nobler sense still is) a linguistic patriot, imbued with the spirit if not the smugness that prompted John Adams to propose his American Academy for Refining, Improving, and Ascertaining the English Language. His linguistic studies began in the exploitation of one of his well-known series of *Prejudices*—as it happens, the most far-reaching prejudice of them all. But Mencken has grown, as anyone having to do with language in an honest way inevitably grows. In the beginning, he was a brilliant amateur, with an amateur's enthusiasms and style, but also with an amateur's technical limitations. As *The American Language* passed through its various editions, the amateurishness, and some of the vehemence, was dissipated. In this book, little is left of earlier attitudes but the unchanged point-of-view which organizes it and the Mencken style, still pungent, still vigorous, and still clean. In all important respects, Mencken is now as professional as a post-doctoral research fellow at Harvard.

There is something quietly ironical about this personal transition of Mencken's. Above all else, this Supplement One is a superb example of compilative and organizational scholarship by one who, in the none too distant past, affected to gibe at scholars if not at scholarship. If, as Sapir used to say, the core of linguistics is careful bookkeeping, then Mencken ranks among the greatest linguists of our time. But, more important than that, he is a writer, and among linguists, writers, or even moderately gifted pedagogues, are rarer than hen's teeth. T. E. Lawrence once alleged to Marshal Foch that soldiers ought to be professionals; generals, amateurs. Even

*From the *Kenyon Review* 8 (Winter 1946): 156–60. Reprinted by permission of the *Kenyon Review* and the author.

more certainly, the professional linguists need to be marshaled by someone like Mencken. As one of those same professionals, I am more than satisfied with his generalship.

The book falls structurally into five parts: (1) The Two Streams of English, (2) The Beginnings of American, (3) The Period of Growth, (4) The Language of Today, and (5) American and English. Considering its subject-matter, it should be regarded less as a sober treatise than a drama in five acts, in which the American David, derided by the British Goliath in the first, achieves stature through two, three, and four, and overcomes the Philistine in the fifth. Like Nathan, Mencken is nothing if not naturally dramatic, and his scenario loses nothing from being so obviously founded on fact. It is fact that British observers, most of them linguistic ignoramuses, criticized and (to use the word they scorned) belittled the nascent American language. It is fact that linguistic traitors abounded within the American camp, that Anglomania attempted what British criticism had failed to achieve, that a deal of prissiness and stuffiness on both sides of the Atlantic obscured the plain truth that a new English was awaking. It is indisputable fact that American English, long ago come of age, has already captured the outer bastions, if not the central keep, of British English tradition. Yet, after all, drama is mimesis, and selective mimesis at that. It cannot hurt, it might even amplify, Mencken's case, to examine one or two aspects of this *mythos*.

The rococo English world of the late 17th and early 18th Centuries was convinced that English had finally crystallized into hard-won perfection. Men like Swift, Nathanael Bailey, and Pope took it for granted, and, like the frenetic Elizabethans under threat of Puritanism, prized it more highly in that it might soon be lost—in this case to a tasteless bourgeoisie. Samuel Johnson, with his usual practical sense, set himself to record the perfection before it was too late; and the result was his *Dictionary* of 1755. Authoritarianism, particularly linguistic authoritarianism, is at best unlovely, but we must give this particular devil his due. Even the prescriptive (and restrictive) grammars of Bishop Lowth and his imitators, aimed primarily at the credulities and pocketbooks of the parvenu middle classes, had in one sense a nobler aim: they attempted to uphold the perfection of Augustan English in a period which had already lost it. Only against this background can the villains in the first part of Mencken's piece be motivated. What Swift in 1702 and Johnson in 1755 had to say about the threatened "corruption" of English, was echoed, much more moderately, by Pickering in 1815:

> It is to be regretted that the reviewers have not pointed out *all* the instances which have come under their notice of our deviations from the *English* standard. This would have been doing an essential service to our literature, and have been the most effectual means of accomplishing what those scholars appear to have so much at heart—the preservation of the English language in its purity, wherever it is spoken.

Men like Pickering and Johnson, and men like Witherspoon, Gifford, Eddis, Cresswell, and Hamilton lived before the scientific study of language had penetrated, if it has ever penetrated, the popular consciousness. There were many fools among them, and some knaves. But it will weaken neither Mencken's scenario nor convictions if we realize that they were fighting, however mistakenly, for a CAUSE.

But devil's advocacy is a profession whose temptations I will not here resist. Nothing in Mencken's book is more illuminating than the section of the last part which anatomizes the differences between American and British English and demonstrates how the direction of linguistic exportation has reversed from east-to-west and is west-to-east. Mencken's two theses, that British English is less word-colorful than American and that American English is making great headway in England itself, are devastatingly complete in their documentation. Yet one wonders whether a list of Briticisms and Americanisms, and even the lively, well-informed discussion that accompanies them, can sufficiently indicate the root-differences between the American and British forms of the English language.

Written British English (and spoken Received Standard British) represents an attempt to achieve a national language as untouched as possible by regional peculiarities, an *Übersprache* poised as securely as possible over the welter of difficult and often mutually incomprehensible British dialects. Since the vast majority of Britons do not and never will speak this language, it is, in a sense, as far removed from the daily life of the average Englishman as Ciceronian Latin from that of a Roman fruitseller. It steadfastly turns its back on the colloquial and the dialectal merely because it is its function, as an instrument of communication, to be non-colloquial, non-dialectal—everyman's language, not anyman's. If we assume, as we must, that it loses a good deal of the spirit of rowdy life because of the empyrean in which it exists, we can underline, from another angle, Mencken's feeling that its inventive founts have dried up.

Yet there is another factor, not considered by Mencken nor, as far as I know, by anyone else. There seems to be a difference of actual stylistic spririt between written American and British English—a difference sufficiently evident, for instance, in a contrast of the *New York Times* or *Christian Science Monitor* with *The Manchester Guardian*. It is not merely a difference of vocabulary, but of the same language, with the same morphological and syntactical resources, being used in contrary ways for quite contrary ends. The best way I can express the difference is that American English functions more morphologically than British English, British English more syntactically than American English. Or, to use another angle of approach, that American English is *chromatic*, British English *achromatic*. In the most typical American writing, sentences seem to be constructs in which the key words function as isolated counters of expression even as they function as part of their syntactical *milieu*. For all that they are combined in a larger unit of expression, they are still sense-units themselves, and often colorful units at that. In British English, individual words, even the key words, seem to be far more submerged into the larger syntactical units of expression. The sense hovers over the whole phrase or sentence, not over the word, which, therefore, decreases in linguistic importance. In the best British writing, the medium itself is translucent, achromatic, self-effacing; one can forget that it exists. In poorer writing, it is merely grey and muddy. My overstatement of the case will not, I think, invalidate the kernel of truth it possesses. That kernel may go a long way towards explaining the superior word-color of American English, its penchant for verbal inventions, its often brilliant utilization of morphological resources, in short, its chromatism. It may also explain the obvious, and to Mencken quite deplorable, sterility of British English in precisely these virtues. Perhaps, after all, it is not the loss of spiritual adventurousness which makes the British verbally impoverished. If Roosevelt was American as a word-maker, is not Churchill typically British as a phrase-maker?

Mencken in Baltimore   Van Wyck Brooks*

In Gertrude Stein's Baltimore, where Henry L. Mencken was a newspaperman, few readers had ever heard of the story *Melanctha* or those other stories about Lena and Anna, the German servant-girls who had also lived in the city where Poe lay buried. In fact, few readers anywhere knew Gertrude Stein in 1910, or Veblen, or Ellen Glasgow, or Theodore Dreiser. The reigning American talents in fiction were Winston Churchill, Booth Tarkington, Richard Harding Davis and James Lane Allen, and most of the authors, already at work and emerging one by one, who interested readers later were still obscure. The playwrights of whom one heard were Augustus Thomas and Clyde Fitch, while the splenetic Paul Elmer More spoke in a measure for a circle of critics who were generally indifferent or hostile to the march of mind. On a lower level but still esteemed by a legion of popularizers, Hamilton Wright Mabie discussed "great books" and "culture," —the last attenuation of the Anglo-American Goethean line by way of Emerson, Arnold and James Russell Lowell. This essayist perfectly fulfilled Leo Stein's characterization of the writing that is "like the running of water down hill," for, possessing no tension whatsoever, it followed the grooves of popular thought, purveying an easy sweetness and an easier light.

While the first shoots of a more vigorous epoch were appearing now on every side, the prevailing tone of the moment was complacent and dull, and a few critics were lamenting already the sterility of the literary scene

*From *The Confident Years: 1885–1915*. Copyright 1952 by Van Wyck Brooks; renewed © 1980 by Gladys Brooks. Reprinted by permission of the publisher, E. P. Dutton, Inc.

and the general flatness and tameness of American writers. John Curtis Underwood observed that Americans had become a machine-made people,
conventionalized, standardized, commercialized in all walks of life, and he
regretted with Percival Pollard that American writers wrote "down to the
public" rather than "up to the art of literature." Percival Pollard was always
asking, "What is wrong with American literature?"—in which one found
scarcely an "ounce of style,"—for so many writers seemed to be "content
with the easy and common phrase" and regarded their work quite simply
as merchandise. It was true that Pollard, in *Their Day in Court*, wrote
without any distinction himself,—both he and the "insurgent" Underwood
were commonplace in style; and Underwood was so far at sea that he
thought David Graham Phillips was a better writer than Henry James or
Howells. But if Percival Pollard, in his own work, did little to quicken the
scene, he delighted in audacity, wit and style in others, and, like Walter
Blackburn Harte, the author of *Meditations in Motley*, he praised Ambrose
Bierce as the "commanding figure" of the time. Like Harte, he wrote also
on Oscar Wilde and others of the "glorious middle nineties" when "savoury
pots were brewing," as Mencken said later, remembering how he had lain
in wait for the sprightly magazine in which Pollard had appeared with
James Huneker when he was a boy. Pollard had written *Masks and Minstrels of New Germany*, a subject that especially appealed to Mencken,
and, as one of the survivors, with Vance Thompson and Huneker, of *M'lle
New York*, he was a hero indeed for this Baltimore friend. He was "like a
truth-seeker in the Baptist college of cardinals," said Mencken who met
Ambrose Bierce through Pollard. But Huneker was the real enlivener for
Mencken as for others, all-curious lover that he was of half a dozen arts, for
his work was a running indictment of what he described as the "mean narrow spirit in our arts and letters." Almost as indifferent as Paul Elmer More
to living American writers and artists—for he was interested mainly in affairs of Europe,—Huneker made art seem, as Mencken said, a "magnificent adventure" and brought this spirit into American criticism. As
Mencken continued, "he was apt to go chasing after strange birds and so
miss seeing the elephants go by,"—he praised brilliantly coloured frauds,
overlooking real talents; but "when his soul went adventuring among
masterpieces . . . it went with vine-leaves in its hair."

Mencken, an offshoot of Huneker's circle with his own "assertive
clang," had been writing for Baltimore newspapers since 1899, and when
Pollard visited the town he planned with this half-German critic a joint
translation of a number of German poems. When Pollard died in Baltimore, Bierce appeared from Washington and he and Mencken were
thrown for a time together, two years before Bierce disappeared,—to "get
the smell of my country," as he said, "out of my nose and my clothing,"
—in Mexico. Bierce had toured the Civil War battlefields as if to retrieve
an experience in which he and the country had felt they were truly alive,
and his disgust with modern America and all things democratic was only

equalled by his hatred of "yokels" and "louts." For Bierce all reformers were "anarchists" and all farmers were "peasants," and much of his choleric thought and feeling drifted into Mencken's mind, which was predisposed to this home-made aristocratism. "Our one genuine wit," as Mencken called Bierce,—forgetting Oliver Wendell Holmes, who was ninety-nine times wittier and much besides,—undoubtedly influenced the man who was always girding at "peasants" and "hinds" and "the quacks who make laws at Washington." Mencken had something in common with Poe, who had also lived in Baltimore and detested the "rabble," the "canaille" and the "progress mongers," and he had found a philosophy in Nietzsche, the subject of his first important book,—the idol-smashing prophet of the "master-races." But Mencken's "boobus Americanus," the hero of an "Eden of clowns" which he also called "this glorious commonwealth of morons," together with his *Americana* and its national imbecilities were oddly reminiscent of the far less genial Bierce. His characterization of the American people as "that timorous, sniveling, poltroonish mob of serfs and goose-steppers" recalled *The Shadow on the Dial*. Mencken shared Bierce's peculiar cynicism.

Now Mencken had inherited, as he remarked, a "bias against the rabble" in his almost exclusively German Baltimore childhood, as the son of a German cigar-manufacturer who had married a German-American wife and who usually took him on Sundays to German beer-gardens. The family barber was a German too and so was the family farm-hand when the Menckens spent sufficient summers in the country to convince the boy that city life was "better," and Mencken had gone to a German school where they sang Geman *volkslieder* and the "pure American children" were regarded as "dunces." If Mencken was later inclined to regard most grown-up Americans as dunces too,—especially the "inferior" Anglo-Saxons,[1]—it was partly because of these impressions that he gathered as a boy, impressions that could scarcely have been dispelled when he briefly attended a Sunday school kept by the author of *What a Young Man Ought to Know*. He acquired early the bourgeois traits that made him a good citizen, methodical, the most orderly of mortals, never late for trains, who never failed to appear in time for dinner, one who respected punctuality and solvency in others and who spent his life in one house in Baltimore. People lost in New York, he said, the sense of "abiding relationships" and the lares and penates that one found in this half-Southern city; and he liked what he described as the Baltimore "tradition of sound and comfortable living." Expressed in terms of a prosperous German cigar-manufacturer's house, this presupposed a contempt for the poor, for the shiftless and for workingmen who did not know their place, the peculiarly German contempt indeed that filled the mind of Nietzsche who regarded them as mere draught-animals to be used as tools. That Mencken should have been drawn to Nietzsche and his notion of the slave-proletariat,—a notion that was alien to Americans,—was preordained, as much as that he should have been drawn to

Huneker if only as a lover of music who sketched for the piano ten or more sonatas. Mencken was a precocious composer of marches and waltzes. He was convinced, as a boy, for the rest, that life was essentially meaningless and that progress, democracy and religion were childish illusions, well summed up in the hullabaloo that amused him on street-corners when he stopped, looked and listened to the Salvation Army. Employed for a while in his father's factory, he went the rounds of cafés and saloons, taking orders for cigars and developing an epicure's palate; then, entering a newspaper-office, he became at eighteen a police reporter and was soon reviewing the theatre and music as well. He picked up the jargon and ways of thought of the city-room. When he came to compile his great work *The American Language,* Mencken was to know whereof he spoke.

Such was the "ruddy snub-nosed youth" with the "small-town roisterer's" air who called upon Theodore Dreiser in his New York office when this novelist, whom Mencken greatly admired, proposed him in 1908 as reviewer of books for the magazine *The Smart Set*. Dreiser had published in *The Delineator* some papers of Mencken's on medical themes and knew him as already a brilliant and forceful writer, one who suggested, in this personal encounter, "Anheuser's own brightest boy,"—as Dreiser said,— "out to see the town." Mencken had read *Sister Carrie* when it appeared in 1900, and Dreiser had impressed him as deeply even as Conrad; and this editor-in-chief of a Baltimore paper who was twenty-eight years old was in fact a voluminous writer in prose and in verse. It was true that Mencken had abandoned the verse in which he followed Kipling and some of the old French forms that were in vogue at the time, for he disliked all fanciful writing, he had no taste for fairy-tales and distrusted poetry as enervating and even as "nonsense." Mencken could see in *Alice in Wonderland* nothing but "feeble jocosity" and he had given up short-story writing, although he continued to write the burlesques that expressed his satirical feeling and his constant and ebullient sense of humour.

The satirical humorist in him had led him to devote his first book, —the first of all books on the subject,—to Bernard Shaw, though he had no sympathy with Shaw's socialistic doctrines; and meanwhile his discovery of *Huckleberry Finn,* which he reread every year, was the "most stupendous event," as he said, of his life. This led him further into the American language. On the whole, his positive mind delighted most in science, and, along with Macaulay, that "first-rate artist," T. H. Huxley was his model in style,—"the greatest virtuoso of plain English who has ever lived." But most of his intellectual gods, as he admitted, were German, from Beethoven to Hauptmann and Ibsen,—"more German than Norwegian,"—and especially Nietzsche, who formed his mind more perhaps than anyone else and whose style, as he put it, was "almost comparable to Huxley's."

In a world in which democracy seemed to be triumphing everywhere and socialism was rising in every country, Nietzsche had become a cult with those who shared Paul Elmer More's disgust with the "canting unreason of equality and brotherhood." More wrote a little book on Nietzsche and W. M. Salter a larger book,—by general agreement the best American study,—while Nietzsche or his ideas appeared in various American novels and a crop of little Nietzsches sprang up in New York. Among these were Benjamin de Casseres, who "danced with Nietzsche," as he said, describing himself as an "intellectual faun," whose "compass," as he also said, had a "thousand needles" and who was always "going in a thousand directions." *The Encounter,* Anne Douglas Sedgwick's novel, was based on Nietzsche's actual life, while Stanford West in *The Man of Promise,* the novel by Willard Huntington Wright, devoted himself to spreading the doctrines of Nietzsche. As an author, Stanford West proclaimed the ideas of the "dancing philosopher,"—which Wright expounded again in *What Nietzsche Taught,*—as Isadora Duncan proclaimed them in terms of her art. Jack London was one of many minds that were torn between Nietzsche and socialism, like the heroes of Max Eastman's *Venture* and Ernest Poole's *The Harbor,* both socialists who were diverted for a while by Nietzsche. Mencken's *The Philosophy of Friedrich Nietzsche,* a book that appeared in 1908, the year in which he began his reviewing for *The Smart Set,* was a lucid presentation of this new group of ideas that were to serve him as touchstones in his work as a critic. Had not Nietzsche regarded himself as a Polish grandee set down among German shopkeepers by an unkind fate? Just so Mencken saw himself as a sort of German Junker whose lot it was to live with American peasants. As Nietzsche had constantly pointed out "what the Germans lack," so Mencken set out to "transvalue" American values,—another Dionysus in a pallidly Apollonian world, a hierophant of idol-smashing and "natural selection."

Mencken's great days were yet to come in the Dionysian twenties, the post-war decade of orgies that recalled *The Bacchae* when writers impersonated the nymphs and satyrs who had formed the train of the god of wine, dancing to the din of flutes and cymbals. The revels of the "jazz age" were in tune with the ideas that Mencken had been spreading in *The Smart Set* since 1908, in his monthly articles reviewing books, in his *Americana* and in other writings including *In Defence of Women.* He was associated with that other Nietzschean Willard Huntington Wright,—the "S. S. Van Dine" of the future,—and with George Jean Nathan, the reviewer of plays, another heir of the Huneker circle,—cosmopolitan minds that were bent on destroying "tradition." The "intelligently emotional" George Jean Nathan,—to apply to himself a phrase of his own,—an opener of the windows of America to the breezes of Europe, was an active apostle of the modern theatre of Hauptmann, Sudermann, Maeterlinck, Ibsen, whom Huneker and Emma Goldman were popularizing. An alert detector of "hokum" himself and as cynical as Cabell, a cockney for whom the country was for "yokels and cows," with a mind as urban as Huneker's or Mencken's, he was wholly an aesthete, unlike Mencken, and indifferent to economics, politics and religion. Mencken, on the other hand, was more interested in these, and in medicine, anthropology, biology, than he was in art, and almost more than in literature, aside from fiction; and he directed his humorous-ferocious assaults at American life in virtually every aspect. At the outset of his career, he said, an ancient had advised him to make his criticism telling at any cost, to "knock somebody on the head every day" with a bladder on a string or, more usually, a "meat-axe." For the way to get rid of obstructive ideas was "not to walk softly before them but to attack them vigorously with clubs." So Mencken laid about him in a slashing style that was full of Nietzschean mannerisms.

Thus, with all the brasses sounding, the great Menckenian campaign began, like the coming of the circus in the springtime, with showers of epithets, attacks on democracy, the "universal murrain of Christendom," and shouts of defiance hurled at the "smuthounds" and the "shamans." According to Mencken, the United States was a "commonwealth of third-rate men" who were in full control of the state and the national standards,— Baptist mullahs scaring the peasantry, Methodist hinds of the "hookworm belt," theological buffoons and commercial brigands. The general average of intelligence, integrity and competence was so low that a man who knew his trade stood out as boldly as ever a wart stood out on a bald head, and the scene was a welter of knavery and swinishness, the operations of master rogues, the combats of demagogues, the pursuit of heretics and witches. It was the greatest show on earth, with Aimee MacPherson, for instance, "caressing the anthropoids with her lubricious coos," and with Orison Swett Marden as the national authority on the art of "getting on in the world as the only conceivable goal of human aspiration." Then there were the Elks and the undertakers who were initiated eighteen times and robed themselves to plant a fellow-joiner in garments that sparkled and flashed like the mouth of hell, who were entitled to bear seven swords, all jewelled, and hang their watch-chains with the busts of nine wild beasts. This race was as barbarous, Mencken said, as the Jugo-Slavs or the Mississippians with its "saccharine liberals," "right-thinkers" and "forward-lookers" and its professors, no longer from New England,—a region that he loved still less,—but now mostly from the land of "silos, revivals and saleratus." They "carried the smell of the dunghill into the academic groves." Nor could one forget the "uplifting vereins" and the countless American delusions and illusions, the notion that American literature was about to produce Walt Whitman's "new and greater literatus order" when it had no prodigies of the first class, few of the second and scarcely even more of the third or the fourth. This literature was colourless and inconsequential, timorously flaccid and amiably hollow, falteringly feeble and wanting in genuine gusto. It lacked salient personalities, intellectual audacity, aesthetic passion, it had an air of poverty and imitation, it evaded the serious problems of life and art; yet what was one to think of Paul Elmer More, who saw it as expiring with Longfellow and Donald G. Mitchell? More's "coroner's inquest criticism" infuriated Mencken, and he attacked the "crêpe-clad pundits, the bombastic word-mongers of the *Nation* school," although, like More, he too was an "incurable Tory." Was he not equally scornful of the "current sentimentalities," socialism, pacifism, deep-breathing and sex-hygiene? But, as he observed, Paul Elmer More preached the "gloomy gospel of tightness and restraint," while he was out to liberate and paganize the country. He seemed to agree with Nietzsche that "the one great intrinsic depravity" was the Christian religion, and his feeling that life, as he said, was "empty of significance" made it the more imperative to eat, drink and be merry.

Now there never could have been any doubt that Mencken played a decisive part in stabbing a flabby society wide awake, in shaking up the American spirit and rousing it out of its lethargy of optimistic fatuity and dull conventions. Mencken's astringent realism seared its adiposity, its provincial self-satisfaction and romantic moonshine, and, reintroducing acrimony into American criticism, he harrowed the ground for the literature and art of the future. As he said, all the benefits that he had ever got from critics had come from those who gave him a "hearty slating," for this led him to examine his ideas, shelve them when he found holes in them and set about hatching others that were better; and was he not right in saying that literature thrives best in an atmosphere of strife? Poe had introduced this three generations before at the dawn of the so-called American Renaissance, and what it really meant was that literary and aesthetic matters were felt to be worth the trouble of a *mêlée* and a combat. Mencken was hardly a literary critic, for his mind was devoid of the feminine traits this type must have in order to be effective. He was a social critic and a literary showman who had taken lessons from Macaulay, as well as from Nietzsche, Huneker and Bierce, and he fought with all his masculine force against the elements in American society that impeded the creative life and stifled its growth. A transatlantic Attila, with his own Teutonic fury, a coarse mind that had undertaken a literary spadesman's work, he accomplished a task that only a coarse mind could do. He was concerned with "numbers,"[2] the big Philistine public that blocked his way and that he attacked with his humour and his rude common sense,—the "Texas Taines," the "policemen of letters," the rural fundamentalists, the"Ku Klux Kritics" that battened in the solid South. In their fear of the new literature that he was fostering, the "cow-state John the Baptists" and their colleagues and supporters were as thoroughly American as the Knights of Pythias or chewing-gum, or Diamond Jim Brady, or Billy Sunday; and, defending what they called the sewage of the mental slums of Chicago and New York, he set the new realistic literature squarely on its feet. His campaign for Theodore Dreiser, a symbol of the rising Middle West, resulted in the general recognition of the other Western writers; and what did he not accomplish too in assaulting the "Sahara of the Bozart"[3] and insisting on a veritable Bismarckian *kulturkampf* there? It was largely thanks to Mencken that "Church" and "State" were separated there, in the sense in which these words meant much to writers,—the republic of letters shook off its clerical controls; and it was more than a coincidence that the birth of the new Southern literature followed the publication of Mencken's essay.[4]

It could scarcely have been questioned that the shifting of forces in American letters which led to the literary dominance of the West and the South,—that this striking phenomenon of the twenties owed much to Mencken, and long before the first world war he had roused the imagination of writers to a sense of the opportunities that America presented. For, along with his abuse, he conveyed a feeling of the 'prodigal and gorgeous life of the country,"—a "circus" to which he awoke each morning with the "eager unflagging expectation of a Sunday school superintendent touring the Paris peep-shows." It was this that kept Mencken at home when the "expatriates" were leaving the country, filling every ship with a groaning cargo, issuing, as he put it, "their successive calls to the corn-fed intelligentsia to flee the shambles." He answered only with a few academic "Hear, Hears" and remained on the dock himself, "wrapped in the flag," for he was happy in a land of grotesques where one could visit Scopes trials and camp-meetings at which preachers denounced the reading of books. He delighted in the "cow-town hell-robbers," the "whoopers and snorters" of prohibition, the pious pornomaniacs listening to radio jazz and stealthily rising and "shaking their fireproof legs," the hill-billy miracle-workers drinking poison and bitten by snakes and the "God-fearing professors laboriously striving to ram their dismal nonsense into the progeny of Babbitts." Mencken was a humorist, a more pungent successor of Artemus Ward, no longer the country showman but the man of the city, and he conveyed an infectious feeling of the spectacle of life in America as a monstrous county fair or museum of freaks. Then he had the pride of craftsmanship that betokened the genuine artist in words, and, "naturally monkish," for all his worldly cynicism, he had much, after all, in common with the professors. His work on *The American Language* showed this in time. He esteemed the man who devoted himself to a subject with hard diligence, the man who put poverty and a shelf of books above evenings of jazz or profiteering; and in all these and other ways he stimulated writers, especially those who appeared after the first world war. If, as he said, these younger writers had a "new-found elasticity," together with a "glowing delight in the spectacle before them,"—a vigorous naive self-consciousness and sense of aliveness,—it was partly owing to the influence of Mencken himself. He had seen an exhilarating prospect for American letters, as he put it in one of his essays, in the exhaustion of Europe.

Still later, after the jazz age passed, when he had become an institution, Mencken's limitations and faults were more generally apparent. It was evident that he had the vaguest of literary standards, that there were no fixed stars in his literary firmament such as sea-faring critics must have in order to sail. In music, with which he was more at home,—conventional as his taste there was, for he hated the "musical felonies" of Ravel and Stravinsky,—he never wavered in his devotion to the "lovely music of Haydn and Mozart" and even went so far as to call Beethoven "noble." This was a word he would never have connected with a writer, for he saw in Dante the "elaborate jocosity" of a satire on the "Christian hocus-pocus" and in *Romeo and Juliet* he found only "tinpot heroics." He called Greek tragedy an "unparalleled bore," he spoke of the "weakness for poetry" as "another hoary relic from the adolescence of the race," and, describing philosophy as "largely moonshine and windmusic," he referred to "metaphysics, which is to say, nonsense." He had no literary scale of values or he could scarcely have spoken of the "harsh Calvinistic fables of Hawthorne" or of Emerson as "an importer of stale German elixirs"; he could never have described Howells as a "placid conformist" because he was indifferent to the "surge of passion" or called Robert Frost a "Whittier without the whiskers." He was so undiscriminating that he spoke of Gertrude Atherton in the same breath with Sarah Orne Jewett, and "Prof. Dr. William James," when Mencken finished speaking of him, was virtually indistinguishable from Orison Swett Marden. He was apt enough when he referred to Veblen's "vast kitchen-midden of discordant and raucous polysyllables," but this did not exhaust the subject of the "geyser of pishposh" even in the matter of style, and his dispraise of American critics lost much of its convincingness when he praised the third-rate Austrian Leon Kellner. Then what was one to say of the absence in him of the sentiment of reverence and the "shudder of awe,"—"humanity's highest faculty," as Goethe called it,—the recognition of certain realities of a spiritual kind upon which all human values are ultimately based? That Mencken really lacked this one saw in his treatment of Bernard Shaw, his early master and one of his early heroes, who became for him the "Ulster Polonius" in 1914, nine years after Shaw had been the subject of his first prose book. Mencken retained so little respect for the man he had admired so much that he said it was Shaw's life-work to "announce the obvious in terms of the scandalous." Mencken remained a child in this region of feeling. He related in his *Heathen Days* how, at thirty-five, in Rome, he had dodged into a crowd of pilgrims who were to be received by the Pope, and, running the risk of detection, obtained the Pope's blessing,—like a village boy squirming under a circus tent.

Mencken once observed himself that his "essential trouble" was that he was "devoid of what are called spiritual gifts." This was an actual trouble indeed, for without these "gifts" one lacks the scale, in the literary and human spheres alike, by which one distinguishes the ephemeral and the small from the great. Mencken's realistic note was admirable and useful, as one saw in his book, for instance, *In Defence of Women,*—women as the logical practical sex, aesthetically responsible, wary, discreet, in distinction from the vainglorious sex to which he belonged. He was as shrewd as Benjamin Franklin there and in other books, the *Treatise on Right and Wrong* and the *Treatise on the Gods,*—in which he admitted the reality of a kind of "progress,"—but elsewhere his arid rationalism blended with a hedonism

that was quite without spirituality and completely fatalistic. It was this tendency of his that blossomed in the jazz age in which so many writers were
influenced by him, an age that also inherited the thinking of William Graham Sumner with his contempt for the idealism and "illusions" of the past.
That life no longer had a purpose was the belief of millions then for whom
the bootlegger became a national hero, and, while man was a "bad mon-
key" for many a scientific mind, others embraced the despair of Eliot's
"waste land." Shakespeare's man, "glorious in reason, infinite in faculty,"
had been dethroned, and Melville's "man noble and sparkling,"—where
now was he? He had been supplanted by Mencken's man, the "king dupe
of the cosmos," the "yokel *par excellence*," the "booby." Much of Mencken's
humour was based upon these denigrations of the "boob" man, "brother to
the lowly ass," whose pretensions he delighted in undoing, and his disdain
of democracy followed from this low view of human nature that struck the
note of the fiction of the nineteen-twenties. If he saw democracy as "the
art and science of running the circus from the monkey-cage," was it not
precisely because he saw men as monkeys and because their continued existence in the world was therefore so inconsequential that one had no reason to assure and facilitate it? Inevitably, from this point of view, philan-
thropy, socialism, pacifism, like the notion of educability, were
sentimental, while Mencken's opposition to birth-control was deadlier even
than his attacks on most of the other aspects of the democratic process. He
said the ignorant should be "permitted to spawn *ad libitum* that there may
be a steady supply of slaves." For the rest, he was convinced that the war
between the haves and the have-nots was an affair of "envy pure and
simple."

With all his reactionary cynicism, Mencken was a liberator who
opened paths for writers and made straight their way by turning many of
their obstacles into laughing-stocks, but his campaign against democracy
lost any glamour it might have had when Hitler murdered seven million
Poles and Jews. While much that Mencken said was true, the inevitable
answer was that all other forms of government had proved to be worse, that
democracy, as Whitman put it, was the only safe system; and, when virtually every thinking German was only too happy to escape to America, Mencken's assaults on the country lost much of their force. Time broke the
lance of the "literary uhlan," as the German-American societies had called
him, and the critic who had said, "Most of the men I respect are foreigners," ceased to be a spokesman for the "mongrel and inferior" Yankees. It
was almost forgotten that he had performed a major work of criticism in
giving the *coup de grâce* to the colonial tradition, while, by fully recogniz-
ing the new interracial point of view, he contributed to the nationalizing of
American letters. More than anyone else perhaps, Mencken broke the way
for writers who were descended from "foreign" stocks and who were not
yet assured of their place in the sun, and it was he who signalized Chicago
as a literary centre and praised the new writers who used the "American

language." Howells had long since welcomed George Ade and many another, but Mencken, who hailed Theodore Dreiser, was foremost in hailing
Ring Lardner and praising with discrimination writers of his type.[5]

As for the question of colonialism,—still a live issue in 1920,[6]—this was
soon to be settled, thanks partly to him; and perhaps it could have been
settled only by a critic of recent immigrant stock whose mind was entirely
detached from the English tradition. Mencken's solution of the question
was in certain ways unfortunate precisely because of this and all it implied,
but he performed an invaluable work in helping to establish the interracial
American literature of the future. Mencken had observed that the distrust
of Dreiser was very largely racial,—he was felt to be sinister because he
was not Anglo-Saxon; and it pleased him to point out how many of the new
novelists and poets might be regarded as sinister for the same reason. But,
he remarked, the "old easy domination of the 'Anglo-Saxon' " was rapidly
passing,[7]—the nation was becoming "transnational," as Randolph Bourne
put it,—and what was the use of attempting to restore, as Stuart P. Sherman wished to do, the Anglo-Saxon tradition in American letters?[8] Mencken
was right in saying that this was a "demand for supine conformity," for, in
fact, the *restoration* of this tradition was by no means the relevant or desirable thing. What was important was the *recognition* of it, the reëstablishing
of a living relation between the future and the past, the sense of which, for
a number of reasons, had been lost. Mencken was the last man to reëstab-
lish this relation, for, having not inherited knowledge of the American past,
he was even antagonistic to its main stream of feeling. He was "frankly
against the Anglo-Saxon," and this led to a confusion he shared with others,
especially during the first world war, when the issue of "colonialism" was
confounded with the issue of "England." One could never tell how far "pro-
German" American writers were opposed to colonialism because of this
hostility to England. But to fight to "throw off the yoke of England's intellectual despotism,"—in the melodramatic phrase of Mencken's friend
Wright,—to settle this age-old question was a service to the country; and
in order to exalt the new "foreign" strains in the American literary world it
was natural enough to depreciate the Anglo-Saxon. The trouble was that
Mencken carried this to impossible lengths, and he indulged in grotesque
misstatements regarding New England, especially, that a serious critic
should have been ashamed to utter. One wonders what the proud "founding fathers,"—or Governor Winthrop or William Byrd,—would have said
to his remark about the first English settlers, that they were "the botched
and unfit"; and what was anyone to say to his statement that "New England
has never shown the slightest sign of a genuine enthusiasm for ideas"? In
"Puritanism as a Literary Force," he said that the literature of the years
1831–1861,—the times of Emerson, Melville, Thoreau and Hawthorne,—
was the "work of women and admittedly second-rate men." It was by assertions of this kind that he "liquidated the American past," as certain of his
admirers praised him for doing, and this was anything but a service to the

country or its writers. But that one could impute these feats to him was a proof of the force of Mencken's mind, and one could leave the balance to be redressed by others.

Notes

1. "Whenever the Anglo-Saxon, whether of the English or of the American variety, comes into sharp conflict with men of other stocks, he tends to be worsted . . . That this inferiority is real must be obvious to any impartial observer."—Mencken, *Prejudices: Fourth Series* ("The American Tradition").

2. See, e.g., in his essay on Dreiser, in *A Book of Prefaces*, the page-long table of statistics of the representation of Dreiser's novels in all the large town libraries in the country.

3. "Nearly the whole of Europe could be lost in that stupendous region of fat farms, shoddy cities and paralyzed cerebrums . . . You will not find a single Southern poet above the rank of a neighbourhood rhymester. Once you have counted James Branch Cabell . . . you will not find a single Southern prose-writer who can actually write . . . In that Gargantuan paradise of the fourth-rate there is not a single picture-gallery worth going into, or a single orchestra capable of playing the nine symphonies of Beethoven . . . In all these fields the South is an awe-inspiring blank."—H. L. Mencken, *Prejudices: Second Series* ("The Sahara of the Bozart").

4. See Vachel Lindsay's comment on "Mencken . . the enemy with whom none of us agree" (in *Letters to A. J. Armstrong*): "A successful tour of Mencken through the South could be the beginning of a new Era for America, because it would set the pace for all the United States in free speech, the thing we abhor the most and the lack of which keeps us behind England all the time."

5. "What amused Mark [Twain] most profoundly was precisely whatever was most worthy of sober admiration—sound art, good manners, the aristocratic ideal—and he was typical of his time. The satirists of the present age, though they may be less accomplished workmen, are at all events more civilized men. What they make fun of is not what is dignified, or noble, or beautiful, but what is shoddy, and ignoble, and ugly."—Mencken, *Prejudices: Fourth Series*.

6. "The American social pusher keeps his eye on Mayfair; the literatus dreams of recognition by the London weeklies; the American don is lifted to bliss by the imprimatur of Oxford or Cambridge; even the American statesman knows how to cringe to Downing Street." —Mencken, *Prejudices: Second Series* (1920).

7. "The fact is too obvious that the old easy domination of the 'Anglo-Saxon' is passing, that he must be up and doing if he would fasten his notions upon the generations to come . . . I am frankly against him and believe, as I have often made known, that he is doomed—that his opponents will turn out, in the long run, to be better men than he is." —Mencken, *Prejudices: Fifth Series*.

8. Stuart P. Sherman was ill-advised,—as no doubt he recognized in time,—in his invidious characterization of the "audience" of Mencken. He said this audience consisted of "children whose parents or grandparents brought their copper kettles from Russia, tilled the soil of Hungary, taught the Mosaic law in Poland, cut Irish turf, ground optical glass in Germany, dispensed Bavarian beer or fished for mackerel in the Skagerrak." But here Sherman was describing the audience of every American writer of the future, and was this not written in the stars of the American past? An "Anglo-Saxon" critic was certainly "doomed," as Mencken would have said, unless he was aware of this and all it implied, and unless he was able to present his tradition as fitting the Americans of the future instead of expecting them to fit his tradition.

This Was Mencken:
An Appreciation
Joseph Wood Krutch*

Everywhere it will be said that the death of H. L. Mencken marks the end of an epoch. But perhaps it is no less true that it marks also the beginning of something—his reputation as a writer. Mencken was a spokesman, a symbol, an embodiment, and all the other things he has been called. But he was first of all a master of the written word and unless the world changes a great deal more than seems likely, that is the only thing which will count in the long run. Men are mentioned in textbooks because they were so right or so wrong and, sometimes, because they were so typical. But it is only because they were great writers that they are read.

Like many another such—like Shaw, for instance—he did everything he could to distract attention from the true character of his gift. On the one hand, he took up all sorts of causes, the less respectable the better, and engaged in all sorts of crusades against whatever was of good report. On the other hand, he identified himself with journalists, spoke contemptuously of what he called "beautiful letters" and violated all the canons of respectable literary taste by sprinkling his pages with outlandish words drawn sometimes from the gutter and frequently from the German—the latter being his favorite foreign tongue less, I suspect, because of his own German ancestry than because, unlike French, it was obviously not genteel. Music was the only art of which he spoke frequently with respect because only a negligible minority of his fellow countrymen respected it; beer was his hippocrene because it was neither elegant like wine nor solidly respectable like whiskey; and he loved to mix beer and music—as he did in the wonderful sketch in which he describes how he and his cronies got so befuddled in the course of their attempt to play all nine of Beethoven's symphonies between dark and dawn that they could never remember whether they finished or not—because under such circumstances not even Beethoven's music could be regarded as respectable. Finally, he built a very solid reputation as a scholar, even among the *gelehrten* whom he loved to ridicule, by a work designed to destroy the authority of all those rules of grammar, syntax and propriety which he himself never violated except with the deliberate artistry of which only a philologue would be capable.

Like Shaw again, Mencken developed a public role which he played so constantly that he may well have ceased himself to know in exactly what relation it stood to his original self. But he at least understood very well what was at any moment appropriate to that role and he had the toughness which enabled him to play it relentlessly even under circumstances which fatally tempt the weakly amiable to concessions. Once when an inoffensive young man asked for some corrections in a story Mencken had written I

*From the *Nation* 182 (11 February 1956): 109–10. Reprinted by permission of the *Nation*.

heard him dismissed with a gay but final, "Journalism is essentially inaccurate" and when, not too long after the First World War, he was about to make a tour of the South, he gave reporters a pronouncement beautifully calculated to constitute a double outrage: "No man over forty loves either his country or his wife." How inevitably a second-rate man would have thought this the proper occasion to say: "I am a Southerner myself."

It may even be that the paradoxes of his temperament and opinions are best resolved by the simple assumption that he took whatever side gave him the best opportunity to exercise his gift. When he maintained that he would rather live in the United States than in any other country in the world because nowhere else was a civilization so absurd, some took this to mean that he was a wicked man who loved to despise his fellows but it may have meant only (and understandably) that, as a certain kind of humorist, he naturally judged a culture by the material with which it provided him.

Those who saw Mencken at the Dayton anti-evolution trial understood this better, perhaps, than anyone else ever could. He was at the height of his popularity and this was a spectacle perfectly designed for his exploitation. Here was a monstrous absurdity which, unlike the monstrous absurdities of our own day, was merely absurd—uncontaminated, that is to say, by anything essentially evil. Mencken was like a schoolboy at a circus. Beaming with sheer delight, unable to believe that anything so like one of his own extravaganzas could really be taking place, he was everywhere at once, hobnobbing with street-corner preachers, charming the rustics with his affability and falling off his chair in the court room when overcome by joy. He was at the moment the happiest man in the United States, for he was not only a boy at a circus, he was also a great writer who sensed that he had his opportunity and he took it to produce what has often been called his masterpiece—his "In Memoriam: W. J. B."—though it did not become fully possible until Bryan died a few days after his declaration on the witness stand that man is not a mammal.

Many of Mencken's admirers were distressed by the attitude which he took in the thirties and forties toward Franklin D. Roosevelt and all other idealists in public life. Perhaps it would not be unfair to say that he continued to see only the absurdity of a world which had become grim and that he refused to acknowledge the existence of problems he was temperamentally incapable of facing.

Certainly it is true that his importance as a spokesman and his popularity with large masses declined as the atmosphere of the world changed. Every literate college boy read him in the twenties, relatively few read him in the forties. His disciples had once been measured by the millions, their numbers shrank into insignificance. And yet, at least when he turned from the questions of the day, he wrote as well if not better than he had ever written before. Not even the Bryan piece is more masterly or more flavorsome than some of the rich happy absurdities in the volumes of reminiscence where such sketches as that about the Italian bands which used to play in Baltimore are in the great picaresque tradition of Rabelais and Smollett.

To mar the portrait which he drew of himself by saying that he was a scholarly and, in certain respects at least, a kindly man is almost a betrayal. But there is no doubt about either the laboriousness of his scholarly work or about the genuineness of his enthusiasm for "beautiful letters." It may very well be that the *Smart Set* under his and Nathan's editorship became the most important "little magazine" in America, though neither of the editors would ever have consented to have it thought of as in the "little magazine" group. In those days at least, no one was more keenly on the look out for new writers and there must have been scores who had reason to be grateful. I, for one, remembered too well the note with which he accompanied the first check I ever received from any publication to be hurt by the words with which he later dismissed one of my books in which he thought he detected the corrupting influence of a kind of nostalgia for God: "After all no one can be expected to come all the way from Tennessee to civilization in one generation." A good many were shocked when, a few years ago, he boasted that he had never admired Theodore Dreiser as a novelist but had used him only as a club against those whom he admired even less. But is that really any worse than Shaw's confession that in his drama criticism he was concerned not at all with the extent to which authors achieved what they wanted to achieve and asked only whether or not they were trying to do what he thought they ought?

If Mencken would not have cared to be praised for moral virtues, he would certainly have liked to have recognized those artistic achievements which were more indubitably his. No doubt it will be some time yet before he will, in all quarters, have lived down his popularity and a lack of gentility more absolute than that which even Mark Twain, his closest analogue, dared exhibit. He founded no worthy school, most of his imitators were contemptible because his style was inimitable and only he could use as a genuine instrument of expression a vocabulary and a rhythm which in other hands stubbornly refused to yield anything except vulgarity. But I risk the prediction that the time will come when it will be generally recognized, as by a few it already is, that Mencken's was the best prose written in America during the twentieth century. Those who deny that fact had better confine themselves to direct attack. They will be hard put to find a rival claimant.

5: Recent Perspectives and Interpretations, 1957–1984

H. L. Mencken's Poetry

Edward A. Martin*

Here, as an example of H. L. Mencken's mature style, are the opening six sentences of his essay on William Jennings Bryan, called "In Memoriam: W. J. B.":

> Has it been duly marked by historians that William Jennings Bryan's last secular act on this globe of sin was to catch flies? A curious detail, and not without its sardonic overtones. He was the most sedulous flycatcher in American history, and in many ways the most successful. His quarry of course, was not *Musca domestica* but *Homo neanderthalensis*. For forty years he tracked it with coo and bellow, up and down the rustic backways of the Republic. Wherever the flambeaux of Chautauqua smoked and guttered, and the bilge of idealism ran in the veins, and Baptist pastors dammed the brooks with the sanctified, and men gathered who were weary and heavy laden, and their wives who were full of Peruna and as fecund as the shad (*Alosa sapidissima*), there the indefatigable Jennings set up his traps and spread his bait.[1]

These sentences appeal most obviously to the ear. We are very much aware of alliteration both of consonant and of vowel as a device for external structural unity. Thus *to catch flies* links rhythmically with *A curious detail*, and the *s'*alliterations add punctuation throughout. Much of the unity and meaning of the sentences turns on the repetition and slant rhymes in *act, catch, fly-catcher, tracked, backways, Baptist pastors dammed, shad, indefatigable,* and *traps.* The main vehicle of meaning is the figurative language and the outrageous comparisons with which the main figure is developed. Bryan is, of course, compared to a big-game hunter whose "quarry" is an animal-insect called *Homo neanderthalensis.* This animal-insect is never precisely identified, but one speaks to it with "coo and bellow" and its habits seem to be amphibian. The male of the species wallows "weary and heavy laden" in ponds whose muckiness is suggested by the "bilge" which these creatures have in their veins instead of blood—and the nature of their habitat is obliquely reinforced by the word "guttered." The female of the

*From *Texas Studies in Literature and Language* 6 (Autumn 1964):346–53. © 1964 University of Texas Press. Reprinted by permission.

species is fishlike in its capacity to reproduce and vaguely bovine in its eating habits, with the exception of "Peruna," a patent medicine popular especially during Prohibition and most noted for its high alcoholic content. The irony, if not the exact nature, of these comparisons is clear, for we see Bryan as hunter pursuing an insect called man—Bryan whose last notable action was to insist that man descended from the angels and was in no way related either to animals or to insects.

What I wish to emphasize about this essay is that in it Mencken is not far from the techniques of the versifier—and those techniques are typical of his best writing. While none of the unflattering cadences and comparisons in the Bryan essay and elsewhere is inherently poetic, one feels that in another era Mencken could have written the heroic couplet with brilliance and that he could easily have fit his metaphors into more rigid metrical forms. Finally, in his essay on Bryan, he created a narrative voice which we hear in much of his best prose. His narrator asks "Has it been duly marked by historians . . . " and then goes on to duly mark in mock-historical rhetoric what Bryan's last secular acts were. One of Mencken's purposes is to debunk Bryan, and to do that he uses the satiric device of a Juvenalian narrator whose extravagance and outrageous comparisons are a calculated source of amusement for sophisticated readers. Mencken's narrator is a journalist-commentator who interprets a broad spectrum of contemporary experiences, a narrator who translates the circumstantial into the meaningful, fact into history, story into myth. An element of parody enters because of our awareness of the discrepancy between the earnestness of the voice and the outrageousness of the subject matter or of the metaphoric and imagistic vehicles for the subject matter. But there is also a genuine seriousness behind Mencken's deft transformation of aspects of the Bryan legend into an American mythology, for Mencken in his time and in his way was attempting to write what Edmund Wilson has called a "poetry of America." It is this aspect of Mencken's prose—its poetic characteristics and the sources of those characteristics—that I intend to explore in this paper.[2]

In 1894, Mencken remembered in a reminiscence, he had been "torn between two aspirations: one to be a chemist and the other to be a poet."[3] He wrote verse, at least until 1903, when his first book, *Ventures into Verse*, was published. He also wrote short stories during these early years;[4] his creative aspirations and expressions were the standard ones for a young man of the middle class with literary interests. Literature was for him a form of release and escape from the mercantile world that his family took for granted. His father, through a combination of affection and firmness, had insisted that he enter into the family cigar-manufacturing business. Mencken did as well as he could for several years in that business out of respect and love for his father. Poetry and literature had to remain partly clandestine activities; Mencken could see no virtue in outright revolt. But when his father died, he effected a compromise between literature and respectable middle-class life by going to work for the Baltimore *Herald*. He was an immediate and precocious success as a journalist, and soon as a columnist and editor; poetry was rapidly sublimated but not forgotten. Journalism was for the young Mencken simply a respectable way to enter the world of literature.

The "poems" in that first book, *Ventures into Verse* were about seafaring, adventuring, war, love, and such miscellany as Christmas vaudeville, soup eating, politics, and the city. A rather maudlin and un-Menckenian sentimentality pervaded many of them; others were modestly facetious or ironic in intent. He tried to leave the sentimentality and seriousness by jesting on the opening pages. The book was subtitled: "Being Various BALLADS, BALLADES, RONDEAUX, TRIOLETS, SONGS, QUATRAINS, ODES and ROUNDELS—All rescued from the POTTER'S FIELD of Old Files and here Given DECENT BURIAL—(Peace to Their Ashes) . . . FIRST (and Last) EDITION . . . Preliminary rebuke [:] Don't shoot the pianist; he's doing his best." Two of the poems were dedicated to Rudyard Kipling. One entitled "A War Song" ended like this:

> For 'tis ever the weak that must help the strong
> Though they have no part in the triumph song,
> And their glory is brief as their work is long—
> (Sing ho! for the saints of war!)[5]

Obviously, there are echoes of Kipling here; many of Mencken's early verses and short stories were imitative of Kipling's style and subjects. Mencken's later prose cadences had part of their source in the rolling and thumping verses of Kipling. He also responded to Kipling's naturalism—that awareness and dramatization of internal and external natural forces which are seen as controlling the destinies and behavior of men and animals. In the quatrain quoted above this naturalism emerges as a simplification and misapprehension of a Darwinian idea: that the weak exist only to help the strong. No one would claim that Mencken had succeeded in giving this idea an effective translation into poetry, or even into ballad. But he was struggling quite seriously with a process that, he hoped, would result in poetry. He had probably not yet discovered—and certainly had not yet interpreted—Nietzsche. It was not until after he read Nietzsche (he published his book on Nietzsche in 1908) that his ideology began to take less sentimental form, and at the same time he abandoned versemaking as an embarrassing, youthful affectation.

The struggle with sentimental commonplaces can be illustrated further in an eight-line poem called "Auroral," first published in 1900—here we find Mencken again attempting to translate naturalistic perceptions into poetry. He used a particular circumstance of modern life (urban existence) as his material:

> Another day comes journeying with the sun;
> The east grows ghastly with the dawning's gleam,
> And e'er the dark has flown and the night is done
> The city's pavements with their many teem.

> Another day of toil and grief and pain;
> Life surely seems not sweet to such as these;
> Yet they live toiling that they may but gain
> The right to life and all life's miseries.[6]

Mencken in this poem (as he himself later on would have admitted with vehemence and, probably, with profanity) was heavy-handed and pompously solemn. There is the promise of a rather startling, typically Menckenian effect in "The east grows ghastly," but that effect is quickly dissipated by the awkwardly "poetic" archaism of "e'er the dark has flown." There is an inept pathos underlying the naturalism of the notion that city dwellers toil only to "gain / . . . all life's miseries." The verses do not survive the sentiment expressed in the line "Life surely seems not sweet to such as these," yet the idea with which we leave the last lines (if we have read that far), commonplace as it is, is one which has been transmuted into poetry by at least one better poet. For example, the underlying idea of William Blake's "London" is similar: life must endure even among the man-created horrors of the city. Blake's rhetoric, unlike Mencken's, is effective; his diction is rich and precise. At no point is the intensity of the poem's imagery weakened by direct thematic statement.

Mencken's verse shows a progression and reflection in itself of Mencken's growing awareness of his failure as a poet. Awareness, not the failure, is the important factor: that Mencken turned away from versemaking and fiction does not mean that his poetic impulses and ways of viewing reality atrophied or changed—only that he sought in journalism what for him were more suitable forms of rhetoric. This progression can be seen clearly in a short poem published in 1905. It was called "On Passing the Island of San Salvador (the First Land Sighted by Columbus)."[7] In it Mencken's narrator had been moved to utterance because the sight of the island had inspired in Columbus "the deathless beauty of a dream come true." But this patriotic sentiment was offset by the rather startling metaphor which described the island as "forgotten offal of the land." Even as a maker of sentimental verses, which meant a special kind of full-blown posturing with "poetic" subjects, Mencken showed twinges of the iconoclasm, the satiric vision, and the irony that later were formed into a muscular prose. The very title of his earlier verses, "Auroral," had expressed a simple irony which the rhetoric of those verses was too obvious in clarifying.

In Mencken's pronouncements on poetry, as in his own brief, early career as a versifier, much is revealed about the nature and development of his rhetoric as a satirist and as one of the most influential critics of American culture. In an essay called "The Poet and His Art" he wrote: "Poetry, then, is a capital medicine. First its sweet music lulls, and then its artful presentation of the beautifully improbable soothes and gives surcease. It is an escape from life, like religion, like enthusiasm, like glimpsing a pretty girl." He described the sickness which the medicine of poetry could cure as arising from the mood "of intellectual and spiritual fatigue, the mood of revolt against the insoluble riddle of existence, the mood of disgust and despair." He observed in the same essay that a "quality of untruthfulness pervades all poetry"; he cited Lincoln's Gettysburg Address as an example of poetry because of its "rippling and hypnotizing words."[8] Nothing quite as clear as a poetics emerges from "The Poet and His Art," yet there is a pattern of ideas and attitudes (Mencken called them "prejudices") consistent with what he wrote about poetry elsewhere. In the essay he expressed the belief that poetry is nonintellectual in its appeal because it lulls the mind away from its normal or routine contemplation of reality; it also has the power to revive a mind weary with the "riddle of existence." Poetry is "artful"; that is, not accidental, and not simply a spontaneous overflow; the poet is fully aware of his techniques and functions. The rhetoric of poetry for Mencken was primary, for poetry could be "untruthful" as long as its language rippled and hypnotized. In citing Lincoln's Gettysburg Address as an example he showed that he was not concerned with any simple, formal distinction between poetry and prose.

Mencken wrote in another essay [9] that prose was the language of truth and that poetry was the language of beautiful lies. Poetry "must soothe the ear while it debauches the mind." He explained that his own prose often had the effect of poetry, for he had eminently succeeded in debauching the minds of many of his readers. He was referring specifically to his bathtub-hoax essay of 1917,[10] which he regarded as poetry because its rhetoric was misleading. His emphasis is significant: the essay was successful *because* "it was poetry, which is to say, a mellifluous and caressing statement of the certainly not true." In the bathtub hoax Mencken had written in mock-serious fashion about the invention of the bathtub in Cincinnati, Ohio, in the year 1842. His statistics seemed authentic, but were, of course, fabrications. For the purposes of the essay Mencken assumed a particular dramatic pose; the narrator speaks with the authoritative voice of the journalist-commentator, one of the everyday, myth-and-legend-making voices of American culture. That some people accepted the voice as authentic was, of course, part of the joke.[11] In that acceptance there was an expression of a desire to see circumstance as history, to translate the trivial into the significant, fact into legend, reality into myth. Those who saw the joke realized that the success of the essay depended on an element of parody: Mencken had imitated that omniscient, myth-making voice with which the journalist-commentator addresses the reader from the editorial section of many newspapers and journals. The bathtub hoax is especially revealing because in it Mencken's rhetoric is *almost* typical: his narrator is authoritarian and omniscient; only the Juvenalian note (which, by destroying the element of parody, would have made the joke too obvious to be effective) is missing. The essay obviously fulfills the requirements of Mencken's theory of poetry: it is untruthful, it is artful, it lulls the mind away from the routine contemplation of reality. When he wrote that he had succeeded through the bathtub hoax in debauching the minds of his readers, he was joking again by indulging in debauchery as a critic, but he was also with an underlying seriousness calling attention to what he himself had defined as the poetic characteristics of his rhetoric. He was aware that poetry, whether satiric or lyric, in one of its aspects circles around the process by which reality becomes myth.

Edmund Wilson, in one of the earliest and one of the best appraisals of Mencken, compared Mencken's evocation of America with Walt Whitman's.[12] Mr. Wilson wrote of the "comic portrait which Mencken has painted of himself," and saw behind that portrait a "critic, an evangelist and an artist." From what he called a Menckenian "prose poem" he quoted a series of descriptions on topics such as: (1) "Aspiration"—"College professors in one-building universities on the prairie still hoping, at the age of sixty, to get their whimsical essays into the Atlantic Monthly. . . . Car-conductors on lonely suburban lines, trying desperately to save up $500 and start a Ford garage"; (2) "Virtue"—"Farmers plowing sterile fields behind sad meditative horses. . . . Methodist preachers retired after forty years of service in the trenches of God upon pensions of $600 a year. . . . Decayed and hopeless men writing editorials at midnight for leading papers in Mississippi, Arkansas and Alabama."[13] As if from an abbreviated Spoon River anthology, many of the images evoked the small town, its loneliness and hopelessness, the small town of E. W. Howe, Sherwood Anderson, and Edgar Lee Masters, all Midwestern realists whom Mencken admired. Mr. Wilson wrote further of Mencken's "gloomy catalogue" as the "poetry of America," comparable to Whitman's "enumeration of another set of visions"—many of Whitman's catalogues would serve for illustration.

The success of the bathtub-hoax essay as satire depended partly on an element of parody—parody which arose out of Mencken's awareness of a myth-and-legend-making compulsion which sometimes affects both the newspaperman and his audience. Since the same kind of compulsion serves poets and versifiers, there is an affinity between Mencken's journalist-narrator who usually, but not always, mocks what he sees and Whitman's narrator who usually, but not always, celebrates what he sees; both narrators are expressions of the myth-and-legend-making impulses of their creators. Mencken as satirist usually dramatized the varied relations between his authoritarian, omniscient, Juvenalian narrator and the setting and culture with which that narrator is in sustained conflict. Whitman as comic poet usually dramatized the identification of his narrator with his setting and culture, a process in which conflict is diminished rather than sustained. But as satirist and comic poet, respectively, Mencken and Whitman had an artistic and dramatic device in common: the narrator in the characteristic works of each is authoritarian, omniscient, individualistic or sometimes libertarian, and prone to hyperbole in expression. Mencken had begun his career with serious aspirations to become a poet. These aspirations survived as he turned from verse to prose. Surely Edmund Wilson was right when he saw that Mencken in his time and in his way—like Walt Whitman—was attempting to write a "poetry of America." Mencken's time and

Mencken's way produced a satirist, where Whitman's time and way had produced a comic poet. The Mencken who had once dreamed of being a poet was a figure the mature Mencken chose to have us forget—but something of that earlier Mencken survived in his prose. He was able to adapt journalism to his needs for self-expression. He had not been a success as a poet or writer of fiction; therefore he chose journalism because as a journalist his talents had proved effective and he was almost immediately able to make his weight felt. His interest in, and writing on, the American language were immediate extensions of his journalism; the journalist's clippings file, scissors, and pastepot were the heart and method of his lexicography. But words were also endlessly fascinating to him because of his intuitive poetic capacities and sensibilities. Language was alive, colorful, absorbing, full of mystery, a kind of ritual central to the lives of all men. These were the attributes of the great religions, and the American language was a church that Mencken honored and helped construct. As he grew older his devotion became chauvinism; in 1948 he wrote: "General American is much clearer and more logical than any of the other dialects, either English or American. It shows a clear if somewhat metallic pronunciation, gives all necessary consonants their true values, keeps to simple and narrow speech tunes, and is vigorous and masculine."[14] As an expert on language he was able to make a devoted bid for respectable academic fame on his own terms. Language studies also were another facet of his individualism, for he liked to think of himself as a linguistic authority in the Johnsonian tradition. But I suspect that his poetic, Whitmanesque sensibility is the main source of the power that generated his writings on the American language. That same sensibility lies behind the startling imagery, the emphatic cadences, and the sharply defined dramatic voice that are the unmistakable, identifying marks of his style in his best writing.

Notes

1. *Prejudices: Fifth Series* (New York, 1926), p. 64.

2. I have tried elsewhere to identify some of the other sources of Mencken's satiric vision, with less attention to his rhetoric: "The Ordeal of H. L. Mencken," *The South Atlantic Quarterly*, LXI (Summer, 1962), 326–338.

3. "On Breaking into Type," *The Colophon*, (February, 1930), 29–36; reprinted in *Breaking into Print*, ed. Elmer Adler (New York, 1937), p. 141.

4. Two typical ones are "On the Edge of Samar," *Criterion*, IV:4 (July, 1903), 17–18 (with Leo Drane) and "The Passing of Sam Ching," *Criterion*, IV:6 (September, 1903), 18–22.

5. "A War Song," *Ventures into Verse* (Baltimore, 1903), p. 10.

6. "Auroral," *New England Magazine*, XXII (May, 1900), 275. Reprinted in *Ventures into Verse*, p. 36, with *city's* in line four changed to *alley*.

7. "On Passing the Island of San Salvador. . . . " *New England Magazine*, XXXIII (October, 1905), 133.

8. "The Poet and His Art," *Prejudices: Third Series* (New York, 1922), pp. 146–170.

9. "Hymn to the Truth," *Prejudices: Sixth Series* (New York, 1927), pp. 194–201.

10. "A Neglected Anniversary," *New York Evening Mail*, December 28, 1917, p. 9; reprinted in *The Bathtub Hoax and Other Blasts and Bravos from the Chicago Tribune* (New York, 1958), pp. 4–10.

11. Vilhjalmur Stefansson, *Adventures in Error* (New York, 1936), pp. 279–299, has recorded evidence that the bathtub-hoax essay was accepted by some as authentic history.

12. "H. L. Mencken," *The New Republic*, XXVII (June 1, 1921), 10–13.

13. "Suite Américane" [*sic*], *Prejudices: Third Series*, pp. 320–324.

14. "The American Language," *Literary History of the United States*, II (New York, 1948), p. 675.

The "Forgotten Man" of H. L. Mencken
Douglas C. Stenerson*

Critics who have damned H. L. Mencken as an arch-reactionary or hailed him as a libertarian have not seen the whole man. The truth is that he was both. His social and political thought is particularly fascinating because it embodies so many conflicting elements in the American heritage. He remained faithful throughout his lifetime to many aspects of the Darwinian revelation as interpreted by such thinkers as Herbert Spencer and William Graham Sumner,[1] but he also derived ideas and values from the tradition of the Enlightenment, the idealized conception of the antebellum plantation society that was widespread in the New South, and the German-American way of life as he had known it in Baltimore. Since he took over concepts from these different sources without attempting to reconcile the assumptions on which they were based, the opinions he expressed in his social criticism are often strikingly inconsistent. Through an analysis of his interpretation of the "Forgotten Man," an image he borrowed from Sumner and adapted to his own purposes, this article will identify and examine some of the major contradictions in his views.

In the first issue of the *American Mercury*, Mencken declared that the reader to whom he and George Jean Nathan wished to appeal was "what . . . Sumner called the Forgotten Man— . . . the normal, educated, well-disposed, unfrenzied, enlightened citizen of the middle minority."[2] Sumner had portrayed the Forgotten Man as "the clean, quiet, virtuous, domestic citizen" who "is independent, self-supporting, and asks no favors."[3] Like this definitely middle-class figure, Mencken cultivated the virtues associated with the Protestant ethic, and for him, as frequently for the Forgotten Man, these virtues had lost all trace of religious feeling. He exhibited, and admired in others, individual initiative, hard work, punctuality, thrift and prompt payment of debts.

*From *American Quarterly* 18 (Winter 1966):686–96. © 1966, Trustees of the University of Pennsylvania. Reprinted by permission.

His approval of these qualities is implied in his description of himself as "a larva of the comfortable and complacent bourgeoisie."[4] In his writings, he scourged not the bourgeoisie as such, but the "booboisie." That is, he resisted and ridiculed only those members of the middle class who were lodge-joiners, back-thumpers, do-gooders and goose-steppers and thus, in his lexicon, qualified as boobs.

Like Sumner and many other social Darwinists, Mencken assumed that the law of natural selection operates in human society much as it does, according to Darwin, among the lower animals. In 1883, Sumner had protested that the Forgotten Man had to bear the expense of laws and agencies designed "to protect people . . . against the results of their own folly, vice, and recklessness." We should not, he argued, spend money for measures that do not really prevent vice, but merely ward off Nature's penalty for it. For "a drunkard in the gutter is just where he ought to be. Nature is working away at him to get him out of the way, just as she sets up her processes of dissolution to remove whatever is a failure in its line."[5] Similarly, when Mencken opposed laws to control "fortune-tellers, layers on of hands, communists, Ku Kluxers, Holy Rollers, . . . heroin addicts, cancer quacks, and a hundred and one other varieties of fanatics and mountebanks," it was partly on the ground that "There is evil, indeed, in every effort to relieve the stupid of the biological consequences of their stupidity."[6]

Both Sumner and Mencken personified Nature as a kind of nemesis for those who fail in the struggle for survival. For Mencken, heredity and natural selection, rather than the cultural milieu and cultural opportunities, were the main determinants of social divisions. Society consisted basically of an elite versus the mob. Apropos of birth control, he argued that we should "promote and not hinder the multiplication of the lower orders, for if they do not multiply then there will be insufficient coal miners, ashmen and curve-greasers in the next generation. . . . "[7] Sometimes he went so far as to maintain that a whole race was far behind in its evolutionary development. After praising a volume of essays by a group of Negro intellectuals, he asserted that one of the chief problems confronting them was that "the vast majority of the people of their race are but two or three inches removed from gorillas. . . . "[8]

For Sumner, the elite—those who presumably proved themselves most fit in the struggle for survival—were the economically secure captains of industry and relatively secure Forgotten Men. Mencken's beliefs carried a kind of tacit approval of these agents of the free-enterprise gospel. On its conservative side, his opposition to big government manifested the sort of economic individualism Sumner advocated when he wrote, "All experience is against state regulation and in favor of liberty."[9] Mencken's admiration for the economic virtues made him recognize similar traits in successful capitalists and industrialists, even though in some respects he might subject them to severe criticism. Henry Ford, for instance, was "the most adept and ingenious manufacturer ever heard of," despite the fact that when "lured into discussing all sorts of public questions, most of them quite beyond his comprehension, . . . he made a fool of himself almost daily."[10]

But Mencken, unlike Sumner, did not define his elite almost exclusively in economic and material terms. For Mencken, the group who paralleled Sumner's captains of industry were the "Tories" who, in the twenties, dominated business and politics and controlled the press. In his opinion, these Tories were an uncivilized plutocracy, not part of a true elite. Even the Forgotten Man, as Mencken described him, was "enlightened" and represented scholars, scientists and artists as well as businessmen. For Mencken, indeed, intellectual and artistic superiority was the prime requisite, with economic security also a desideratum, but in second place.

The social and political realism stressed in the first *Mercury* editorial had a forerunner in Sumner's observations "that cupidity, selfishness, envy, malice, lust, vindictiveness, are constant vices of human nature." Much as Sumner counseled "that if you learn to look for the Forgotten Man and to care for him, you will be very skeptical toward all philanthropic and humanitarian schemes,"[11] Mencken editorialized that in politics "utopianism is not only useless; it is also dangerous, for it centers attention upon what ought to be at the expense of what might be."

> Yet in the United States politics remains mainly utopian—an inheritance, no doubt, from the gabby, gaudy days of the Revolution. The ideal realm imagined by an A. Mitchell Palmer, a King Kleagle of the Ku Klux Klan or a Grand Inquisitor of the Anti-Saloon League, with all human curiosity and enterprise brought down to a simple passion for the goose-step, is as idiotically utopian as the ideal of an Alcott, a Marx or a Bryan.[12]

Although Mencken was as fervent as Sumner in opposing Liberal or Radical reformism, he differed from Sumner in being as skeptical of "utopianism" on the right as of "utopianism" on the left. He saw no reason why Americans should fear Radical doctrines and persecute their advocates. He ridiculed the widely held assumption that leftist agitators seriously threatened American capitalism. Americans, he held, were full of delusions running directly counter to those of the Radicals. Because Americans refused to admit they might be "doomed to life imprisonment in the proletariat," they always hoped to move upward economically and socially. As a result, they suffered from "the delusion that class barriers are not real." They were even likely to believe "that the interests of capital and labor are identical—which is to say, that the interests of landlord and tenant, hangman and condemned, . . . are identical." Capitalism would endure in the United States as long as the notion that any bright boy can rise to the top remained part of the national religion.[13]

It seemed to Mencken that the Forgotten Man, representing "the middle minority," was always in danger of being victimized by the dominant social and political groups. If the Forgotten Man indulged in a harmless bottle of wine, he ran the risk of trial and imprisonment. If he spoke up vigorously on behalf of the Bill of Rights, he might be denounced as an agent of the Bolsheviks. Neither the Liberals nor the Tories could offer him any real help. "There is no middle ground of consolation," Mencken claimed, "for men who believe neither in the Socialist fol-de-rol nor in the principal enemies of the Socialist fol-de-rol—and yet it must be obvious that such men constitute the most intelligent and valuable body of citizens that the nation can boast."[14]

When his individualism operated in the context of the harsh competitive world envisaged by Sumner, with Nature siding with a self-styled elite and inexorably stalking the allegedly unfit, Mencken often gave the impression that only he and the enlightened minority could lay claim to true individuality. At such times, he tended to stereotype a whole group unfavorably as "the nether rabble of cowherds, lodge-joiners and Methodists," or the like. If Swamp Root hastened the death of the yokels who drank it, so much the better; they were merely reaping "the biological consequences of their stupidity." The elite, meanwhile, could preen themselves on the superior intelligence which prompted them to take their medical problems to a doctor.[15] The logical outcome of this attitude is an atomistic and inhumane individualism, with its pitting of the rights of the privileged few against efforts to help what Sumner called "the nasty, shiftless, criminal, whining, crawling, and good-for-nothing people."[16] To the extent that Mencken carried the outmoded assumptions of social Darwinism into his analyses of socio-economic problems, he overlooked the possibility "that the life of man in society, while it is incidentally a biological fact, has characteristics which are not reducible to biology and must be explained in the distinctive terms of cultural analysis."[17]

Mencken's seeming callousness reflected the harshness of the dogmas of social Darwinism, but it was also in part an impression created by his literary technique. Stereotyping is a form of exaggeration with considerable value for writers who, like Mencken, specialize in invective and ridicule. Such an author wants his readers to share his animus against a particular group or a type representative of the group. Stereotyping enables him to ignore all the differences among the members of the group which make them unique personalities and which might enlist his readers' sympathies with his victims. If he has the stylistic resourcefulness, he can portray the evil traits he attributes to the group so vividly that he succeeds in making many readers accept his judgments. The danger is that stereotyping may become not a conscious technique but a habitual manner of thought.

Although Mencken sometimes seemed to assume that his stereotypes summed up the whole truth, his quick response to anything vital and colorful in individuals saved him from consistently taking his own sweeping generalizations at their face value. Whenever he looked upon the yokels or the boobs as individuals, not mere ciphers, the more humane aspects of his social and political thought began to emerge. He then realized that even "the Rotarian and his humble brother, the Kiwanian," "the Americanizers, the

Law Enforcers, the boosters and boomers" have aspirations distinctly and appealingly human. They glimpse "a dim and disturbing mirage of a world more lovely and serene than the one the Lord God has doomed them to live in." What they lack is "the vision of Liberty" which would give them "a rational conception" of what this lovelier world "ought to be, and might be."

Liberty, as Mencken defined it here, featured not economic individualism and free enterprise, but the right to moral and spiritual self-determination:

> I preach reaction. Back to Bach! . . . The Fathers, too, had a Vision. . . . What they dreamed of and fought for was a civilization based upon a body of simple, equitable and reasonable laws. . . . The thing they imagined was a commonwealth of free men, all equal before the law.

Although convinced that "some of their primary assumptions were false," Mencken accepted their "premiss [sic] that the first aim of civilized government is to augment and safeguard the dignity of man."[18]

Responding sympathetically to Hamilton's aristocratic bias and distrust of the mob, Mencken did not accept all the implications of this liberal faith in human dignity. He rejected Jefferson's belief in the wisdom of the common people as having "a sweep and scope that took it far beyond the solid facts." To explain his point of view, he made a distinction between two kinds of political liberty:

> There was, first, the liberty of the people as a whole to determine the forms of their own government, to levy their own taxes, and to make their own laws—freedom from the despotism of the King. There was, second, the liberty of the individual man to live his own life, within the limits of decency and decorum, as he pleased—freedom from the despotism of the majority

"We have got the [first] half of liberty," he commented, "but the other half is yet to be wrested from the implacable fates. . . ."

> Minorities among us have no rights that the majority is bound to respect; they are dragooned and oppressed in a way that would make an oriental despot blush. Yet behind the majority . . . there is always a sinister minority, eager only for its own advantage and willing to adopt any device, however outrageous, to get what it wants.[19]

In several respects, however, Mencken's concept of liberty was closer to Jefferson's than it was to Hamilton's. His elite resembled Hamilton's only superficially. Hamilton sought to preserve the powers and prerogatives of an economically privileged group, but Mencken wanted a guarantee of the moral and spiritual liberties which make it possible for the civilized minority to be civilized. Despite his preference for an aesthetic and intellectual elite and his distrust of "the lower orders," he acknowledged "that it is worth nothing to be a citizen of a state which holds the humblest citizen cheaply, and uses him ill."[20] He praised Jefferson's "complete integrity," "immense intellectual curiosity, profound originality, and great daring."[21] Mencken's libertarianism was strongly Jeffersonian in tone because it insisted that *all* persons, not only members of the elite, have inalienable rights, and that any interference with these rights by either an agency of government or community mores is intrinsically evil.

Closely linked with the liberal aspect of Mencken's individualism were his concepts of honor and "common decency." Like his libertarianism, these values had an absolute validity for him. They transcended the materialism and dog-eat-dog ethic so resolutely expounded by Sumner. The Forgotten Man emerged, at this juncture, as a gentleman of humane sensibilities—a role which further transformed Sumner's image of him. In addition to intelligence, a concern for the arts, and courage, the gentleman upheld decency and honor. He knew that he must not violate privately commitments that he had made publicly. For example, he would not advocate Prohibition, thus encouraging invasions of the rights of his wet friends, and then accept hospitality from those friends.

The ideals of honor and decency also suggested the pattern Mencken would have liked society to take. To the "good American," who felt that "the notions of propriety . . . held by the mob are good enough for the state, and ought, in fact, to have the force of the law," he opposed the citizen "who views the acts and ideas of his fellows with a tolerant and charitable eye, and wishes them to be free and happy."

> For the thing that makes us enjoy the society of our fellows is not admiration of their inner virtues but delight in their outward manners. It is not enough that they are headed for heaven, and will sit upon the right hand of God through all eternity; it is also necessary that they be polite, generous, and, above all, reliable. We must have confidence in them in order to get any pleasure out of associating with them. . . . It is the tragedy of the Puritan that he can never inspire this confidence in his fellowmen. . . .

Mencken and his Forgotten Man wanted a stable, orderly society dominated by an elite to which they would belong, but they wanted everyone to have the right to self-determination. They wanted all members of the society to have the opportunity to act as men of honor, maintain the social amenities and take an innocent enjoyment in the pleasures of the senses— "the non-puritanical acts and whimsies that make life charming."[22]

A close relationship exists between Mencken's Forgotten Man and his idealized conceptions of the antebellum colonial planter and of the late-nineteenth-century bourgeois German-American—two other images that formed focal points for his values.

His strong provincial pride as a Baltimorean and a Marylander made

him susceptible to an idyllic interpretation of the colonial plantation society. Many of his essays contain hints of this interpretation, but a striking
example occurs in "Maryland, Apex of Normalcy" (1922). After describing
the early planters of Maryland as leading "a life of peace, tolerance, and
ease," he declared that "out of their happy estate there grew a civilization
that, in its best days, must have been even more charming than that of
Virginia."

> That civilization was aristocratic in character, and under it the bonds of
> all classes were loose. Even the slaves had easy work, and plenty of time
> for jamborees when work was done. . . . The upper classes founded their
> life upon that of the English country gentry, but they had more money,
> and, I incline to think, showed a better average of intelligence. They de-
> veloped their lands to a superb productiveness, they opened mines and
> built wharves, they lined the Chesapeake with stately mansions—and in
> the hours of their leisure they chased the fox, fished the rivers, visited
> their neighbors, danced, flirted, ate, and drank. . . . Nor were they mere
> guzzlers and tipplers. Annapolis, down to Washington's presidency, was
> perhaps the most civilized town in America. It had the best theater, it
> had the best inns, and it also had the best society. . . . [23]

This nostalgic portrait is in the tradition of those southern writers who used
standards drawn from the myth of the Old South to disparage the crudities
of the increasingly industrialized New South.[24] In the eighteenth-century
Tidewater, especially as represented by such figures as Washington and
Jefferson, Mencken found a close approximation to his ideal society. The
remark that in colonial culture "the bonds of all classes were loose" suggests his belief that a firmly established aristocracy can permit more freedom to all—especially more freedom of speech—than can a democracy,
threatened as it always is by the tyranny of the mob. But how much freedom did the slaves have? In the classic manner of apologists for the Old
South, Mencken evaded this issue by evoking the stereotype of the happily
irresponsible bondsman shifting quickly from his "easy work" to joyful
"jamborees."

    Nostalgia also dominated Mencken's memories of the German-Ameri-
can way of life as he had known it when he was growing up in the Baltimore of the eighties and nineties. He was convinced that the kind of prosperous German-American burgher typified by his own father had affinities
with the colonial planter. If, as the context clearly justifies, we take "the
authentic Baltimorean" in the following passage as including—and, indeed,
emphasizing—the bourgeois German-American, such an equation of the
two patterns of life is strongly implied:

> . . . The authentic Baltimorean, . . . the Baltimorean lifted above all
> brute contact and combat with the native blacks and the invading Goths
> and Huns . . . is a fellow who touches civilization at more places, per-

haps, than any other American. There is a simplicity about him which speaks of long habituation to his own opinions, his own dignities, his own class. In a country so largely dynamic and so little static that few of its people ever seem (or are) quite at home in their own homes, he represents a more settled and a more stately order. There yet hangs about him some of the repose, the air, the fine superiority of the Colonial planter, despite the pianola in his parlor and his daily journey to a skyscraper. One sees as the setting of his ultimate dream, not a gilded palace and a regiment of servitors . . . but only his own vine and fig tree and the good red sun of Maryland beating down.[25]

The true Baltimorean might work in a skyscraper or manage a factory, but his concern with having "his own vine and fig tree," with "the good red sun of Maryland beating down," had distinctly agrarian overtones. He and the colonial planter had in common a strong sense of family and class loyalty, an appreciation of comfort and repose, and a desire to maintain stability in the social order. Mencken attributed to both types such traits as competence, decency and honor, courage, a capacity for joy, and a corresponding anti-puritanism. From this composite figure of the Baltimore burgher merged with the Tidewater planter, it is not a long step to the Forgotten Man invoked in the *Mercury*.

Mencken's nostalgia for the past and his distaste for many of the social and political trends of the twenties reinforced each other. His emphasis on a free and assertive individualism, decent and honorable behavior, and joy in life presented a counter-image to the mechanizing and standardizing forces that were shaping "normalcy" as he saw it developing. America, he believed, formerly produced many men who were forcefully themselves if not always men of integrity, but in the twenties most men fitted a pattern. Americans once loved liberty, but now only scattered voices spoke up in its behalf. Mencken would not ally himself with any of the existing political parties, but he identified himself imaginatively with such statesmen as Washington, Hamilton and Jefferson. During the Revolution and the early national period, gentlemen could enter politics and not be forced to compromise their honor. The dilemma of modern American politics was that, with few exceptions, gentlemen would not assume political duties, and even when they did, they could not long remain gentlemen. The "worst curse of democracy . . . is that it makes public office a monopoly of a palpably inferior and ignoble group of men. They have to abase themselves in order to get it, and they have to keep on abasing themselves in order to hold it."[26]

As for government generally, Jefferson was right in seeing "that it tended inevitably to become corrupt—that it was the common enemy of all well-disposed, industrious and decent men."[27] Since 1914, in particular, Jefferson's worst fears had been realized. Although Mencken sometimes treated the events of the First World War in a tone of ironic detachment, his real feelings came out in an editorial note in which he spoke of the war as causing "the appearance of organized and malignant Babbittry, and the complete destruction of all the old American ideas of freedom."

> Down to 1914, the United States was a refuge for the oppressed of all lands; now they are barred out, and the government is engaged gloriously in the oppression of its own citizens.[28]

At times, Mencken's opposition to government verged on anarchism. In the widespread evasion of the efforts to enforce Prohibition, he saw "the first glimmers of a revolt that must one day shake the world—a revolt, not against this or that form of government, but against the tyranny at the bottom of *all* government."[29]

Although his aggressive manner has led some critics to classify Mencken as an almost entirely destructive force, his negative "prejudices," as the preceding analysis has shown, implied a considerable number of positive, though contradictory, standards. He accepted, for example, much of the conservative creed of the American middle class, with its confidence in capitalism, its equation of natural and economic laws, its stress on the utility of the Protestant virtues, its skepticism about Liberals and Radicals. In part, like Sumner, looking down scornfully upon those who failed in the economic struggle, he called on the middle class to live up more fully to its ideal of self-reliance. In part, since he identified the Forgotten Man with an intellectual and artistic elite, he condemned the middle class for its philistinism and anti-intellectualism. In other instances, he measured American life by norms he believed had formerly prevailed but were now neglected, as when he contrasted the integrity and courage of Washington and Jefferson with the venality of politicians in the twenties. As a staunch libertarian, he opposed any interference with individual rights.

In its mixture of conservatism and liberalism, orthodoxy and iconoclasm, Mencken's social commentary showed the shrewdness of his judgments about the interests and needs of the middle-class Americans who formed the bulk of his audience. It also embodied his two logically incompatible sets of standards. As a partisan of Sumner's Forgotten Man, he complacently ignored or accepted as inevitable some types of economic and social inequalities and injustices. He distrusted sudden innovations and proposals for transforming society and the existing political system. Although he was kind and generous to individuals in need, he simply took both poor and rich for granted, and adopted as his norm of good living a middle-class competence beyond the reach of most men. At the same time, as the champion of his more humane version of the Forgotten Man, he asserted his libertarianism. On behalf of "common decency," he attacked real evils: gentility, ignorance, philistinism, bigotry, intolerance, suppression of individual rights. What united his conflicting attitudes was the mood generated by his insistence that the individual counts more than the group. With all the strength of a powerful ego, he resisted the forces, both cultural and legal, which tended to impose conformity on him and his contemporaries.

His affirmation of the right to dissent, and the gusto and artistry with which he expressed it, are the two most durable aspects of his work as a social critic.

Notes

1. Sumner was Spencer's main American disciple. In a letter to Albert G. Keller, dated Jan. 5, 1932, Mencken said, "The books of your old chief, Dr. Sumner, made a powerful impression on me when I was young and their influence has survived. I only wish that such things as 'The Forgotten Man' could be printed as circulars in editions of millions." (*Letters of H. L. Mencken*, ed. Guy J. Forgue [New York, 1961], p. 337.)

Sumner's philosophy typified the kind of social Darwinism which most strongly affected Mencken during his formative years. The scope of this article does not permit discussion of the related influences on him of Thomas Huxley, another of the favorites of his youth, or of Friedrich Nietzsche, whom he studied after his basic "prejudices" were already formed.

2. "Editorial," *American Mercury*, I (Jan. 1924), 28. Hereafter this magazine title will be abbreviated *AM*.

3. "The Forgotten Man" (lecture delivered before the Brooklyn Historical Society on Jan. 30, 1883), *Sumner Today*, ed. Maurice R. Davie (New Haven, 1940), pp. 15, 11.

4. "Preface," *The Days of H. L. Mencken* (3 vols. in 1; New York, 1947), I, viii.

5. *Sumner Today*, p. 14.

6. "Editorial," *AM*, II (May 1924), 26.

7. "Birth Control," in Nathan and Mencken, "Clinical Notes," *AM*, IV (Apr. 1925), 452.

8. "The Aframerican: New Style," *AM*, VII (Feb. 1926), 255.

9. *Sumner Today*, p. 15.

10. "Babbitt as Philosopher," *AM*, IX (Sept. 1926), 125–26.

11. *Sumner Today*, pp. 6, 25.

12. *AM*, I (Jan. 1924), 27.

13. *AM*, I (Jan. 1924), 28.

14. *AM*, I (Jan. 1924), 29.

15. *AM*, II (May 1924), 26.

16. *Sumner Today*, p. 25.

17. Richard Hofstadter, *Social Darwinism in American Thought, 1860–1915* (Philadelphia, 1945), p. 176.

18. "Editorial," *AM*, VIII (July 1926), 287–89.

19. "The Heroic Age," *AM*, VII (Mar. 1926), 382–83. Illustrating how "a sinister minority" could force through restrictive legislation, Mencken added, "Law Enforcement becomes the new state religion. A law is something that A wants and can hornswoggle B, C, D, E and F into giving him—by bribery, by lying, by bluss and bluster, by making faces. G and H are thereupon bound to yield it respect—nay, to worship it."

This argument was one of his favorites and was drawn from Sumner. See *Sumner Today*, pp. 4, 17 and Sumner, *What Social Classes Owe to Each Other* (New York, cop. 1883), pp. 123, 132. On the latter page, Sumner uses the argument to show how prohibition laws worked a hardship against the Forgotten Man.

20. *AM*, VIII (July 1926), 289.

21. *AM*, VII (Mar. 1926), 382.

22. "Editorial," *AM*, VIII (May 1926), 34.

23. *Nation*, CXIV (May 3, 1922), 518.

24. Valuable accounts of how southern writers after the Civil War made use of the myth of the plantation appear in Jay B. Hubbell, *The South in American Literature 1607–1900* ([Durham, N. C.], 1954), pp. 738–43, 789–804 and *passim*; Gregory Paine, "Introduction," *Southern Prose Writers: Representative Selections* (New York, cop. 1947), pp. lxxxvii–xciii, cv–cviii; Francis P. Gaines, *The Southern Plantation: A Study in the Development and Accuracy of a Tradition* (New York, 1925), pp. 62–94.

25. "Good Old Baltimore," *Smart Set*, XL (May 1913), 112.

26. "Editorial," *AM*, VIII (Aug. 1926), 416.

27. "The Immortal Democrat," *AM*, IX (Sept. 1926), 124.

28. "Editorial Notes," *AM*, IX (Sept. 1926), xxxvi.

29. "Editorial," *AM*, IV (Feb. 1925), 160; Mencken's italics.

Rhetoric and Vision in Mencken's Satire: The "Medieval" Mob   M. K. Singleton*

Henry Louis Mencken achieved celebrity during the 1920's as an enemy of sumptuary legislation, academic pussy-footing, "Victorianism," Wilsonian idealism, Harding "normalcy," Coolidge paltriness, and most cultural manifestations of gentility, Christianity, and Democracy. His vogue as iconoclast led some to call the decade following the First World War "the Age of H. L. Mencken." Catering to a mood of fashionable disillusionment, he took the side of the modernists—the so-called "civilized minority"—against the pressures of an increasingly standardized and arrogant Babbittry.

At present, however, most of Mencken's immense output has been shelved as strident and dated, and close study of his rhetoric is lacking. To be sure, Mencken has certain modest claims to historical importance. In a period when the more genteel makers of literary opinion brought to their craft only "church membership and an honest face," Mencken's support for such emerging authors as Theodore Dreiser and Sinclair Lewis was as timely as it was unmodulated; and his great contribution to lexicography, *The American Language*, with its several revisions and supplements, is still consulted. Likewise unforgotten is his swashbuckling editorial conduct, with the help of George Jean Nathan, of *The Smart Set* and *The American Mercury*; these two reviews, popular with urban sophisticates, made such engaging sport of the "booboisie" that satire became one of the parlor diversions of the self-consciously "emancipated." That satire today, for many critics, is a *genre* ranking well below comedy and only slightly above topical journalistic scavenging is unfortunate, because with satire Mencken was able, as Jim Tully observed in 1927, to teach "a million thinking people the value of fundamentals."

*Reprinted by permission of the publisher from *In the Twenties: Poetry and Prose*, ed. Richard E. Langford and William E. Taylor (Deland, Fla.: Everett/Edwards, 1966), 74–77.

Nevertheless, if Mencken is to be established as an accomplished stylist in satire, criticism of him must become both wider and deeper than it has been for a number of years. Much recent discussion of his work adds up to little more than a scolding of him for his anti-New Deal politics. More potentially fruitful lines of approach are anticipated by early tributes to his prose: in 1926, Edmund Wilson discerned that the writing style of his Baltimore colleague gave "a certain literary satisfaction" based on "most attractive eighteenth century qualities of lucidity, order and force." And F. Scott Fitzgerald, also writing in 1926, hailed Mencken's invective as equal to that of Jonathan Swift, and as "the most forceful prose style now written in English." The word *force*, so frequently met in statements about his style, shows the respect of Mencken's contemporaries for the power of bluntness, but of the sort of invective created by Juvenalian indignation Mencken is relatively free. After all, he was not, even by implication, attempting to correct vice; and even his famous name-calling is conducted with an almost Horatian mellowness. A major reason for his *force* has been hitherto undefined: his recurrent and extensive use of "medieval" figures of speech and diction to define his satiric panorama. Any inquiry into his mastery of satiric form must take account of this part of the satiric landscape and its use in some of his *Prejudices*.

A surprisingly pervasive body of metaphor in the *Prejudices* is drawn from "medieval" tropes—or, more precisely, from the stereotyped language used by Enlightenment and progressivist nineteenth-century authors to describe the benighted era of the "Dark Ages." Although Mencken had next to no knowledge of, or interest in, the actualities of medieval history, he had a good familiarity with Mark Twain's several books exploiting medieval settings to elaborate Twain's anti-clerical, progressivist hostility to survivals of European "feudalism," and Mencken borrowed from Twain the "Dark Ages" diction and phraseology that Twain, in turn, had lifted from such liberal historians of the nineteenth century as W. H. Lecky and Jules Michelet. With such quaint, archaic, or otherwise historical epithets drawn from Twain's medieval tableaux did Mencken embroider his own tapestries: *peasantry, yeomanry, Berserker, knave, paladin,* and *Vandal.* Denounced in such essays as "Roosevelt: An Autopsy," "On Being an American," and "Chiropractic" are such follies as *sorcery, demonology, credulity, superstition, mountebankery, medieval despotism, charlatanry*—all in their modern guise, of course, but still freighted with derogatory "Dark Ages" connotations. Individuals are also likened to personages from the Middle Ages: Theodore Roosevelt, feeling mettlesome, swells into a "national Barbarossa," and when he denounces a political enemy, it is with "the wildest interdicts of a medieval pope;" Jackson, with his "merry men," breaks down the barriers against popular democracy; Wilson serves the "holy crusade" of Prohibition as its "Peter the Hermit;" and Harding, in the eyes of the credulous, becomes a "Charlemagne." Generalized types are also satirized in a pseudo-medieval frame: the prairie demagogue, aspiring to dictatorship, is likened to "that Pepin the Short who found himself mayor of the palace and made himself King of the Franks." Genteel literary critics meet in "ponderous conclave," issue "bulls," and, if New Humanists, are "of the apostolic succession." Evangelical Methodism is burlesqued as "the Only True Christianity," its "secular arm" is the Ku Klux Klan, and it issues "excommunications" in large number, because, to the "rabble of peasants" all discussion of ideas must take the form "of a pursuit and scotching of demons;" after all, "anything strange is to be combatted," "is of the Devil," and one "cannot think of a heresy without thinking of a heretic to be caught, condemned and burned." William Jennings Bryan, despite his defeat with Free Silver and his temporary set-back at the Scopes trial, is "a protean harlequin" still able to lead the "motley horde" (or "fabulous mob") of Fundamentalists because the "mysticism of the mediaeval peasantry gets into the community view" of its heroes. Indeed, the more one reads Mencken, the more one is willing to accept his personal admission of a "medieval but unashamed taste for the bizarre and indelicate."

At times Mencken rolls up scathing catalogues of his countrymen and their follies, catalogues reminiscent of the hundreds of now-amusing ancient "catch-all" ordinances passed during the Middle Ages against sturdy beggars, fornicators, actors, goliards, harlots, buffoons, jugglers, rogues, minstrels, and mountebanks; and other compilations recall the delightfully indignant compilations by Burton in his *Anatomy of Melancholy.* In a number of his surveys of boobus americanus, Mencken sets forth mock-medieval compendia of "the most timorous, sniveling, poltroonish, ignominious mob of serfs and goose-steppers ever gathered under one flag in Christendom since the end of the Middle Ages," a mob whose daily measure of communal follies includes "unending processions of governmental extortions and chicaneries, of commercial brigandages and throatslittings, of theological buffooneries, of aesthetic ribaldries, of legal swindles and harlotries, of miscellaneous rogueries, villanies, imbecilities, grotesqueries, and extravagances . . . steadily enriched with an almost fabulous daring." By such listings, Mencken stressed the multitudinous nature of folly by images which define vast and unremittingly panoramic nonsense. (At times the burgeoning mobs of gaping peasants resemble the numerous credulous and childish folk depicted so comically in Dan Beard's illustrations for the first edition of Twain's *A Connecticut Yankee in King Arthur's Court*). Mencken's mobs, mobile in choice of error, but fixed in susceptibility to it, proliferate ridiculously: the incurable optimists and reformers, for example, are a host: "Thousands of poor dolts keep on trying to square the circle; other thousands keep pegging away at perpetual motion." Despite the fact that these "Dark Ages" metaphors in themselves are nothing more than rubber-stamps, Mencken's use of them for his ridicule of the "mediaevalism at home" (as he called it) imparts a sort of metaphoric unity to the satiric landscape, yet it also gives a comically disheveled air to his essays by showing, as do some of the teeming scenes in Rabelais' *Gargantua and Pantagruel*, the undignified scramblings of the nether herd.

At times, though, Mencken employed medieval figures of speech in a somewhat more delicate way than indicated above, skewering the rustics rather than clubbing them. In his brilliant essay "The Husbandman," he runs through several kinds of mocking comparisons; initially the farmer is burlesqued by a lavish rehearsal of the immense praise he commonly receives. First given are assorted "Common Man" tributes; next advanced are comparisons of the farmer with classical personages, such as the Gracchi and high priests at the altar of Ceres; then the satirist, after waggishly pretending to have lost sight of his subject ("submerged in rhetorical vaseline, so that it is hard to tell which end of him is made in the image of God and which is mere hoof") moves from heavily Biblical tributes (*Laborantem agricolam oportet primum de fructibus percipere*) into a seething denunciation grounded in reductive animal tropes ("simian," "mammal," etc.). Finally Mencken utilizes his stock of "medieval" metaphor by envisioning the American intelligentsia as "beleaguered in a few walled towns" by a swarm of errant Fundamentalists armed with dung-forks and determined to put God into the Constitution. The satirist warns the city dweller—the aristocrat in his castle—that, if the rural religionists triumph, "then *Eoanthropus* will triumph finally over *Homo sapiens*. If [they do triumph], then the humble swineherd will drive us all into his pen." This climactic sentence, with its very ambiguous use of *humble*, is utterly contemptuous: the swineherd is truly "lowly," but certainly not "deferential"; in fact, he is outrageously "pushy," without any of the virtues of humility (cf. St. Thomas Aquinas on the proper attitude of swineherds). This key sentence is clearly an embodiment of the farmer for cautionary purposes because his "Dark Ages" barnyard theology is dangerously anachronistic to the besieged aristocrats peering down in alarm from the crenelated ramparts of their towns. Mencken's phraseology suggests the lineaments of rustics painted by Pieter Bruegel: Bruegel's canvases of lumpish Flemish peasants, heavy in their leathern aprons and stupidity, happy in their sparse and coarse possessions, were painted for the amusement of the wealthy burgher. Bruegel's antipastoral paintings, with their hundreds of dense, lumbering, and happy oafs, share the fundamental haughtiness of Mencken's essays; and both imply an approach quite different from that, say, of Gay's *Beggar's Opera*. Gay's work was intended, as William Empson points out (*Some Versions of Pastoral*), to describe the lives of "simple" low people for an audience of wealthy and refined persons in a way so as to make it appear that " 'this is true about everyone' and then 'this is specially true about us' "—a sleight-of-hand transfer of associations highly flattering to both classes—and starkly antithetical to Mencken's terms of approach. Mencken's readers, he assumed, were aristocratic in temperament, skeptic in thought, able to remember with nostalgia the native exuberances of the nineteenth-century

German-American saloon, yet sophisticated about Continental elegances. The Baltimore author tried to be of service to this community of superior men by, on the one hand, encouraging their willingness to "dance with arms and legs" in the Dionysian and Libertarian fashion, and, on the other hand, by helping these free spirits, scoffers, and bibuli to resist what Nietzsche called *Herdenmoral*: the jealous effort of the congenitally inferior democratic man to reduce to his own frumpy level, by the enactment of "Puritan" legislation, the happier, superior, individualistic, "first-caste" man.

Certainly Mencken did not write primarily to "stir up the animals," as is frequently charged. His essays were intended for the amusement and instruction of his cronies and the intelligent minority. Although his work features, on occasion, a number of "constructive" suggestions, these were intended for the sophisticates besieged in their "walled towns," or, more specifically, for mellow and civilized professional men such as Mencken's friends in the Saturday Night Club, which met for many years in Baltimore. When his written opinions fell into the hands of the *chandala*, the author could be mildly interested in the ensuing howls; but, as he sardonically admitted, *The Saturday Evening Post* was appropriately edited for "just folks," and to attempt to snare its ample following would have been, in its way, as immoral an interference with "divine will" (by which he meant "natural selection") as if chiropractors were prevented from freely ministering to the "botched."

Seen in perspective, the "medieval" phase of the satiric landscape is only a part of a thoroughly eclectic vision. Mencken's assumptions about life were drawn from several quarters. Many of his general attitudes were grounded on "Augustan" or "eighteenth-century" viewpoints. For example, his preferences in architecture were based on his esteem for "the principles which went into the English dwellinghouse of the Eighteenth Century," so, as he expressed it, he simply borrowed them "with a clear conscience." Of the merits of the Enlightenment, he had little doubt: "It got rid of religion. It lifted music to first place among the arts. It introduced urbanity into manners, and made even war relatively gracious and decent." And important for Mencken's materialistic, even mechanistic, view of nature, was the eighteenth century's encouragement of science, which it turned "to the service of man, and elevated . . . above metaphysics for all time." Moreover, he often expressed pleas for normative agreement among gentlemen on matters of the "fundamental decencies," "sound sense," and honor, dignity, and decorum. In his description of the vision which inspired the Founding Fathers of the Republic, Mencken set forth something of his own values: "the Fathers, too, had a Vision. . . . What they dreamed of and fought for was a civilization based on a body of simple, equitable and reasonable laws—a code designed to break the chains of lingering medievalism, and set the individual free." Onto this background of "Augustan" or Enlightenment attitudes, he projected more particular ideas derived from such nineteenth-century writers as Nietzsche, Spencer, Darwin, Huxley, Twain, and Shaw. His immense respect for biology and medicine as sciences, his hunkerous *laissez faire* social philosophy, and his bellicose tone were adapted from these thinkers in his pantheon.

As for the twentieth century, it provided him, especially during the 1920's, with responsive readers. In justification of his right to lecture these readers, Mencken clearly felt that, as the most efficient spokesman for two great and enlightened centuries, he had a secure mandate to criticize any resurgence of the "Dark Ages." That his purview was simplified and eclectic was immaterial to him; but that many thinkers of the twentieth century would have thoughts and second-thoughts of their own about the concept of progress, eventually became bewildering to the Sage of Baltimore. By 1932, his Libertarianism, so heady to the "scofflaws" of the 1920's, appeared to the younger set of the 1930's as too generalized and too nostalgic for their needs. Most of the intellectuals during the grim 1930's saw Mencken's yen for Libertarianism as similar to Don Quixote's love of chivalry: at best, laughable antiquarianism; at worst, political reaction. But for many old-timers—and a growing number of youthful fans—Mencken's exhortation to forget our "brummagen Grails for one week. . . . Let us have a Common Decency Week" is, though perhaps "generalized," worth remembering whenever public esteem for the fundamental decencies has worn perilously thin.

The Impact of Mencken on
American Linguistics   Raven I. McDavid, Jr.*

. . . . In discussing *The American Language* in the less urbane precincts of this Great Republic, I have had to explain what it was in Mencken's background that qualified him to write so effectively on American English—a subject that no academic linguist, no professional lexicographer, no sociologist or historian had dared tackle in extenso. In Baltimore, however, we can take this background information for granted. No one in this audience needs to be reminded of the rich complexity of surrounding cultures including the Susquehanna Valley, the Eastern Shore, the old tobacco plantations, and what HLM fondly called "that great protein factory, the Chesapeake Bay." No one needs to be reminded of the variegated economic and social history of a city that has evolved from an outpost of the Virginia aristocracy through the cradle of the clippers, to the industrial center symbolized by the works at Sparrows Point. No one, I hope (despite the xenophobic idiocies of 1917), needs to be especially reminded of the

*Reprinted by permission of the author from *Menckeniana*, no. 17 (Spring 1966):1–7. This was the second annual Mencken lecture delivered at the Enoch Pratt Free Library, Baltimore, 21 October 1965.

civilizing effect that the German emigrés of 1830 and 1848 had on all American cities, or of the fact that by helping prevent the secession of Kentucky and Maryland and Missouri, they may have tipped the balance toward preserving the Union in its days of peril. No one who knew Henry Mencken needs to be reminded of the fact that, however much he delighted in ridiculing *homo boobensis Americanus*, he took equal delight in recording the variegated and often fantastic behavior of the species, especially its use of language—the most intimate and habitual and characteristic of human activities. None of you who come together tonight under the auspices of this institution needs to be reminded how important it is to a boy of bookish inclinations and free-wheeling tastes that he have untrammeled access to a rich collection of reading materials. All this background information, however, fails to explain genius, though it may help us to understand it.

Nor do occasion and opportune leisure explain the success of *The American Language*. It is true that the times were ripe for it; Thornton had just issued the monumental two volumes of his *American Glossary*; George Philip Krapp was gathering his evidence toward *The English Language in America*; the editors of the Oxford Dictionary were glacially grinding their way toward the completion of this greatest of all historical dictionaries—and in the process, assembling evidence that would soon lead one of them, Sir William Craigie, to conclude that the English of the Western Hemisphere had diverged so greatly from the English of the Mother Country that it needed a separate historical treatment. The bumptiousness of the returning AEF—and the even greater bumptiousness of those who had cheered them from the privileged sanctuaries of shipyards, assembly lines, and propaganda mills—began to make itself felt in a new cultural self-respect: if our soldiers had been good enough to tip the balance of war on the Continent, our sailors—merchant and naval—good enough to throttle the U-Boats, our language was a legitimate subject for serious investigation and the speakers of its cultivated varieties owed no apologies to anyone. It is also true that many other Americans of German descent—not to speak of Irish, Scandinavians, and the rest—suffered in 1917–18 and after from the national intoxication with a sense of virtue. To cite only one example: my mentor Hans Kurath recalls with wry humor the witch hunt by the Texas legislature when he was an instructor under Edward Prokosch, later to be his father-in-law. "Is it true, Mr. Prokosch," snarled the chairman of the committee, "that you said that English was a German dialect?" "No, sir." "Then what did you say?" "I said it was a low German dialect." And so the Texas legislature—despite the role of the German-Americans in the Lone Star Republic and the early days of statehood (one of their descendants being Admiral Chester Nimitz, of whom a few of us heard tidings during the early forties)—voted to proscribe the study of German and things Germanic in all Texas institutions.

Yet one cannot explain *The American Language* on the grounds of national self-consciousness, enforced leisure, or the gradual accumulation of materials on which the study could be made. Something more was needed—a person who could pull the strands together into a pattern whose significance might be appreciated—whether it was or not—by even the least sophisticated reader. Here is Mencken's essential contribution. . . .

Having seen that the influence of *The American Language* cannot be explained by happy circumstances or Mencken's flair for the dramatic, let us approach its virtues through the experience of a few linguists who were associated with Mencken.

Allen Walker Read, characterized by Mencken as "America's most indefatigable reader of old newspapers"—and probably the most frequently cited contemporary in *The American Language*—not only has served on the editorial staff of the *Dictionary of American English* but has explored many interesting linguistic and cultural byways of the American scene, ranging from the pronunciation of the *Show-Me State (Missourah* or *Missouree)* to a monograph privately printed in Paris (this before Mme. de Gaulle) on *Lexical Evidence from Folk Epigraphy in Western North America*. Read decided in the late thirties that the record of the English language would not be complete without a historical study of Briticisms; it is necessary to have dictionaries showing the development of English in the United States, Canada, Australia, New Zealand, South Africa, and the West Indies—to say nothing of Scotland and Ireland—but it is equally necessary to show the independent development of the language in its original habitat—the things that the English of England do not share with other varieties, and that are manifestly borrowings from England when they appear in other climes. Through Mencken's encouragement, Read found a publisher for his work. . . . It is no doubt Read's gratitude for Mencken's help, and for Mencken's interest in his earlier identification of *O.K.* and *Old Kinderhook* (Van Buren) in the 1840 campaign, that led to the recent outpouring of articles in which *O.K.* is definitively explored in all its relationships, except possibly with the Polish question.

In the thirties Kurath, then director of the Linguistic Atlas project, was seeking funds to complete the Atlas field work on the Atlantic seaboard. Since no one else knew so well both the resources of the Free State and the significance of the project, he wrote Mencken, whom he had admired for his understanding of the American scene ever since the appearance of the 1919 edition of *The American Language*. After sessions at the Maryland Club and at 1524 Hollins Street (where Kurath was surprised and delighted to find the best private linguistics library in the United States), they launched a campaign which resulted in the completion of the investigations in this critical transitional commonwealth.

Einar Haugen, now professor of linguistics at Harvard, is author of a magnificent study, *The Norwegian Language in America*, and probably the most distinguished student anywhere of the theoretical and practical problems of bilingualism. He grew up in a Norwegian-American community in Iowa, went to the University of Illinois during the bright morning of the

Mercury, and read Mencken's earliest sketches of the development—in the American setting—of other languages than English. The *Mercury* confirmed his scientific rebellion against the ecclesiastical prejudices of his community; the sketch of Norwegian-American—"the kind of language I'd been hearing at home all my life"—conveyed the surprising knowledge that serious students were interested in something that people at home took for granted, and were even a bit ashamed of.

My own experience is on record; let it suffice here that Mencken was for me a catalyst, an appreciative audience when such audiences were not too common. And if I have done anything for the next generation of investigators it has been to serve as an appreciative audience for the interested and intelligent beginner. Moreover, at least one interest of mine—with awesome potentialities for our national health—I owe to H. L. M. The most interesting current development in the teaching of English within this Great Republic is the plan to adopt methods of teaching foreign languages for the purpose of teaching the standard language to those whose slum dialects—among other things—doom them to menial labor or support at the public charge; the first suggestion of the need for such a program is found in Chapter Nine of Supplement Two.

We finally come to five qualities in *The American Language* that explain its influence.

1. There is accurate observation, in so far as Mencken's experience permitted. (We are all creatures of our experience—and all are capable of making categorical statements that are ridiculous to a person in possession of more data. A few years ago one of my fellow linguists publicly took me to task for including *tomatoes* in a discussion of the "broad A" words, on the ground that "nobody says *tomattoes*," providing me with a delightful opportunity to say that there were plenty of Americans who used that pronunciation, and that evidence on their usage was available within fifty feet of where he was standing, in the ample archives of the Linguistic Atlas.) We now have the data to make some of Mencken's early statements seem naïve—but often because those early statements made many of us investigate what the actual state of affairs happened to be. If he assumed that local Baltimore terms were generally in use throughout the United States—*espantoon* for a policeman's nightstick comes to mind—he can be pardoned for lacking information that nobody else had at the time, and for relying on the usage of the practicing policemen he knew best.

More important, though, was his observation of the state of the field. This is nowhere more clearly pointed out than in the preface to the first edition, where he explained that too often he had to run the lines himself because no professional scholar had provided the evidence:

> a. On Americanisms, the one treatise of any authority was by a person whose native tongue was neither British nor American, and it had long been out of print [here he was probably referring to Schele de Vere's

treatise of 1871; Thornton's glossary had actually appeared, but the edition was small and the work was poorly advertised].

b. On American pronunciation, almost nothing.

c. On American spelling, showing many significant variations from British practice, again almost nothing.

d. On American grammar, less than nothing.

And what is more, a large proportion of the pitifully poor evidence we had was devoted to the incredible thesis that there were really no significant differences between British and American usage after all.

It is interesting to examine the reviews of the first edition. The unfavorable ones usually missed the mark entirely: they berated him for his lack of academic training (a lack he had freely conceded) and chided him for daring to write what academicians were afraid to undertake. The more favorable ones came from such giants as George O. Curme of Northwestern, the greatest historical grammarian that has yet appeared in this country, and Brander Matthews of Columbia, a sensitive observer of Americanisms. Far from deploring Mencken's work, these men accepted it on its merits as a synthesis of available information, a set of conclusions based on that information, and an appeal for more research. The response to this appeal is shown by the appearance of the following works:

1. The Craigie-Hulbert *Dictionary of American English* (1938–44).

2. The M. M. Mathews *Dictionary of Americanisms* (1951). A supplement is now in preparation.

3. George Philip Krapp's *The English Language in America* (1925), especially valuable for its evidence on the history of American pronunciation.

4. J. S. Kenyon's *American Pronunciation* (1924) and the subsequent works of C. K. Thomas (1947) and Arthur Bronstein (1960).

5. *The Linguistic Atlas of New England* with its accompanying Handbook (1939–43). Editing of the materials for the Middle and South Atlantic States has just been resumed. In the meantime, there has been a steady succession of articles derived from the Atlas materials, plus three large-scale studies: Kurath's *Word Geography of the Eastern United States* (1949); Atwood's *Survey of Verb Forms in the Eastern United States* (1953); Kurath and McDavid's *Pronunciation of English in the Atlantic States* (1961). Kurath's *Phonology and Prosody of Modern English* (1964) draws heavily on Atlas materials.[1]

6. Field work and other gathering of data in other parts of the United States, yielding many interesting articles and monographs and one first-rate book, Atwood's *The Regional Vocabulary of Texas* (1962). Work has also progressed toward linguistic atlases, dialect dictionaries, and historical dictionaries in Canada, Newfoundland, and Jamaica.

7. Many studies of the language practices of American authors, against the background provided by the DAE and DA.

8. A reëxamination of usage, notably in Fries' *American English Grammar* (1940).

To the end, Mencken was staking out territory for future investigators. Among the areas regretfully untouched in Supplement Two was the language of gesture; in the last decade we have had a monograph on the sign language of the deaf and another by the incredible Ray Birdwhistell (echoing Dana of the New York *Sun,* "Yes, Virginia, there *is* a Ray Birdwhistell.") on *Kinesics*—the role of gestures and other body movements in human communications (1952). And Mencken's laments on the lack of serious study of American proverbs and American political terms have been at least partially met, by Wayland Hand and by Hans Sperber.

2. The second characteristic of Mencken's work is familiarity with source material and scholarship in the field, and an attempt to keep informed on both. As we know, there was a limited amount available when the first edition was written, and the lack of proper bibliographical tools made it not too easy for scholars to find even what was available. The space devoted to footnotes grew with each edition, until they filled more than half the space for Supplement Two. (In the making of the 1963 edition, footnotes were cut more drastically than any other part, but still totaled some sixty thousand words; documentation was revised seriously in galleys and occasionally even in page proof.) Part of this came from his own wide-ranging reading, part from the services of clipping bureaus, part from the correspondence of readers—amused or indignant—who wished to set the record straight. If there is one field where Mencken neglected what was available, it was in the new theoretical and technical linguistics of the forties; but as one of the brethren, in tolerable standing, I can appreciate his dissatisfaction with the cult of opacity so much in vogue then and since. By any standards, his familiarity with the materials was remarkable.

3. The third characteristic is intellectual flexibility. As he read and assayed the evidence, HLM frequently changed his earlier opinions. The most striking example was the change in emphasis from the first edition of 1919 to the fourth of 1936. In 1919 he had asserted that the force of linguistic change would soon make English and American mutually unintelligible; in 1936 he observed that improvement in communication was bringing the two streams of English closer together so that in the future one might well study "English" as a dialect of American. In this same spirit Mencken was continually alert to alter, expand, or delete particular statements in the light of new evidence. This quality was especially noticeable when I came to collating the 1936 edition with the 1945 and 1948 supplements: though Mencken specifically stated that the supplements were not revisions, but merely addenda to be "hooked on" at specified places, it often happened that he had to revise the original statement in order to make the addenda meaningful. If this practice created difficulties for the subsequent editor, it could only increase the editor's respect for the work he was editing—as

something organic, growing, and changing as new evidence and more accurate evidence became available. Whenever a scholar pointed out a lapse, Mencken made the correction promptly. This virtue, too, has had its embarrassments: in Chapter X, I was called to account by the styling editor for my handling of diacritics on Slavic proper names. Fortunately, in addition to my own knowledge, I could point out that I was working from a corrected printing of the 1936 edition, while he was looking at a house copy of the uncorrected first printing.

4. A fourth quality of *The American Language* is that it is well written. I do not refer merely to such entertaining passages as the etymology of the verb *to goose* (239–40) or the history of the coinage of *ecdysiast* (349–50) as a polite name for a strip-teaser. Nor do I mean the wonderful footnotes, full of social and aesthetic criticism, such as the one on *obituarize* (243 n).

> I had hardly got this paragraph [on verbs in *ize*] on paper when someone sent me a copy of the *Literary Supplement* of the London *Times* for June 7, 1934, with the ghastly verb to *obituarize* marked with a red circle. Worse, I discovered on investigation that it was in the OED, credited to the London *Saturday Review* for October 17, 1891. If I may intrude my private feelings into a learned work, I venture to add that seeing a monster so suggestive of American barbarism in the *Times* affected me like seeing an archbishop wink at a loose woman (243, fn. a).

What I have in mind is the deftness with which he could condense a world of sound linguistic information into a few clauses, as in his treatment of English noun inflections (526).

> The primordial Indo-European language had eight cases of the noun; in Old English they fell to four, with a moribund instrumental, largely identical with the dative, hanging in the air; in Middle English the dative and accusative began to decay; in Modern English the dative and accusative have disappeared altogether, save as ghosts to haunt grammarians (526).

Mencken's style is so lucid that by comparison even the best writing by technical linguists for a popular audience seems awkward or patronizing. As embarrassing as is this admission, Mencken's style nonetheless serves as a touchstone for critics in the profession: if he was able to write so well about the phenomena we discuss every day, why can't we do the same?

5. A fifth quality of Mencken's work as a linguist was his generosity. He was prompt in acknowledging even the most trivial contribution from the rankest amateur. To be sure, he was not always able to "embalm" in his book the interesting casual contributions he received, such as the Negro undertaker's sign in Clarendon County, South Carolina: "Let L. P. Brock wash you and dress you and prepare you to meet your God" (fitly but not as poetically paralleled by the sign I saw in Beacons Field, England—"Edward Tilbury and Son: Builders, Decorators, Sanitary Engineers; Complete Funeral Service"). Nevertheless, he was scrupulous to document the

sources from which he reached his conclusions—a practice I wish had been followed by certain contemporary academicians. In the long run, of course, this care only enhanced Mencken's own reputation, as I found out recently in running down the myth (offered with some skepticism in the 1936 edition and repeated in the 1948 supplement) that *Levy* is the second most common surname in New Orleans. A little detective work revealed that Mencken—as any scholar might have done—had simply followed the statements of an article by Howard Barker, described as "the foremost authority on American surnames"—and Mr. Barker had not cited specific sources, which for this detail did not exist. In the short run this generosity created a wonderful corps of Hollins Street irregulars, only too happy to send in information in the hope of finding themselves cited (even today my academic friends enjoy counting references to themselves in the 1963 edition). And some of these went on to become professionals, like Ethel Strainchamps, who went from the Ozarks to newspaper work in Springfield, Missouri, and is now helping with the new edition of Perrin's *Index to English*.

6. Finally, and perhaps most important, Mencken never lost sight of the fact that a language is a living and developing organism, used by actual people in their interactions. All efforts—and such efforts are commendable—to reduce language to a set of formulas, whether analytical or generative, come up against this hard fact: languages are used by living people, each the resultant of all kinds of experiences, in highly complicated situations. There is no other book on language that so effectively brings us back to the real situation as does *The American Language*. If I have had one thought in mind throughout my association with the work, it has been to preserve that quality. . . .

Notes

1. Professor McDavid wanted to add at this point a reference to the *Linguistic Atlas of the Upper Midwest*, 3 vols., ed. Harold B. Allen (Minneapolis: Univ. of Minnesota Press, 1973–1976) and the information that this and similar surveys for most other regions are available on microfilm.—Ed.

Mencken as a Magazine Editor   Carl Dolmetsch*

On July 10, 1923, H. L. Mencken wrote to his future wife, Sara Haardt, as follows:

> Confidentially, I am making plans to start a serious review—the gaudiest and damnedest ever seen in the republic. I am sick of *The*

*Reprinted by permission of the author from *Menckeniana*, no. 21 (Spring 1967):1–8. This was the third annual Mencken lecture delivered at the Enoch Pratt Free Library, Baltimore, 13 October 1966.

Smart Set after nine years of it, and eager to get rid of its title, history, advertising, bad paper, worse printing, etc.

A few weeks later (on July 30) he echoed these sentiments to his friend Max Brödel,[1] thus:

> I am preparing to assassinate *The Smart Set* and to start a new magazine—something far grander and gaudier—in brief, a serious review but with undertones of the atheistic and lascivious. . . . Altogether, the prospect makes me young again.

These statements are among the very earliest portents of what was to be a momentous double event in American publishing history: the demise of one venerable periodical of enormous literary significance and the founding of another which, in its own way, would have just as great an impact in other areas, such as politics and social thought. There is ample evidence that even at that very moment both Mencken and his coeditor, George Jean Nathan, were quite aware of the significance to literary history of the "assassination" of *The Smart Set* and the founding of *The American Mercury*. One may see this, for example, in the somewhat grandiloquent broadside in which, with characteristic self-dramatization, they officially announced (on October 10, 1923) their decision that " . . . they are withdrawing from the work so long carried on together because they believe that, insofar as it is accomplishable at all, the purpose with which they began in 1908 has been accomplished. That purpose was to break down some of the difficulties which beset the American imaginative author, and particularly the beginning author of that time—to provide an arena and drum up an audience for him, and to set him free from the pull of the cheap, popular magazine on the one side and of the conventional 'quality' magazine, with its distressing dread of ideas, on the other—above all, to do battle for him critically, attacking vigorously all the influences which sought to intimidate and regiment him. This work is obviously no longer necessary."[2]

That this work of liberation was truly "no longer necessary" and that, in consequence, Mencken had grown "sick of *The Smart Set*" and eager for combat in new fields, was owing in large measure to the success of the editorial program HLM and Nathan had evolved during their collaboration. To my mind, this is one of Mencken's finest and most enduring achievements and the area of his greatest impact upon American literary history. Nevertheless, such has been the blinding glare thrown off by Mencken the linguist, Mencken the journalist, Mencken the pundit and stylist, even Mencken the literary critic, that the real significance of Mencken the workaday magazine editor has been at least partially obscured. I can only hope that my book about *The Smart Set* and what I have to say here tonight will help to correct our focus in seeing the great and many-faceted career of HLM in its proper perspectives. There is some comfort, too, in the thought that the next generation (*ca.* 1990) may get to read the fourth volume of HLM's memoirs, dealing with his editorial days (believed to be among his restricted papers), and will thus be able to evaluate his career as editor even better than we now can.

Meanwhile, what we have had so far constitutes only a partial portrait of HLM the editor—a composite, with sundry ornamentations and elaborations, that may be abstracted from the three biographies to date (Goldberg, Kemler, and Manchester), from Singleton's book about the *Mercury*, and from the scurrilously vindictive memoirs of Angoff. The general impression one gets from these books is of Mencken and Nathan as a pair of irresponsible freebooters merrily hijacking their way through the world of periodical journalism in the teens and twenties. It was all, so we are told in these accounts, a "harlequinade," a "hoisting of the Black Flag," a romp, a lark (or, at least, "an adventure") carried off *sforzando* with the left hand while the editors were busy being influential literary and drama critics. These books abound in descriptions of the "high camp" decor of the "Editorial Galleries" of *The Smart Set* and *Mercury*, in the spoofing, the fanciful pseudonyms (Owen Hatteras, Janet Jefferson, *et al.*), the complaints of "Heinie" to "The Professor" about his extracurricular love-making duties with lady novelists, the parody acceptance letters to Untermeyer, the burlesques (such as "Suggestions to Our Visitors"), etc. No one could possibly take it very seriously even if, along the way, an astonishing number of really good writers were somehow "discovered."

Now, I will try not to deny here (as I have not in my book) that there is some essential truth to this picture. There can be no doubt that Mencken and Nathan extracted every ounce of possible pleasure from their collaborations as editors of *Smart Set* and, in the early months at least, in the founding of the *Mercury*. As they both pointed out more than once, they got little enough out of their editorial chores other than pleasure. The collaboration would not have lasted as long as it did had they not enjoyed it so much. As someone has said of the Austrians in World War I, one gets the impression that their situation was often hopeless, but never serious, so lighthearted were they in facing some of their most horrendous editorial problems. But this, I repeat, is only a *partial* view of the matter—not the whole story. To take the part for the whole is obviously to distort literary history and to do a great disservice to both men.

What is the rest of the story? It is, in a word, that editing *The Smart Set* and—to a lesser extent—the *Mercury* was an incredibly difficult task carried out against odds that, in this degenerate hour, would make an editor turn in his IBM cards. To be sure, there are plenty of editors today—as in yesteryear—struggling to keep so-called "little" magazines afloat and producing good material. But neither *The Smart Set* nor the *Mercury* was in any sense a "little" magazine, despite their relatively limited circulation. Both were distinctly commercial ventures (*i.e.*, designed to make money). The problems of editing Mencken encountered in both were, though infinitely more acute, precisely those encountered by, say, George Horace Lorimer, his great contemporary on that commercial of commercials, *The*

Saturday Evening Post. The appearance Mencken and Nathan carefully cultivated of not giving a damn, of saying, for instance, that "one civilized reader is worth a thousand boneheads" (a cover motto on their first issue), was as much a matter of whistling in the dark as it was of bravura. The truth is that Mencken and Nathan faced their editorial nightmares with an equanimity, a deftness, and a resourcefulness that must surely rank them among the great editors in the history of American periodicals.

Mencken came to magazine editing almost by accident and almost despite himself. He left it, some nineteen years later, in much the same way, that is, by force of circumstance. He did not choose it as a "career" and he obviously did not look upon it as such. Yet, during an important period of his life, it claimed his major attention. Given his Germanic sense of thoroughness, efficiency, and order, it claimed his loyalties far more than he intended. The story has often been told of Eltinge Warner's chance encounter with Nathan aboard the S.S. "Imperator" in July, 1914; of how, when Warner learned a few weeks later that he had "acquired" *The Smart Set*, he offered Nathan the editorship; and of how Nathan accepted only on provision Mencken would come in as coeditor. But for the duplicity of a London tailor (who sold both Warner and Nathan the same model topcoat), so the improbable story goes, neither Nathan nor Mencken might ever have edited "The Magazine of Cleverness" nor, perhaps, have founded *The American Mercury.*

Fantastic as it is, it happens to be a true and completely documentable story! On two (perhaps three) previous occasions Mencken had refused the editorship of *Smart Set* under John Adams Thayer, a vacillating opportunist who had acquired the magazine in 1911 and, even earlier, under that superb old mountebank, Colonel William D'Alton Mann, who had founded the magazine in 1900 and had, in hard times, unloaded it upon the unwary Thayer. Now, in the late summer of 1914, Mencken was constrained to accept a coeditorship on condition he could remain in Baltimore and on Warner's promise to give him and Nathan *carte blanche* in editorial policy—a promise that, as we shall see, Warner came to regret and, after nine years, to break disastrously.

August, 1914, was hardly an auspicious time to begin the editorship of a nearly-defunct magazine. The great "explosion" in American magazine publishing which began in the last two decades of the nineteenth century as the result of increased literacy and affluence, of the massive application of technology to publishing (*e.g.*, Mergenthaler's Linotype, electric rotary presses, photogravure) and of the rise of modern advertising had begun to dissipate in the first decade of the twentieth century. There was a final, almost convulsive, upsurge in magazine publishing again under the impact of muckraking in the first decade of the century but this, too, had ebbed. By 1914, the boom was decidedly over. One generalized statistic may be worth mentioning here: between 1870 and 1900 the numbers of American magazines increased decade by decade by almost geometric ratios, as did the expansion of the magazine-reading public. Since 1915 the total number of magazines published in America and the percentage of magazine readers in the total population have remained relatively the same. Thus, Mencken and Nathan began their editorial regime at the onset of what might be called an ebb tide, or at least a period of consolidation, in American magazine history. It was not a time when anything less than a bold new venture could succeed spectacularly.

Even without these general conditions in magazine publishing, the events of the moment would certainly have given even the least judicious editor pause. The outbreak of war in Europe had sent the American financial community into something akin to panic and publishing into a tailspin. It was, in fact, this very circumstance that prompted Thayer to dump *The Smart Set* on his creditors and head for the woods of Westport. Moreover, as World War I dragged on, month after weary month, the publishing world felt increasingly acute shortages in almost all materials. Inflation set in, advertising declined sharply, wartime taxes and increased postal rates for periodicals proved a heavy burden. Large segments of the reading public, dislocated by conscription or war industries, did not renew their subscriptions to magazines. At least one long-established periodical, *Harper's Weekly*, fell victim to these circumstances. Almost all American magazines felt a greater economic pinch then than they have during any other war in our history.

Smart Set was a sinking ship when Mencken and Nathan were brought in as salvage captains. It had reached its peak circulation in 1906 at around 165,000. In that year it had been hard hit by the scandal that attended the libel suit of its publisher, Colonel Mann, who had been accused of running a High Society blackmail operation in its sister-publication, *Town Topics*. When the Colonel lost his libel suit and was arraigned for perjury, the public unaccountably transferred an undeserved reputation for "perfumed pornography" to "The Magazine of Cleverness," which declined in circulation inexorably throughout the next eight years. By the time Mencken and Nathan took command, the circulation and reputation of the magazine had been further damaged by the reckless, if brilliant, experiments of Willard Huntington Wright, its editor during 1913. Mencken described the situation graphically on April 29, 1915, in an exasperated letter he wrote to Dreiser, in rebuttal of the latter's criticisms:

> I grant you that there has been a decided lightness in the magazine—but we had a condition, not theory, before us. The experiment with whores and horrors [Wright's "daring" policies] had failed; the experiment with cheap melodrama had failed; we had to try a new tack or go down. On August 15 The Smart Set owed $24,000 and was losing more than $2,000 a month. The circulation was cut to pieces; there was no advertising at all; we actually had to borrow money to pay interest on the debt. We guessed that satire would save it, *and we guessed right.*"[3]

The measure of the courage with which Mencken and his colleague faced these difficulties is that, during the same week, he could write another letter (to James Joyce), stating baldly: "We have to go slowly, but it is our aim ultimately to make it *the best magazine in America*."[4] If there has ever been such a Sisyphean task attempted in the history of American magazines, I do not know of it!

Why, I am often asked, did not Warner, Mencken, and Nathan at this point simply change the name of the magazine and, salvaging what assets they could, start over? The answer to this is somewhat complicated, but reduced to its simplest terms, it was not legally possible either then or later without declaring bankruptcy and liquidating all of the assets of The Smart Set Company. The principal purpose of this legal proviso was to protect the contractual arrangements with the English Smart Set Company, which published a London edition of the magazine and always enjoyed a modest but steady profit. So, stuck with a soiled name, a teeth-rattling debt, and a dwindling circulation at the outset, the coeditors simply had to make the best of it. And this they did—superbly!—HLM from his bastion at 1524 Hollins Street, Nathan in the various offices the magazine occupied in midtown Manhattan during their nine-year coeditorship. The two met at their monthly "harlequinades" in New York when each issue was "put to bed."

I need not delve into the details of the famous and unique system of editing by which Mencken and Nathan each exercised a complete veto over the contents of their magazine. The system worked splendidly until the famous disagreement (on the *Mercury*) over O'Neill's *All God's Chillun Got Wings* which effectively ended the collaboration after eleven successful years. The upshot of the "double veto" system was that HLM, as first reader, wrote most of the rejection letters, Nathan most of the acceptances (signed, however, "The Editors"). Quite early in his editorial career, Mencken developed a style of terse, yet friendly, rejection that pinpointed the objections to a manuscript at the same time it encouraged the author to keep writing and submit more material. Look, for instance, at what this rejection (to Vincent Starrett, a Chicago writer, in 1917) conveys in exactly fourteen words: "Unluckily, nay. It is a bit too pianissimo for us. Haven't you something else?" To be sure, most of Mencken's rejection notes were a bit longer than this, but typically never more than a paragraph typed on a half sheet. The late Lillian Foster Barrett, a frequent *Smart Set* contributor from Newport, Rhode Island, echoed the sentiments of dozens of correspondents when she wrote me in 1955 that "Mr. Mencken could usually tell you more about what was wrong with a piece in one sentence than most editors could impart in pages of analysis. To a young writer this was exhilarating. You knew *exactly* what he wanted and he gave you the confidence that you could give it to him!"

After the first year or so on *The Smart Set*, there was very little "tinkering" with contributions, as Mencken called editorial improvements. If it

did not suit, a manuscript was returned with a precise editorial suggestion—and with amazing alacrity, since Mencken made it a rule to "grade
his papers" the day they arrived and fire off the returns. Thus, HLM became *malgré lui*, an unexampled schoolmaster of the literary arts to a great
many (perhaps fifteen hundred) of the younger generation of writers.

In later years, Mencken often tried to shrug off this schoolmastering
as having been a virtue made of necessity. In his recorded interview with
Donald H. Kirkley[5] he specifically disavowed the claims made for him of
having "discovered" writers like F. Scott Fitzgerald, James Branch Cabell,
Ruth Suckow, *et al*. In August, 1955, he reiterated to me personally his
feeling that the writers who forged successful literary careers from their
first publication in *The Smart Set* or *Mercury* "would have made it inevitably" through some other means had these magazines not existed. I am inclined to doubt this and to think it an uncharacteristic piece of modesty.
True enough, the pinched pockets of *Smart Set*, with its traditional cent-a-
word rate for prose, for example, made it quite impossible for Mencken
and Nathan to compete in the marketplace for the services of established
authors of the first rank. But they were not satisfied, as many of their predecessors in the days of Thayer and Mann had been, to take what they
could get from well-known contributors of the *second* rank. They wanted
the best writing they could get. The best then, as in most eras, came from
young writers, however rough-cut some of their gems might be. *Ergo*: their
cultivation, verging almost upon paternalism, of the rising generation—the
untried, the unknown, and the scorned—and their announcement, in October, 1921, of this set of *Smart Set* aims which I, for one, am willing to accept at face value:

1. To discover new American authors as they emerge, and to give
   them their first chance to reach an intelligent and sophisticated audience;
2. To present the point of view of the civilized minority;
3. To introduce the best foreign authors to America;
4. To leaven the national literature with wit and humor; and
5. To encourage sound poetry.

A current joke among the *literati* in 1922 went something like this:
"Writing for *The Smart Set*, says Mr. Mencken, is more fun than being
paid for it." But even the pittance the "Aristocrat Among Magazines" could
then afford to pay would not have been forthcoming had Mencken and
Nathan not succeeded so spectacularly with the "louse" ventures—as
Mencken denominated *Parisienne, Saucy Stories,* and *Black Mask*. These
three cheap pulps were launched with Warner between 1916 and 1919 and
later sold out to Warner and Colonel Crowe (his silent partner) at a profit
that, Mencken once half-jokingly claimed, "freed Nathan and me from
work permanently thereafter." The strategy in operating these magazines
was quite simple: they were wastebaskets, made up (at least in the begin-

ning) of material found promising but unsuitable for the parent magazine. Sometimes, as in the case of contributions to *Parisienne*, there had to be a bit of "tinkering," as all of the stories in this magazine were given a French locale and a French flavor. Nevertheless, this provided the young *literati* with an even wider market for their talents than *Smart Set* could afford— and at slightly better rates of pay. They also afforded editorial jobs for some young *Smart Set* contributors: Wyndham Martyn, for example, edited *Parisienne* for a time, as Louis Wilkinson did *Saucy Stories* and Florence Osborne *Black Mask*. All of them worked under the aegis and initial editorial supervision of Mencken and Nathan. No less illustrious a career than that of S. N. Behrman was launched in the pages of *Parisienne*, as he tells in the charming reminiscence he wrote as an introduction to my book. Another contributor, Carl Glick (until very recently professor of writing at California Southern University, San Diego) fondly recalls his beginnings as a writer and critic under the guise of "Captain Frank Hawley," a pseudonym concocted by HLM and used for a time to review whodunits in *Black Mask*, an all-mystery magazine. When Mencken turned over this job to Glick, he recalls, it was with this piece of advice: "Never waste extended praise. If a book is good, say so flatly and leave it at that and be careful not to find too many that are good. The public loves good round denunciation and will respect you for it but they'll think you don't know your business if you praise too much." One more instance of Mencken's editorial schoolmastering.

This is not to say that Mencken enjoyed the "louse" ventures. He and Nathan detested their editorial chores on these "parasites," although, in retrospect, it would be fairer to say that *Smart Set* was really the parasitical one. It could not have survived World War I financially without subsidies from these pulps.

The saddest part of *The Smart Set* story for me is the way in which it was "assassinated" or, better, sold down the river. It seems evident that Mencken and Nathan had no intention of abandoning the magazine when they first decided to found the *Mercury*. Instead, they intended to run it as an all-fiction sideline, as they had the "louse" ventures earlier. But a piece of satire or a parody obituary that Mencken and Nathan composed following the death of President Harding in San Francisco and the organization of a cross-country funeral train (shades of Lincoln!) aroused the ire of Eltinge Warner, their conservative publisher, and a fearful row ensued. It seems that Warner kept a "spy" (a compositor) in the Charles Francis Press, where the magazine was printed, to alert him if anything really objectionable should show up in print. It was a frustrating business for Warner because he had promised to keep out of the magazine's editorial affairs, yet he really did not like the editorial policies Mencken and Nathan were pursuing. The piece on the Harding funeral train, however, proved too much and Warner broke his silence. He demanded its removal. When Mencken and Nathan stood their ground, as they had every right to do, the publisher announced flatly, *"The Smart Set's* for sale!"* and stormed out of the office. In the end, Nathan vetoed the piece himself but the damage had been done. The seeds were sown for the dissolution of the editorial partnership two years later. In October, 1923, Morris Gilbert, a young regular contributor, was brought in as editor. Mencken and Nathan turned their attention to the new *Mercury* and by the spring of 1924 Warner had found a buyer—William Randolph Hearst. He quickly turned the old "Magazine of Cleverness" into a subliterary moneymaker, a cynical datum of HLM's epigram, "Nobody ever went broke underestimating the taste of the American people."

Obviously, I know a great deal more about *The Smart Set* than I do about *The American Mercury*. Indeed, I must frankly confess I have never been able to work up enough interest in the *Mercury* to probe deeply beneath its olive green surface and its splendid typography. Perhaps because of this, I have never felt that, aside from the great blow for freedom of expression struck in the "Hatrack" Case, the *Mercury* represented a great editorial achievement. It was, as Mencken predicted, a "serious review" in every sense of the word, with its proportion of belles-lettres to nonfiction commentary in almost inverse ratios to those of *Smart Set*. It did not cultivate young writers. Indeed, it did not accept unsolicited contributions unless they were extraordinary in some way. With fewer—far fewer—financial problems, the *Mercury* always seemed to me to be an institution, not a magazine. It institutionalized many of the ideas and insights that were fresh in "The Aristocrat Among Magazines." As I have said many times before . . ., I do not regard the *Mercury* as *The Smart Set*'s successor. If it had a successor at all, it was *The New Yorker*, founded the following year when, at a Saturday night poker session in Manhattan, Harold Ross and Raoul Fleischmann fell to lamenting the passing of the old *Smart Set* (the "new" one was then still very much in evidence) and decided to start a magazine of their own that would be like it, "only better." Thus, in Ross's successful policies, the influence of those of Mencken and Nathan endured and, in time, *The New Yorker* came to wield the same kind of power and influence in the American literary scene as *Smart Set* once did.

When Mencken left magazine editing in 1933, the Great Depression had begun to create some of the same problems for *The American Mercury* that he had encountered at the outset of his coeditorship of *The Smart Set* nineteen years earlier in World War I. Like Huck Finn, Mencken "had been there before." Now he had no stomach to tussle with a magazine's financial woes and declining circulation. He moved on to his monumental linguistic studies and to his great volumes of autobiography—perhaps his two most enduring achievements, after all. Nevertheless, his editorial accomplishments are not to be passed over lightly. They were enormous, as I have tried to show. In an age that produced some great American editors— Lorimer, Ray Long, Frank Crowninshield, Edward Bok, and Ellery Sedgwick among them—H. L. Mencken ranks among the best.

Notes

1. Anatomical illustrator, Johns Hopkins University, 1870–1941.

2. The date given here (1908) for the beginning of the Mencken-Nathan collaboration is erroneous. Mencken joined *The Smart Set* as book reviewer in 1908, but Nathan did not appear in the magazine until October, 1909.

3. Guy J. Forgue, ed. *The Letters of H. L. Mencken* (Knopf, 1961), p. 70. The italics are mine.

4. *Ibid.*, p. 65.

5. Recorded at the U.S. Library of Congress, 1948; also issued by Caedmon Records.

Private Voices of Public Men:
The Mencken-Dreiser Inscriptions   Vincent Fitzpatrick*

When Theodore Dreiser and Henry Louis Mencken met for the first time in the spring of 1908,[1] the novelist was editing the *Delineator*, and the Baltimorean was ghostwriting articles on child care for a pediatrician at Johns Hopkins. The ensuing friendship was long, tumultous, and mutually beneficial. For more than twenty years, these robust individuals laughed and played and drank together and sometimes fought bitterly. This was the most significant literary relationship, as well as one of the more important friendships, in each man's career. It was also one of the more intriguing and influential alliances in American literary history.[2]

A knowledge of the Mencken-Dreiser correspondence, which began in 1907 and ran to about 1,200 items—letters, notes, postcards, and telegrams—is essential for an understanding of the relationship. But some of the other items that passed back and forth in the mail can, at times, prove equally informative. The inscriptions in the books and pamphlets the authors exchanged, for example, serve, like the letters, as a barometer for the relationship. Ranging from off-hand camaraderie to calculated insult, these inscriptions also, at times, reveal what the correspondence and the writing intended for publication do not.

Dreiser's inscriptions began on Thanksgiving Day, 1909, in a copy of the Dodge, 1907 *Sister Carrie*: "To H. L. Mencken. In honor of breweries, witches, materialism, Mark Twain and all the winds of doctrine. Let's fill up the glass." Such good feeling was in keeping with the then-present mood of friendship and professional respect. Dreiser had already offered Mencken a position on the *Delineator*, which he refused. Mencken, who

*A retitled and revised version of "Gratitude and Grievances: Dreiser's Inscriptions to Mencken," *Dreiser Newsletter* 12 (Fall 1981):1–16, published by permission of the *Dreiser Newsletter* and the author.

at that time was also helping Dreiser with the *Bohemian* magazine, sent two books to New York, one of which was his own *The Philosophy of Friedrich Nietzsche* affectionately inscribed: "To Theodore Dreiser:—In memory of furious disputes on sorcery & the art of letters." This year also saw Mencken's first remarks about Dreiser in a national forum—fittingly enough in the *Smart Set*,[3] for Dreiser had been influential in getting Mencken hired as a book reviewer for the magazine.

After being dismissed from his editorial post in 1910, Dreiser had more time for *Jennie Gerhardt.* Mencken repeatedly urged Dreiser to complete the novel and then praised the manuscript when it arrived in Baltimore. (Astonishingly, Mencken went so far as to say that, with the single exception of *Huckleberry Finn*, this was the best American novel ever written.)[4]

Mencken favorably reviewed *Jennie Gerhardt* in the *Smart Set*, the Baltimore *Evening Sun*, and the Los Angeles *Times* and also wrote a small pamphlet which Harper used for advertising. On October 19, 1911, Dreiser warmly inscribed the novel: "My Dear Mencken: What shall I say in this first copy that I have secured? Oh, yes. May your good opinion of it never change. And may you live long and prosper." Mencken proceeded to use his "Free Lance" column in the Baltimore *Evening Sun* to run three blurbs praising the novel and also spoke highly of Dreiser the man and writer in correspondence with third parties.

From January, 1912, to November, 1916, Dreiser published six books, all inscribed to Mencken and reviewed by him. Mencken matured as a critic and came to view his friend more objectively. For the first time, Dreiser felt the sting of Mencken's pen. Likewise, Dreiser became more detached in some of his inscriptions. It was unfortunate that a bad novel and a worse play changed the relationship irrevocably.

In late August, 1912, Dreiser wrote that he had nearly finished with the galleys of *The Financier*. Having read the proofs, Mencken recognized that, while the novel was definitely flawed, Dreiser needed encouragement. Despite his reservations, Mencken played up the novel in three "Free Lance" columns. On October 24th, Dreiser sent to Baltimore his graciously inscribed first copy of the novel: "To H. L. Mencken, from Dreiser, in grateful friendship." Mencken was equally effusive in a copy of *The Artist. A Drama Without Words* (a spoof originally published in the *Bohemian*): "To Theodore Dreiser, in admiration and affection." Mencken proceeded to review *The Financier* favorably and, in his correspondence, went so far as to claim that unfavorable reviews had been written by those who had not read the novel.[5]

Later in 1912, Mencken offered to edit *A Traveler at Forty*. After reading the page proofs, he found the travelogue burdened by useless detail, yet he still waxed enthusiastic. The book was published on November 25th, three days before Dreiser sent Mencken the first copy: "To my beloved Henry L., in honor of beer, art and in spite of Italy." (Mencken had objected especially to Chapter XXXII, "Mrs. Q. and the Borgia Family," for he thought that the information contained there was common knowledge.) Mencken returned the favor by sending Dreiser the revised edition of *The Philosophy of Friedrich Nietzsche* and inscribing it affectionately.

Events in March, 1914, further strengthened the relationship. In his reviews of *The Financier*, Mencken had played up *The Titan*, the forthcoming second volume of the *Trilogy of Desire* featuring Frank Cowperwood. Despite advertising the novel and printing 8,500 sets of sheets, Harper reneged on the contract.[6] As Mencken saw things, Harper's squeamishness was yet another example of the moral mania plaguing American letters. He advised Dreiser to sign with Doran and offered to write the publisher on the novelist's behalf.

Mencken, once again letting his enthusiasm conquer his critical judgment, informed Dreiser that *The Titan* was "the best thing [he had] ever done with the possible exception of 'Jennie Gerhardt.' "[7] On May 13, 1914, nine days before *The Titan* was published, Dreiser sent Mencken a copy inscribed: "To Henry L. Mencken, from Theodore Dreiser—to add to his collection of Dreiseriana." Mencken's reviews were far less restrained. In *Town Topics*, for example, Mencken proclaimed that Cowperwood is "a memorable figure in a memorable book. People will be reading 'The Titan' thirty years from now. It is the sort of thing that refuses to be forgotten."[8] Such enthusiasm brought a generous response. Dreiser offered the Baltimorean the handwritten copy of any manuscript he chose, and Mencken opted for *Sister Carrie*.

In August, 1914, after Mencken and Nathan had agreed to co-edit the *Smart Set*, Mencken wanted to run several chapters from The *"Genius,"* which he had not yet seen; Dreiser refused. In early December of that year, Mencken read the manuscript and suggested revision. This autobiographical novel was Dreiser's favorite—and perhaps his worst. Blind to the book's flaws, he rejected Mencken's advice.

On September 27, 1915, five days before *The "Genius"* was published, Dreiser sent Mencken a copy with a tepid inscription: "To Henry L. Mencken from Theodore Dreiser. Without change but with best wishes just the same." Mencken's far more lively *Smart Set* review, entitled "A Literary Behemoth," depicted Dreiser as a buffoon. The *"Genius,"* for example, does not merely lack form; rather, it is "as shapeless as a Philadelphia pie woman. It billows and rolls and bulges out. . . . " Mencken does not merely say that the prose is turgid; instead, the parched Baltimorean declares that "a greater regard for fairness of phrase would be as the flow of Pilsner to the weary reader in his journey across the vast desert, steppes and pampas of the Dreiserian fable."[9] Dreiser, who never found it easy to laugh at himself, was not amused. And his mood did not brighten when this, up to that time his most successful novel financially, was suppressed by John S. Sumner, secretary of the New York Society for the Suppression of Vice.

Mencken played a major role in the events which followed, including the organizing of the Dreiser Protest—events which have been admirably explained by both Dreiser and Mencken scholars. By the time this episode was over, Mencken was disenchanted with his friend, as was evident in a later inscription. When Mencken and Nathan began the *American Mercury* in January, 1924, they included a regular department entitled "Americana." Consisting of excerpts from newspapers and magazines nationwide, this feature was designed to show the imbecility of the American mind. In 1925 Mencken published, under the same title, a volume collecting some of the choicer remarks and sent the novelist a copy inscribed: *"Theodore Dreiser.* Here we have the effect of reading 'The Genius' upon the American mind. In brief, go to hell!"

On December 13, 1916, several months after the uproar over *The "Genius"* had begun, Dreiser mailed to Mencken *The Hand of the Potter*, a play whose title alludes to a passage describing God's creation of mankind in Edward Fitzgerald's translation (1859) of the "Rubaiyat of Omar Khayyam." The Potter's hand shook badly in shaping Isadore Berchansky, Dreiser's protagonist, who rapes and murders an eleven-year-old girl. As a work of art, the play is disastrous. But what infuriated Mencken was Dreiser's insistence on publishing a play defying conventional moral standards while *The "Genius"* case, so important for the freedom of American letters, still had not been settled.

Once again, Mencken showed his displeasure in an inscription. After the play was published in 1919, Dreiser sent a copy, apologetically inscribed, to Baltimore: "H.L.M.—In some dark corner of your shelf—perhaps—you will make room for this very reprehensible member of the Dreiser family." The following year, Dreiser received a copy of *Heliogabalus, A Buffoonery in Three Acts*, co-authored by Mencken and Nathan. "Dear Dreiser," reads Mencken's inscription, " 'The Hand of the Potter' set me to itching for the glory of the boards. This is the lamentable result." This inscription conveys more than humor, for Dreiser's "tragedy in four acts" had generated Mencken's "buffoonery in three." It became increasingly clear that there were fundamental differences between the men.

Unlike Dreiser, Mencken rarely changed his mind. His tastes in literature were never eclectic, and, from the beginning of his career, Mencken most admired and wrote most intelligently about mimetic fiction—precisely the sort of writing at which Dreiser was most proficient. There was a strong strain of mysticism in Dreiser, however, and he believed, perhaps correctly, that Mencken was far too much the rationalist. Such mysticism was patent in several plays in *Plays of the Natural and the Supernatural*. In his gracious inscription, though, Dreiser did not allude to this difference. "For Henry L. Mencken from Theodore Dreiser. With all good wishes." While Mencken tried to explain away the mysticism in four plays, his impressionistic *Smart Set* review was, in the end, a staunch defense of Dreiser against the moralists.

A *Hoosier Holiday*, a travelogue more admirable than *A Traveler at Forty*, appeared in November, 1916, and Dreiser's inscription, dated October 27th, showed an affectionate irony between old friends and graciously acknowledged Mencken's editorial services: "To Henry L—from Dreiser. Thou scoundrel!—This night shalt thou be compelled to once more glance it through." Mencken more than reciprocated. "The Creed of a Novelist," a five-page review full of approbation, appeared in the *Smart Set* more than two months before *A Hoosier Holiday* was published.

In November, 1916, Mencken sailed to Germany as a war correspondent for the Baltimore *Sunpapers*. Both Dreiser, a first-generation American of German descent, and Mencken, whose paternal grandfather left Germany in 1848, suffered badly at the hands of jingoistic critics during World War I. (Mencken's battles, on Dreiser's behalf and his own, against critics such as Stuart Pratt Sherman need not be recounted here.) When Mencken returned to Baltimore in March, 1917, he was welcomed by a pamphlet containing "Life, Art and America," one of Dreiser's most significant essays. "To my first (critical) love Henry L.—on his return from the fatherland," reads the affectionate inscription.

Such solidarity was interrupted, however, by the publication of Mencken's first, and last, volume of literary criticism, *A Book of Prefaces*, which contained an essay entitled "Theodore Dreiser." Dreiser had already responded favorably to the three lengthy columns which appeared in the Baltimore *Evening Sun* during the summer of 1916; all three contained material reprinted in *A Book of Prefaces*.[10] In May, 1917, Mencken informed Dreiser that the essay was being revised. That same month, Mencken sent "Theodore Dreiser," or at least part of it, to the novelist, who returned the manuscript in July.[11] Apparently, Dreiser became angry before *A Book of Prefaces* was released in the fall.

The copy Dreiser received bore a frigid inscription: "To Theodore Dreiser." One would expect something more effusive, for this essay of more than eighty pages offered what was at the time the most comprehensive treatment of Dreiser's life and art.[12] The Dreiser-Mencken correspondence, which had broken off in July, 1917, did not resume until May of the following year. In his letters to third parties, Mencken's comments about Dreiser grew more caustic. And in late August, 1918—more than a year after this tiff had begun—Dreiser's inscription in *Free and Other Stories* bore a marked coolness: "For Henry L. Mencken from Theodore Dreiser." Mencken, in turn, wrote a tepid review.

Throughout the remainder of 1918 and the early months of 1919, Mencken urged Dreiser to complete *The Bulwark*. But Dreiser pushed ahead with another project, and Mencken exulted over *Twelve Men*, the character sketches published in April, 1919. "For Henry L. Mencken—" reads Dreiser's inscription, "acknowledging many courtesies and services." Mencken responded unequivocally that the portraits of Paul Dresser and Muldoon ("Culhane, the Solid Man") were the best writing Dreiser had ever done. Two days later, Mencken called for a companion volume to be entitled *Twelve Women*.[13] He inscribed the first edition of *The American Language* as follows: "To Theodore Dreiser, with veneration." Moreover, Mencken applauded *Twelve Men* in both the New York *Sun* and the *Smart Set*. Never again, however, would Mencken respond this favorably to a new piece of writing by Dreiser.

In fact, Mencken's remarks about *Hey-Rub-a-Dub-Dub*, in which he hooted at the Hoosier's clumsy attempts to write metaphysics, comprised the Baltimorean's most unsympathetic review of a book by Dreiser. Far more than in his burlesque of *The "Genius,"* Mencken enjoyed himself thoroughly at the novelist's expense. Dreiser came to wonder if Mencken were not a Philistine anaesthetic to art lying outside his narrow circle. Mencken, in turn, thought that Dreiser was dissipating his talents by writing about what he did not understand and by having such a messy personal life. Dreiser, on his part, found the Baltimorean managerial and overly conventional.[14]

Nonetheless, Dreiser asked Mencken to edit *A Book about Myself* and to search for chapters that could be sold to magazines. Mencken suggested several changes in the manuscript. On November 28, 1922, Dreiser inscribed the book in a quasi-German which has defied all attempts at translation and pasted inside the front cover a note acknowledging the revisions. Mencken's gift to Dreiser in 1922—*Prejudices: Third Series*—carried a perfunctory inscription: "Dear Dreiser: Once again." And in his *Smart Set* review of March, 1923, Mencken gave only cursory attention to Dreiser's autobiography.

On April 13th, Dreiser sent to Baltimore *Douze Hommes*, the French translation of the character sketches, with a stilted, perhaps ironic, inscription that did not bode well: "For Mencken from Dreiser. Bows. Genuflections. Hand-Kissings." And when *The Color of a Great City* was published on December 6th, 1923, Dreiser wrote only: "For Henry L. Mencken— his first edition." Mencken reviewed these sketches only in the Baltimore *Evening Sun*. The fact that Mencken chose not to discuss *The Color of a Great City* in the *American Mercury*, whose first issue appeared the same month as the *Sunpapers'* review, showed his low esteem for Dreiser's current writing.

The manuscript of *An American Tragedy* was approximately one million words. In July, 1925, Dreiser cut the manuscript to 385,000 words and sent it to the printer.[15] As late as November 28, Mencken had not received the page proofs. In his letter of that day, Mencken promised to review the novel in "a höflich [courteous] and able manner." It is certain that he performed no editorial services upon the novel, and it is probable that he did not see *An American Tragedy* before it was published on December 17, 1925.

On January 14, 1926, Dreiser wrote: "I'm sending you a signed and numbered and personally inscribed copy of *An American Tragedy* whether you want it or not. If you don't want it give it to your worst enemy. My regards. My Pontifical indulgence." Mencken replied amiably that he would be delighted to have the book.[16] Certainly, he was not delighted when he received the novel and saw Dreiser's inscription: "Dear Heinrich: As my oldest living enemy I venture to offer you this little pamphlet. Don't mind if it emits a destructive gas. Us Germans—you know."[17]

Mencken wrote on January 28 that his review was finished. Forthright as usual, he said he had attacked *An American Tragedy* as well as praised it. He explained further, in his letter of February 5, that the trial and execution of Clyde were well handled but that the events up to and including Roberta's death "made me shed some sweat." Significantly, Mencken closed on an amiable note: "I hear that the book is selling well." Thoroughly enraged, Dreiser vilified Mencken three days later: "As to your critical predilections, animosities, inhibitions—et cet. Tosh. Who reads you? Bums and loafers. No-goods. We were friends before ever you were a critic of mine if I recall. And,—if an [*sic*] humble leman may speak up—may remain so despite various—well—choose your insults."[18] Mencken chose not to respond in kind, and the correspondence ceased for more than eight years.[19]

During the estrangement, Mencken chose to comment publicly upon only some of Dreiser's books. He decided not to review the three books published in 1927: a revised edition of *The Financier*; a collection of short stories entitled *Chains* (three of which Mencken had run in the *Smart Set* and the *Mercury*); and an edition of an old nemesis, *The Hand of the Potter*. Mencken did, however, acquire the first two books, and he also obtained *The Songs of Paul Dresser* (New York: Boni and Liveright), for which Dreiser had written the Introduction.

In 1928, Mencken failed to acquire both *Moods: Cadenced and Declaimed* and *Dreiser Looks at Russia*. In 1929, Mencken obtained the four-page "Catalogue of an Exhibition of Paintings by Jerome Blum," with a Foreword by Dreiser, and *A Gallery of Women*, the two-volume collection of fifteen sketches published after a gestation of more than ten years. This was the first book by Dreiser which Mencken chose to review after the rift. "Ladies, Mainly Sad," a perfunctory review of about a page, appeared in the *Mercury* of February, 1930.

Dawn, the second volume of Dreiser's autobiography to be published although the first in chronological order, appeared in May, 1931. Perhaps for old-time's sake, Mencken reviewed the book. The untitled review of barely more than 200 words, Mencken's briefest for any volume by Dreiser, was printed in the July *Mercury*. The polemical *Tragic America* was published in December, 1931, and Mencken received a copy in February, 1932. If he read the book carefully, he was undoubtedly incensed by Dreiser's politics. In any event, he did not respond in print to *Tragic America*. *Dawn*, in fact, proved to be the final new book by Dreiser which Mencken reviewed.

Late in 1934 some ill-tempered comments by Burton Rascoe provided the occasion for a reconciliation between Dreiser and Mencken. Rascoe, who had been editing *The Smart Set Anthology* in collaboration with Groff Conklin, was upset because Mencken refused to allow any of his work to be reprinted. In his Introduction, circulated in pamphlet form for advertising purposes, Rascoe asserted that, according to Dreiser, Mencken split with the novelist because Dreiser refused to contribute to a fund for defending the *Mercury* in a censorship case involving "Hatrack."[20] (This story by Herbert Asbury about a small-town prostitute was in the April, 1926, issue.) Dreiser wrote several letters protesting against this misinterpretation of his remarks, and also sent a conciliatory letter to Mencken, who replied in the boisterous vein of the good old days. When the two men got together in New York in December, 1934, they struggled under the weight of this first reunion,[21] for there were still profound differences between them.

Nonetheless, Mencken resumed some of his former roles and offered advice. When *The Living Thoughts of Thoreau*, with an Introduction by Dreiser, came out in March, 1939, Mencken received a copy warmly inscribed: "For Henry L. Mencken in gratitude for much." In December, Mencken gave Dreiser a copy of *Happy Days*, the first volume of the Baltimorean's congenial and highly successful autobiographical trilogy.

In August, 1940, Dreiser asked for help on a manuscript tentatively entitled *America, Keep Out*.[22] Despite the deep conflict between radical and reactionary, Dreiser and Mencken could agree upon several issues. Both were, at heart, isolationists. Both hated what they viewed as British imperialism and believed that England was using the United States for its own self-interest. Finally, both thought that President Franklin Roosevelt wanted to enter World War II as quickly as possible because his New Deal economics had failed miserably. The long and effusive inscription to *America Is Worth Saving*, published in January, 1941, was the last Dreiser would write for the Baltimorean: "For Henry L. Mencken from (and with the enduring affection of) Theodore Dreiser. In trade, as you might say, for those ten realistic years of your youth. No concealed attempt at proselytizing because of no hope of so doing."

In 1944, there was a serious falling out over Dreiser's decision to accept an award from the American Academy of Arts and Letters. In Mencken's eyes, Dreiser had profaned the cause for which they had fought so long and ardently, and Mencken chastised the novelist in correspondence with third parties. But the friendship now proved more resilient than it had in early 1926, and the men continued to correspond amiably enough. On December 27, 1945, Mencken wrote in a facetious, even ribald, manner about their first encounter more than thirty-five years before. Ominously, he closed the letter with intimations of his own mortality, but it was Dreiser who died first—the very next day, in fact. Two of America's most prolific writers, Mencken and Dreiser never took the opportunity to say two simple words: good-bye.

The inscriptions used in this essay clearly indicate Mencken's propensity for laughter as opposed to Dreiser's fundamental seriousness. They reveal not only a deep-seated affection and mutual respect but also a contentiousness resulting from radical differences in temperament and outlook. While none of the inscriptions are especially profound—one should not expect them to be—they do show the breadth of the relationship and help to suggest its importance in American literary history. In this way, these private voices—often congenial but sometimes caustic—complement both the correspondence and the writing done for publication.

Notes

1. The author wishes to thank Dr. Neda M. Westlake, Curator of the Rare Book Collection at the University of Pennsylvania, for permission to quote from Dreiser's unpublished writing, and the Enoch Pratt Free Library in Baltimore for permission to quote Mencken's inscriptions and letters.

The books and pamphlets Dreiser gave to Mencken are in the Enoch Pratt Free Library. Both the material Mencken gave and his letters to Dreiser are at the University of Pennsylvania. The New York Public Library holds the letters from Dreiser to Mencken. Unless otherwise noted, the letters referred to in this essay are in these collections.

2. The Mencken-Dreiser relationship has been discussed by many biographers and critics. W. A. Swanberg examines it in detail in his *Dreiser* (New York: Scribner's, 1965) and more briefly in *Menckeniana*, 15 (Fall, 1965). See also Donald Stoddard, "Mencken and Dreiser: An Exchange of Roles," *Library Chronicle*, 32 (Spring, 1966), and Thomas P. Riggio, "Dreiser and Mencken: In the Literary Trenches," *American Scholar*, 54 (Spring 1985).

My article in the *Dreiser Newsletter*, 12 (Fall, 1981), an earlier version of this essay, contains some information on Mencken's relations with Helen Dreiser after her husband's death. I have discussed aspects of the Mencken-Dreiser friendship in the *Dreiser Newsletter*, 10 (Fall, 1972) and *Menckeniana*, 60 (Winter, 1976). My dissertation, "Two Beasts in the Parlor: The Dreiser-Mencken Relationship" (State University of New York at Stony Brook, 1979), includes a comprehensive bibliography.

3. Mencken, "The Books of the Dog Days," *Smart Set*, 29 (September, 1909), 157; and " 'A Doll's House'—with a Fourth Act," *Smart Set*, 29 (December, 1909), 153.

4. Mencken to Dreiser, 20 September 1911, in *Letters of H. L. Mencken*, ed. Guy J. Forgue (New York: Knopf, 1961), p. 14. In a letter of 15 September 1911, Mencken had even said that *Jennie Gerhardt* was the best American novel ever written.

5. Mencken to Dreiser, 7 January 1913.

6. Swanberg. *Dreiser*, p. 172.

7. Mencken to Dreiser, 23 March 1914, in Forgue, *Letters of H. L. Mencken*, pp. 43–44.

8. Mencken, "The Literary Show: Dreiser and His Titan," *Town Topics*, (18 June 1914), 17–18.

9. Mencken, "A Literary Behemoth," *Smart Set*, 47 (December, 1915), 150–154.

10. Mencken, "Theodore Dreiser," Baltimore *Evening Sun*, 26 July 1916, p. 6; "More Dreiseriana," Baltimore *Evening Sun*, 1 August 1916, p. 6; and "Two Dreiser Novels," Baltimore *Evening Sun*, 4 August 1916, p. 6.

11. See Stoddard, "Mencken and Dreiser: An Exchange of Roles," p. 133. Professor Stoddard says that Dreiser saw the entire essay before it was published.

12. Several critics have praised the essay. See Stoddard, "Mencken and Dreiser: An Exchange of Roles," p. 133; Swanberg, *Dreiser*, p. 223; and Robert Elias, *Theodore Dreiser: Apostle of Nature* (Ithaca, New York and London: Cornell University Press, 1970), p. 378.

13. Mencken to Dreiser, 3 April 1919 and 5 April 1919.

14. See especially Dreiser, *The American Diaries, 1902–1926*, eds. Thomas P. Riggio, James L. W. West III and Neda M. Westlake (Philadelphia: University of Pennsylvania Press, 1982), p. 169. In this, his diary entry of 2 August 1917, Dreiser calls Mencken a "cautious conventionalist." Mencken's mistress, Marion Bloom, was the sister of one of Dreiser's mistresses, Estelle Bloom Kubitz. It bothered Dreiser that Mencken was so secretive about the affair.

15. Swanberg, *Dreiser*, p. 295.

16. Dreiser to Mencken, 14 January 1926; Mencken to Dreiser, 20 January 1926.

17. Quoted in Carl Bode, *Mencken* (Carbondale, Illinois: Southern Illinois University Press, 1969). p. 185.

18. Mencken to Dreiser, 28 January 1926; Mencken to Dreiser, 5 February 1926, in Forgue, *Letters of H. L. Mencken*, p. 289. The passage in Dreiser's letter concluding with "No-goods" is quoted by Edgar Kemler, *The Irreverent* Mr. Mencken (Boston: Little, 1950), p. 172; he does not give his source. "Who reads you? Bums and loafers. No-goods" is quoted by Bode, *Mencken*, p. 325, with Kemler credited as the source.

19. The question of what factors other than those already mentioned may have helped generate Dreiser's strong language is debatable. I have argued elsewhere (in my dissertation, for example) that Dreiser, at the time of this letter, could not have seen "Dreiser in 840 Pages," the review Mencken wrote for the *American Mercury*. It is certain that Dreiser could not have seen the published review, since the March, 1926, issue of the *Mercury* had not been released by February 8. But Professor Thomas Riggio has kindly suggested that I reconsider the letter of January 28 in which Mencken told Dreiser that a proof of the review was being sent to the novelist's editor at Boni and Liveright. Although Dreiser, in his letter of February 8, did not say he had seen the proof, and did not quote or paraphrase the review, it is conceivable that he may have seen the proof by that time. Moreover, the review printed in the *Mercury* would not have been changed substantially, if at all.

20. Burton Rascoe, " 'Smart Set' History" (New York: Reynal and Hitchcock, 1934), p. 33. This error was corrected before the Introduction was published in *The Smart Set Anthology*.

21. Dreiser to Mencken, 20 November 1934; Mencken to Dreiser, 21 November 1934. The meeting at the Ansonia is discussed by Arnold Gingrich, "How to Become the World's Second-Best Authority on Almost Anything," *Esquire*, 55 (April, 1966), p. 6; and by Swanberg, *Dreiser*, pp. 425–426.

22. Dreiser to Mencken, 22 August 1940, quoted by Swanberg, *Dreiser*, pp. 469–470.

"This Hellawful South": Mencken and the Late Confederacy
Fred Hobson*

H. L. Mencken, dean of American letters and rebellion in the 1920s, occupies a strange position in the cultural life of that decade. A conservative, in the twenties he attracted mostly liberals to his side. A writer given

---

*This essay was written for this volume and is published by permission of the author.

to racial slurs—"coon" and "darky," "blackamoor" and "niggero"—he numbered many black writers among his friends and, more important, played a central role in the Harlem Renaissance of the twenties. He called the vast region beneath the Potomac and Ohio the "hellawful South," a cultural and literary "desert," yet he influenced dozens of southern writers and intellectuals and played a leading role in the first phase of the Southern literary renascence.[1]

Of all Mencken's love-hate relationships, perhaps that with the American South is the most famous. And of all his targets in the 1920s and 1930s—and he took on nearly every American institution, ideal, and region at one time or another—the late Confederacy was perhaps the most vulnerable. He devoted to its failings perhaps his most famous single essay, "The Sahara of the Bozart" (1920). I quote liberally from that essay, because—as his friend Gerald W. Johnson once said—"how the man could write." Of the American South Mencken wrote:

> It is, indeed, amazing to contemplate so vast a vacuity. One thinks of the interstellar spaces, of the colossal reaches of the now mythical ether. Nearly the whole of Europe could be lost in that stupendous region of fat farms, shoddy cities and paralyzed cerebrums; one could throw in France, Germany and Italy, and still have room for the British Isles. And yet, for all its size and all its wealth and all the "progress" it babbles of, it is almost as sterile, artistically, intellectually, culturally, as the Sahara Desert. There are single acres in Europe that house more first-rate men than all the states south of the Potomac; there are probably single square miles in America. If the whole of the late Confederacy were to be engulfed by a tidal wave tomorrow, the effect upon the civilized minority of men in the world would be but little greater than that of a flood on the Yang-tse-kiang.

And Mencken had hardly warmed up yet, had not yet turned to the primary focus of his essay—the scarcity of beaux arts (i.e., "bozart"), particularly good literature, in the South:

> In all that gargantuan paradise of the fourth-rate there is not a single picture gallery worth going into, or a single orchestra capable of playing the nine symphonies of Beethoven, or a single opera-house, or a single theater devoted to decent plays. . . . Once you have counted Robert Loveman (an Ohioan by birth) and John McClure (an Oklahoman) you will not find a single southern poet above the rank of a neighborhood rhymester. Once you have counted James Branch Cabell . . . you will not find a single southern prose writer who can actually write. And once you have—but when you come to critics, musical composers, painters, sculptors, architects and the like, you will have to give it up, for there is not even a bad one between the Potomac and the Gulf. Nor an historian. Nor a sociologist. Nor a philosopher. Nor a theologian. Nor a scientist. In all these fields the south is an awe-inspiring blank—a brother to Portugal, Serbia and Esthonia.[2]

The response to Mencken's indictment—which appeared as a nine-teen-page essay in his volume *Prejudices, Second Series*—proved that Southerners, if they did not write, at least read. "The Sahara" shocked professors, editors, politicians, poetasters, and old maids of both sexes. Soon professional southerners were speaking up from the Potomac to the Rio Grande. The southern offensive was led, as other charges were to be led throughout the twenties, by Arkansas—a particular favorite of Mencken, as it had been of Mark Twain. One newspaper charged that Mencken had ties with Germany, another wrote that "Herr Mencken" was "a self-appointed emissary of the Wilhelmstrasse" and further "an insufferable excrescence on the body of American literature." But the most poignant plaint came from an editor who first called Mencken an "infernal and ignorant mounte-bank," a "miserable, uninformed wretch," then stopped to wonder: "What has the South done to Menneken?"[3]

A fair enough question. What *had* the South done to Mencken, and why did he unleash such a barrage of criticism against it? First, one must consider what the South thought of itself in the year 1920. It considered itself, quite simply, the American seat of civilization, the land of the greatest poets, statesmen, political philosophers, and orators. Were not four of the first five American presidents Southerners? Was not Robert E. Lee the noblest general America had produced? And so on. The point is that southerners were not only angry but genuinely puzzled. And many non-southerners who read Mencken's essay were probably puzzled as well. For in the year 1920 the South in the American imagination was not all that benighted. Certainly it *had* been during the period of Civil War and Reconstruction, and certainly it would be again after 1920; but from the late 1870s until the aftermath of World War I one finds an era of relatively good feelings in American regional relations. The 1870s, 1880s, and 1890s were characterized by local color in American literature, and Southern writers such as Thomas Nelson Page described a harmonious neverland befo' the war, a land inhabited by brave gentlemen, gracious ladies, and content and grateful slaves. Southerners created the myth, but northerners bought it. They too believed Robert E. Lee was the noblest general the country had produced. They too had seen *The Birth of a Nation* and had sympathized with southern whites fighting to restore white rule. For the most part, the rest of America turned its eyes from the contemporary South, the land of Jim Crow and Judge Lynch, demagogy and illiteracy and hookworm. They preferred instead to see that antebellum paradise that was becoming not only a southern but an American ideal.

But if H. L. Mencken hated anything, he hated frauds, and he saw the South as it existed in 1920 as fraudulent—smug, complacent, and lying to itself. What made matters worse was that Mencken believed the South *had* been at one point precisely what it now claimed to be—the American seat of civilization. What it had experienced was "the drying up of a civilization," a decline "impossible in all history to match." As Mencken explained in "The Sahara":

> I say a civilization because that is what, in the old days, the south had, despite the Baptist and Methodist barbarism that reigns down there now. More, it was a civilization of manifold excellences—perhaps the best that the Western Hemisphere has ever seen—undoubtedly the best that These States have ever seen. Down to the middle of the last century, and even beyond, the main hatchery of ideas on this side of the water was across the Potomac bridges. The New England shopkeepers and theologians never developed a civilization. . . . They were, at their best, tawdry and tacky fellows, oafish in manner and devoid of imagination. . . . But in the south there were men of delicate fancy, urbane instinct and aristocratic manner—in brief, superior men—in brief, gentry.[4]

What had wiped out this civilization, Mencken believed, was the Civil War. He was wrong there, since the civilization he admired—the southern civilization which was broad and tolerant and valued ideas—had begun to decline in the early 1830s, thirty years before the war. With the beginning of the great national debate over slavery in the 1830s (or the accelerated phase of that debate) the old Jeffersonian spirit of free inquiry departed and the South turned nearly all its intellectual energy to a defense of its peculiar institution.

But if Mencken had not been specifically right, he was right in general—except that he should perhaps have substituted "Virginia civilization" for "southern civilization," since it was the Old Dominion that contained most of what Mencken admired in the Old South. In any case, he contended, the Southern aristocracy had been wiped out in the war and its aftermath and the "poor whites" had taken control of Dixie. The "poor whites" were an almost separate race as Mencken described them, and the contemporary South they controlled was nearly fabulous. He wrote in "The Sahara" of a faraway land, a wasteland, a country of "shoddy cities and paralyzed cerebrums." This land lay not just across the Potomac, but seemed to exist rather on some distant continent: and Mencken, like Gulliver, having investigated an unbelievable culture and having returned, felt obligated to report his truth. Dixie was "a vast plain of mediocrity, stupidity, lethargy, almost of dead silence," a land of "barbarism," of "unanimous torpor and doltishness." It possessed "a curious and almost pathological estrangement from everything that makes for a civilized culture." The natives of one particularly despicable region, Georgia, were descended from "the most degraded race of human beings claiming an Anglo-Saxon origin that can be found on the face of the earth." Even in the twentieth century, these people, like Gulliver's yahoos, were "but little removed from savagery."[5]

Did Mencken mean all this? He meant it in the way Gerald Johnson had in mind when he later wrote that the effect of "The Sahara" could be "attributed to Mencken's mastery of the cardinal principal of dramaturgy, namely, that nothing else produces as smashing an effect as the truth magnified by ten diameters."[6] Mencken meant it, too, as a corrective to excessive southern claims: southerners had so exaggerated their virtues that exaggeration on the other side was necessary to balance the scales.

But it was not only because Mencken was an Old South romantic who bitterly protested the southern fall from civilization that he unleashed his wrath against Dixie in "The Sahara of the Bozart" and other essays. He blasted the South, too, because by 1920 he had come to see the southern states as the repository of almost everything he detested about the United States as a whole. His greatest targets for the eight or ten years preceding "The Sahara" were puritanism in American culture, the "Anglo-Saxons" in America, the attendant pride in the English cultural tradition to the exclusion of all other traditions, and, finally, during World War I, England itself. Pride in "pure Anglo-Saxon blood," Mencken felt, was stronger in the South than in any other part of the country—particularly in the early twentieth century when the Northeast and other regions had received great numbers of European immigrants but the South had not. With Anglo-Saxon "blood" (which, in fact, as Mencken pointed out, was often Celtic rather than Anglo-Saxon) came a pride in English heritage. And, with the war, that pride translated into strong support for England against Germany—the ancestral home of the Menckens.

It would be hard to estimate the effect the First World War had on Mencken, not only on his attitude toward the South but toward America in general. He was intensely proud of his German ancestry—of German music, German literature, German food, German beer—but Germany, and German-Americans, were under attack in wartime America. For a time Mencken was forced to remain silent about the war and his pro-German sentiments. And when the war was over and he was free once again to write what he wished, his distaste for England—and for those Americans who had vilified Germans—was extreme. A good number of those detractors inhabited the South, the most heavily English part of the country.

Also connected to Mencken's dislike of the British Isles was his hatred of puritanism, that habit of belief and conduct that had sprung up in England in the early seventeenth century but had taken root in New England and—by the mid-nineteenth century, Mencken believed—in the American South. "There is nothing but empty nonsense," he wrote in 1915, "in the common superstition that Puritanism is exclusively a Northern, a New England madness. . . . In 1757 a band of Puritans invaded what is now Georgia—and Georgia has been a Puritan paradise ever since." He then quoted historian John Fiske: "In the South today there is more Puritanism surviving than in New England." "If you doubt it," he added, "turn to prohibition and the lynching-bee (the descendant of the old Puritan sport of witch-burning), or run your eye over any newspaper published South of the Potomac."[7]

Mencken's understanding of puritanism, and particularly southern puritanism, was never very exact. The raw Calvinism of the backwoods South, in fact, was very different from the structured, highly intellectualized religion of Massachusetts Bay. Neither did puritanism as an American cultural force deserve all the abuse Mencken gave it. What he had in mind when he blasted "puritanism" was more nearly an American version of Victorianism. Genteel standards in literature, American reticence about discussing sex, a movement toward prohibition, a distrust of hedonism, the American passion for "decency" and "respectability": these Mencken denounced as "puritanical." They were more nearly Victorian.

But such distinctions matter little: the South in the early twentieth century was also the most Victorian part of America, and Victorianism was also English.[8] Thus whatever Mencken saw in Dixie he disliked: prohibition, demagogy, evangelical religion, sentimentalism in literature, white racial attitudes—and finally democracy itself. Mencken had long been a critic of democracy, and the Southern brand of democracy he saw as the worst kind of populism, or mob rule. Southern governmental powers had been "transferred to what the old South called the 'poor white trash.'. . . . Its ideals and habits have fallen to those of the mob."[9]

"The Sahara of the Bozart," then, should not have been quite the bombshell it was to those who read Mencken in 1920; it was but the logical result of many of the views he had expressed for the previous decade. Three years earlier, in fact, he had published a much shorter newspaper article under that same title—and in that article had blamed the South's cultural sterility on its "astounding orgy of puritanism."[10]

Nor was Mencken through with Dixie after "The Sahara." Spurred by the reaction he drew from angry southerners, he continued to attack southern prejudices and mediocrity in essays in the *Baltimore Evening Sun* and the *Smart Set*. But he soon discovered that his attacks were attracting a different kind of southern reader, one who agreed with rather than disputed his findings. There has long been a debate about Mencken's intentions in "The Sahara." Oscar Cargill has suggested that he meant the essay to stir up young southern writers and intellectuals, that it was to be the first step in a "crusade" to bring about a southern literary renascence.[11] This is very doubtful, since Mencken himself seemed unaware at the time of an incipient renascence of the southern spirit and later wrote that he was "astonished" at the first fruits of a southern awakening in 1920. But if he was not a crusader at first, he became one when certain southerners praised his attacks and pledged to join his forces in a war of southern liberation.

Among those writers and would-be writers who became southern Menckenites in the early 1920s were Paul Green, an aspiring playwright in North Carolina who would win the Pulitzer Prize for drama in 1926; Green's former classmate Thomas Wolfe, a twenty-year-old Tar Heel who was studying literature at Harvard when he read "The Sahara" and immediately began scribbling into his notebook ideas about the "puerile nature of intellectual life" in the South;[12] Allen Tate, a young poet at Vanderbilt University who went around with Mencken's *American Mercury* under his arm; Julia Peterkin, a South Carolinian whom Mencken advised to write stories about Gullah Negro life; and Frances Newman, an Atlanta librarian whom Mencken inspired to write the controversial satirical novel, *The Hard-Boiled Virgin* (1924). Literary groups in Richmond and New Orleans, inspired by Mencken's boldness, founded little magazines in which they dispensed Mencken's idea of a benighted South. The editors of both magazines, *The Reviewer* and *The Double Dealer*, kept in close contact with the Sage of Baltimore. Other Southerners, such as those writers who founded the Poetry Society of South Carolina in 1920, did not precisely agree with Mencken, but they were challenged by him and set about to prove him wrong by producing a literature he would applaud.

Mencken's influence was so immense and widespread that by 1922 Menckenism had become in the South nothing short of a literary and intellectual force. "It is my opinion," wrote Edwin A. Alderman, president of the University of Virginia, that "practically every intelligent member of the University, in the student body and in the faculty, has read Mencken's essay on 'The Sahara of the Bozart.' " "You have no idea," he wrote an acquaintance in 1925, "the enormous vogue [Mencken] has among students." Although Alderman was not an admirer of Mencken, he believed Mencken's "very daring and irreverence [were] causing him to reveal a picture" that southerners "ought to see." Addison Hibbard of the University of North Carolina wrote that Mencken had become an "institution" in the South, and Frances Newman, in a lead article in the *New York Herald Tribune Books*, attributed the new literary activity in the South to Mencken's attacks, insisting that he had "dug all the violets out from the Sahara's sands with [his] own Corona."[13] By the year 1922, then, it was clear that Mencken had given rise to a certain southern frame of mind—one characterized by an extreme distaste for southern tradition, a belief that southern culture (at least since 1830) was severely deficient, a disavowal of all literature, poetry or prose, written in the South since the Civil War, and above all, characterized by a tone, a gleeful irreverence that liked nothing better than mocking the old gods.

What Mencken called for in southern literature was realism and satire, and a "Confederate Sinclair Lewis" was the writer he hoped to find. He already deeply admired one southern writer, the satirist James Branch Cabell of Richmond (the only prose writer he had excepted from the indictment of "The Sahara of the Bozart"), and he hoped that Cabell, as well as the midwesterner Lewis, would serve as a model for other southerners. His admiration for Cabell, in fact, betrays much about Mencken's overall attitude toward the South. Cabell was, to him, the last aristocrat—"a lingering survivor of the *ancien régime*," the last elegant, refined artist left in a Dixie that had otherwise been taken over by poor whites. Cabell is a writer nearly forgotten today, but he was in 1920 a leading American novelist—

"one of the great masters of English prose," Vernon Louis Parrington wrote in 1921, "the supreme comic spirit thus far granted us." Cabell was best known as the author of *Jurgen* (1919) and other novels which created the mythical realm of Poictesme and told the story of Manuel, a swineherd who became redeemer, and of his descendants through seven generations. Since Cabell wrote of Poictesme he was often charged with escapism, but the story of human foibles he told was also a story of Richmond, of Virginia and the American South. At the center of his fiction was the whole complex of myths upon which his fellow southerners based their lives. His most consistent targets were chivalry and hero-worship, southern religion and oratory. Mencken understood this: it was "the grotesque quasicivilization in which, coming to manhood, [Cabell] found himself" that "sent him flying to Poictesme," and it was "that civilization which he depicts from his exile there." Mencken understood as well, however, that Cabell was not only a contemporary satirist but also a writer committed to art for the sake of art in a way no other southern writer was. He was, finally, that variety of artist Mencken had earlier championed in Theodore Dreiser and others—the writer as outcast, isolated from his immediate culture, the writer operating in a "sort of social and intellectual vacuum." Cabell was not sentimental, he was irreverent toward southern tradition, and he had been condemned by reviewers, within and without the South, for *Jurgen*, which had been judged a "lewd, lascivious, indecent . . . book."[14] To Mencken he was, at one and the same time, victim, iconoclast, holdover gentleman from the Jeffersonian days of free southern inquiry, and model for younger southern writers.

But Mencken attracted not only southern novelists and poets to his side in the early 1920s but also a host of journalists and social commentators who saw his method of close observation and attack as the best way to correct southern ills. In fact, Mencken saw the first harbinger of a southern renascence not in the belletrists but rather in a sociologist, Howard W. Odum, and Odum's *Journal of Social Forces* in Chapel Hill. In the *Journal*, he wrote, Odum was "scientifically" approaching social problems that had been left unexamined in the South for half a century. He was not completely right, but he was close. Except for George W. Cable of Louisiana, Walter Hines Page of North Carolina, and some few other native critics, the South had dwelled under the rule of what one of Mencken's later apostles was to call "the savage ideal"—that code under which all criticism and dissent were suppressed.[15] Odum, a Georgian who had come to teach at the University of North Carolina in 1920, sought to change that.

He had help from a group of iconoclastic journalists, the most notable of whom was Gerald W. Johnson of the *Greensboro* [N. C.] *Daily News*. The young Carolinian approached the southern scene with Menckenian irreverence and glee. He developed a prose style similar to Mencken's, he employed the same metaphors, and he was equally incisive as a critic. As another of Mencken's North Carolina correspondents wrote him, Johnson was a " 'realistic' critic—of your school, preferring the axe and the bludgeon, particularly after the spear and the rapier have failed to 'go home.' "[16] Mencken agreed, enlisted Johnson as one of his most frequent contributors to the *American Mercury* in the 1920s, and in 1926 brought him to Baltimore to write for the Sunpapers.

He encouraged and influenced numerous other southern journalists, including Julian and Julia Harris of Georgia, Grover Hall of Alabama, and Nell Battle Lewis of North Carolina, but his greatest apostle was young Wilbur J. Cash, an editorial writer for the *Charlotte News* and future author of *The Mind of the South*. A Carolinian whose background was similar to Johnson's, Cash began to write for the *Mercury* in 1929, the month Johnson left off, and he, even more consciously than Johnson, mastered the Mencken style. His vocabulary was unashamedly Menckenesque: "blackamoor," "Ethiop," "shamans," "holy men," "civilized minority," and "below the Potomac." His view of southern culture in his *Mercury* articles of the late 1920s and early 1930s was precisely Mencken's: the South was a fraudulent society, dominated by preachers, demagogues, and poor whites. Later, in the mid-1930s, Cash began to depart, to some extent, from the influence of Mencken, and by the time he finished *The Mind of the South* (1941) he seems to have found his own voice. But that book, still the classic work on the plain white southerner, was nonetheless characterized by Menckenian assumptions: that southern history was essentially a struggle between aristocrats and poor whites, that puritanism was the curse of the South, that puritanism and hedonism in fact ran parallel in the same southern society, and that the South was essentially an uncultured land.

Although by the mid-1920s Mencken's influence in the South was established, he still had not actually visited any of the southern states except Virginia. But in July 1925 he would find reason to visit the heart of the southern Bible Belt, and it was the most celebrated trip into Dixie he ever made. John Thomas Scopes, a high school science teacher, had taught his students about Darwinian evolution, and when the state of Tennessee took him to trial for his heresy—and signed William Jennings Bryan for the prosecution—Mencken decided the event was too good to miss. Earlier that year he had persuaded Clarence Darrow to undertake Scopes's defense, and in early July he and more than a hundred other journalists from across the United States and from Europe descended on Dayton, Tennessee. The Dayton trial epitomized to Mencken most of the southern failings he had observed for more than a decade—the narrow-mindedness of religious fundamentalism, a fear of ideas, a hostility to outsiders. "On to Dayton," he had written Howard Odum in June 1925. "The greatest trial since that before Pilate!"[17]

Mencken thoroughly enjoyed the trial. He debated with fundamentalists in front of the courthouse, passed out handbills announcing the appearance of "Elmer Chubb, LL. D.," and, near the end of his stay, nearly became the victim of the same sort of mob he had often described in his essays. But his satirical writing about Dayton, while it drew the admiration of his fervent disciples, lost him the support of some of his early followers. Notably, the Fugitives of Nashville—particularly Allen Tate and Donald Davidson—were offended that Mencken made their state the butt of national ridicule. Already somewhat disenchanted with Menckenism, they charged that Mencken's complete dismissal of religious fundamentalism betrayed a limited vision on his own part. Davidson bitterly resented Mencken's comic portrait of rural southerners and charged that he could see them only as types, as abstractions, not as individuals with individual hopes, fears, plans, and human dignity.

The rebellion of Davidson and other influential Fugitive poets was significant: they were the first young southerners of the highest intellectual respectability who challenged Mencken. John Crowe Ransom was a former Rhodes Scholar, Tate a brilliant poet and critic who was usually assumed to be a modernist, and Davidson himself had solid credentials as a literary critic. These were hardly the backwoods preachers and editors and pedagogues who had attacked Mencken earlier. Throughout the late twenties they wrote essays for various magazines, national and southern, defending the traditional southern way of life against the charges of the outsider Mencken. And in the year 1930 they joined with Robert Penn Warren, Stark Young, Andrew Lytle, and other southerners to produce a remarkable volume of essays, *I'll Take My Stand: The South and the Agrarian Tradition.*

I'll Take My Stand affirmed virtually everything Mencken had denied. It defended the antebellum South—and not just the Tidewater South of aristocratic grace Mencken had in mind when he had celebrated the Old South. Rather it was the trans-Appalachian South, the hinterland, most of the Agrarians championed, and the yeoman as much as the planter they had in mind—the "poor white" of Mencken's imagination. Primarily they disagreed with Mencken about the idea of culture. Mencken had always meant by "culture" a high culture, measured by symphonies, art museums, libraries, and an appreciation of the best Western man had thought and written. To most of the Agrarians "culture" was that, but it was also much more. It was also folk culture, the organic expression of the experience of a people, and culture in this sense included folk music, tale-telling, folk arts and crafts and so on. A backwoods southerner, given the Agrarians' definition, might be uncouth, illiterate, and completely ignorant of Beethoven—and still be "cultured."

I'll Take My Stand appeared ten years to the month after the appearance of "The Sahara of the Bozart," and although it would be too much to claim that the latter volume would never have been written if Mencken had not blasted the South, the Agrarians later acknowledged that they were forced to reexamine their tradition partly because one so powerful and so eloquent as Mencken had dismissed it so completely. But most reigning southern intellectuals remained, at least generally, in Mencken's camp: Gerald Johnson, Cash, and Mencken's other associates summarily put down the Agrarians, and most other influential southern editors and writers followed their lead. Mencken himself got in numerous jabs at the "neo-Confederates," as he came to call them, particularly in an essay, "Uprising in the Confederacy," in the *American Mercury* and a later article, "The South Astir," in the *Virginia Quarterly Review.*[18]

After the controversy with the Agrarians in the early and mid-1930s, however, Mencken seemed to lose the serious interest in the South he had demonstrated in the 1920s. Franklin D. Roosevelt took the place of the late Confederacy as the target of his most vicious barbs. Indeed, in the summer of 1930, he had married a southerner, Sara Haardt of Montgomery, Alabama, and in the 1930s and 1940s he occasionally visited Montgomery and, more frequently, the mountains of North Carolina. Although in essays he still remarked on the "moron South" and its religious superstition, the fire had gone out of it.[19]

But what had been the larger meaning of Mencken's confrontation with the South between 1915 and 1935? What had he done to or for Dixie? The assumption that he played a central role in bringing about the Southern Renascence in literature of the 1920s and 1930s is partly true. He played perhaps *the* central role in the first phase of that renascence—the 1920s phase which stressed a critical examination of southern life, and which manifested itself, in belles lettres, in the realism of T. S. Stribling and Julia Peterkin, the satire of Francis Newman, and the boldness of the little magazines. But the reign of southern realism and satire was a brief, if touted, reign, and it was succeeded in the 1930s by a southern literature which saw a value in myth, religion, folk life, and southern tradition that Mencken never recognized. In 1929 Mencken's early apostle Thomas Wolfe wrote a novel, *Look Homeward, Angel,* which—though sometimes Menckenesque in spirit—was anything but Menckenesque in form. The same year William Faulkner produced *The Sound and the Fury.* Mencken, still believing realism and satire were the way of the future in southern letters, ignored both books—although both were to become American classics.

But to recognize and evaluate great literature was not precisely Mencken's role as critic. His role, rather, was to stir the potential southern writer out of his lethargy, to challenge the world of his fathers so that the writer would see that world more critically and more honestly. "Before the creative artist of genuine merit can function freely," Mencken had written in the 1920s, "the way must be cleared for him, and that clearly is best effected by realistic and unsentimental criticism."[20] Mencken, then, offered detachment, and if the southern literature he influenced in the 1920s was largely the literature of protest or of sociological observation, the literature that followed was greater because of the groundclearing work that had gone before. The Mencken phase of the renascence had abolished the ancestor-worship, challenged the tradition, and brought a new perspective to the South.

If Mencken did not fully recognize the great southern literature he had predicted and he himself had helped to create, that was characteristic of a certain blindness he had toward the South. His attitude toward Dixie was always fraught with paradoxes. He blasted "Anglo-Saxon blood" and the English cultural tradition in the South, yet championed no writer (save perhaps Dreiser) more than James Branch Cabell who he acknowledged was "an absolutely pure Anglo-Saxon" of "pure English stock on both sides." He blasted southern Methodists and Baptists for practicing a "barbaric religion," yet found his greatest early followers—and the leaders of the critical awakening of the 1920s—in Howard Odum, of backwoods Methodist stock, and Gerald Johnson, son of the editor of a Baptist newspaper. He blasted the South in general, yet often spoke of himself as a southerner.[21] He denounced the South, yet married a southerner—and greatly admired the style of those Virginians who had come to Baltimore, with abundant charm but empty bellies, during his childhood.

"Why do I denounce the southern *kultur* so often and so violently?" Mencken asked in 1921. "Send a postcard to Professor Dr. Sigmund Freud, General Delivery, Vienna, and you will get the answer by return mail." Although Mencken was having fun, there is much truth in his statement. Indeed, his case was precisely the opposite of Faulkner's frequently psychoanalyzed character, Quentin Compson, who ends the novel *Absalom, Absalom!* by protesting, "I dont hate it. . . . *I dont. I dont!*"[22] If Quentin could not bring himself to admit he hated the South, Mencken found it difficult—except on rare occasions—to admit publicly that he, in fact, held a high regard for many things in Dixie, and Dixie *since* 1865. "I don't love it. I don't," he might have protested. And he would have been no more convincing than Quentin Compson.

Notes

1. See Charles Scruggs, *The Sage in Harlem: H. L. Mencken and the Black Writers of the 1920s* (Baltimore: Johns Hopkins University Press, 1984), and Fred Hobson, *Serpent in Eden: H. L. Mencken and the South* (Chapel Hill: University of North Carolina Press, 1974).

2. H. L. Mencken, "The Sahara of the Bozart," *Prejudices, Second Series* (New York: Alfred A. Knopf, 1920), 136–39.

3. "To Ask Congress to Probe Rantings Against South by N. Y. Magazine," *Arkansas Democrat*, 3 August 1921; and "Menace of Herr Mencken," *Little Rock Trade Record*, 3 August 1921.

4. Mencken, "The Sahara of the Bozart," 137.

5. Ibid., 136, 137, 141–43, 147.

6. Gerald W. Johnson, Foreword to *Serpent in Eden*, x.

7. Mencken, "The Literature of a Moral Republic," *Smart Set* 47 (October 1915):152–53.

8. See Daniel J. Singal, *The War Within: From Victorian to Modernist Thought in the South, 1919–1945* (Chapel Hill: University of North Carolina Press, 1982).

9. Mencken, "The Free Lance," *Baltimore Evening Sun*, 1 December 1914.

10. Mencken, "The Sahara of the Bozart," *New York Evening Mail*, 13 November 1917.

11. Oscar Cargill, "Mencken and the South," *Georgia Review* 6 (Winter 1952):373.

12. Richard S. Kennedy and Paschal Reeves, eds., *The Notebooks of Thomas Wolfe* (Chapel Hill: University of North Carolina Press, 1970), 1:4–5.

13. Edwin A. Alderman, letter to John Barton Cross, 4 February 1925, Alderman Collection, University of Virginia Library; Addison Hibbard, "Literary Lantern," *Greensboro Daily News*, 26 September 1926; and Frances Newman, "On the State of Literature in the Late Confederacy," *New York Herald Tribune Books*, 16 August 1925, 1.

14. Mencken, "Violets in the Sahara," *Baltimore Evening Sun*, 15 May 1922; Mencken, "The Sahara of the Bozart," 138; Vernon Louis Parrington, "The Incomparable Mr. Cabell," *Pacific Review* 2 (December 1921):366; Mencken, "A Comedy of Fig-Leaves," *American Mercury* 12 (December 1927):510; Mencken, "The National Letters," *Prejudices, Second Series*, 54; and affidavit against Cabell, by the New York Society for the Suppression of Vice, quoted in Padraic Colum and Margaret Freeman Cabell, eds., *Between Friends: Letters of James Branch Cabell and Others* (New York: Harcourt Brace and World, 1962), 157.

15. W. J. Cash, *The Mind of the South* (New York: Alfred A. Knopf, 1941), 93–94.

16. Archibald Henderson, letter to Mencken, 21 December 1922, Mencken Collection, New York Public Library.

17. Mencken, letter to Howard W. Odum, [June 1925], Odum Papers, Wilson Library, University of North Carolina.

18. Mencken, "Uprising in the Confederacy," *American Mercury* 22 (March 1931):379–81; and "The South Astir," *Virginia Quarterly Review* 11 (January 1935):47–60.

19. Mencken, quoted by Roger Butterfield in "Mr. Mencken Sounds Off," *Life*, 5 August 1946, 51.

20. Mencken, "Is the South a Desert?" *Southern Literary Magazine* 1 (October 1923):4.

21. Mencken, unpublished preface to a collection of American short stories to be translated into German, 1923, Mencken Collection, Enoch Pratt Free Library, Baltimore, printed in *Menckeniana*, no. 20 (Winter 1966):1–7; and Mencken, "Notes of a Poetry-Hater," *Smart Set* 58 (April 1919):143; "Conversations," *Smart Set* 64 (April 1921):92; and "Nordic Blond Art," *Smart Set* 71 (May 1923):138.

22. Mencken, "Conversations," 92; and William Faulkner, *Absalom, Absalom!* (New York, 1936; Vintage Books, 1964), 378.

H. L. Mencken and James Weldon Johnson: Two Men Who Helped Shape a Renaissance

Charles Scruggs*

I

Anyone who has ever read Richard Wright's fictional autobiography *Black Boy* remembers the scene in which a lonely youth of nineteen first encounters the works of H. L. Mencken. One day, while waiting to go to

*This essay was written for this volume and is published by permission of the author.

work, Wright wandered into a bank lobby, and, perfunctorily, he picked up a nearby newspaper. As he glanced through it, he suddenly fixed his attention upon a startling article. Here was a vicious personal attack in a Southern newspaper upon a man who was not a Negro, and yet the vehemence of the language was the kind usually reserved for Negroes. His curiosity pricked, he borrowed a white friend's library card and forged a note: "Will you please let this nigger boy have," it said to the librarian in charge, "some books by H. L. Mencken." Handed *A Book of Prefaces* and a volume of *Prejudices*, Wright returned to his boarding room and read late into the night. It was an experience he would never forget, one that shaped his own life as an author. He was struck by Mencken's "clear, clean sweeping sentences," his Gargantuan rage, his Olympian ridicule of "everything American." To Wright, Mencken was a warrior, "fighting with words . . . using them as one would use a club." But the thing that "amazed" Wright most about Mencken "was not what he said, but how on earth anyone had the courage to say it."[1]

There is a curious historical irony in Wright's isolated experience of discovering Mencken's works in Memphis in 1927, because by that year an older generation of black writers had already made the same discoveries about Mencken—and in almost the same precise terms. By 1927, the members of the Harlem Renaissance recognized Mencken as a striking presence in the American scene and in their own literary movement which, at that very moment, was in full swing. They too had singled out those facets of Mencken's personality and writings that had appealed to Wright: humor, clarity, honesty, and courage. For instance, in 1927 Countee Cullen had called Mencken "the intrepid Mr. Mencken"[2] in the *Pittsburgh Courier* and only a month later, in the same black newspaper, George Schuyler had praised the Sage of Baltimore for "telling what God loves."[3] So too in that same year, Kelly Miller and W. E. B. DuBois had admired his objectivity. Said DuBois: "there can be no question of H. L. Mencken's attitude toward Negroes. It is calmly and judiciously fair."[4] And Miller added a literary touch: when it comes to describing the Negro, Mencken, "like Shakespeare . . . holds the mirror up to nature."[5]

But to Harlem's intellectuals fairness was not Mencken's chief virtue— Mencken was fun. Both George Schuyler and Theophilus Lewis had been "avid" readers of the *Smart Set*[6] and tried to copy his brash, iconoclastic wit in their own columns in the *Messenger*. Indeed, Mencken had encouraged the black writer in general to lampoon the lily-white Americano: "He looks ridiculous even to me, a white man myself [Mencken wrote to the *Crisis* in 1926]. To a Negro he must be a hilarious spectacle. . . . Why isn't that spectacle better described? Let the Negro sculptors spit on their hands. What a chance."[7] And when he became editor of the *American Mercury* in 1924, Mencken intended to give that "chance" to the black writers, for he solicited articles from them on all conceivable subjects—politics, religion, folklore, black newspapers, music, and even the race's "inhibitions."

Yet what he wanted most, as he told the *Crisis*, was for the black writer to pay the white man "in his own coin." Hence he often urged George Schuyler to do "something realistically and fearlessly" for the *Mercury* "like your excellent stuff in the *Pittsburgh Courier*."[8] When Schuyler finally did do something for the *Mercury*, Mencken must have liked what he saw, for in his ten-year tenure as editor (1924–33), he published more articles by Schuyler (nine) than by any other contributor, white or black.[9]

As aficionados know, Walter Lippman called Mencken in 1926 the "most powerful influence on this whole generation of educated people."[10] Not quite as well known as Lippman's statement is white novelist Carl Van Vechten's portrait of Mencken in his bestselling *Nigger Heaven* (1926). Here Mencken is an equally powerful presence in a novel about Negro life set in contemporary Harlem. In creating the portrait of Russett Durwood (Mencken), the editor of the *American Mars* (*Mercury*) who has an interest in black literature and black writers, Van Vechten was only drawing on the facts. For in real life Mencken had not only befriended black writers in the *Mercury*, but had previously published articles by Walter White, Eric Waldrond, and W. E. B. DuBois in the *Smart Set* at a time when black writers had trouble getting published anywhere outside their own periodicals.[11] Moreover, Van Vechten knew that both publicly and privately Mencken had helped these intellectuals in other ways. In his own humorous and sometimes pontifical manner, he had taken time to give them advice on what needed to be done in order for them to create a great and abiding literature. Hence, Van Vechten's portrait is of a hard man (Durwood) with a soft heart, who, while feigning indifference, is quite upset with a young black writer for betraying his talent. For the young man has squandered his energies on a cliché-ridden story about an interracial love affair gone awry, and yet he is living in Harlem, a world teeming with variety and vitality. Write about the untold riches around you, says the frustrated editor to the young man, and leave "all the old clichés and formulas" to the "Nordic blonds who, after all, never did know anything about the subject from the inside."[12]

Writing about black life from the inside was a favorite Mencken theme, and Van Vechten's source for this episode in *Nigger Heaven* may have come from a *Smart Set* review in which Mencken had outlined what he believed to be the proper focus of the Negro novel. In "Gropings in Literary Darkness" (October, 1920), Mencken noted that the darker brother is a "shrewd observer." He knows much more about the white man than the latter knows about him. The black novelist, implied Mencken, must redirect this power of observation from outward to inward: "The thing we need is a realistic picture of the inner life of the negro by one who sees the race from within—a self-portrait as vivid and accurate as Dostoyevsky's portrait of the Russian or Thackeray's of the Englishman." Working with a specific character, "presented against a background made vivid by innumerable small details," the Negro novelist can illuminate a culture virtually unknown to most Americans: "He will force the understanding that now seems so hopeless. He will blow up nine-tenths of the current poppycock."[13]

As Van Vechten knew, many black intellectuals had been impressed with Mencken's review, and one in particular, Walter White, had set out to put its lessons into practice. Indeed, according to White, Mencken himself had written to the young Negro from Atlanta, asking him to write a realistic novel, told from the inside, about what it was like to survive in the heart of darkness known as Georgia.[14] And in *The Fire in the Flint* (1924), White used a small town, Central City, as a background for a tragedy of a doctor who naively thinks that he can remain free of the racial tensions that plague his hometown.

And Van Vechten also knew—for he had gotten the story from White—that Mencken's help went beyond giving advice. When White had trouble finding a publisher for his novel, Mencken took the manuscript to Knopf and almost singlehandedly got it published.[15] Hence by 1926, the year of Van Vechten's portrait, Mencken's reputation among the black intellectuals was an established fact; and Van Vechten expected his readers, black and white alike, to see the black hero of *Nigger Heaven* as something of an anachronism. By 1926, "realism" had carried the day, and Van Vechten believed that Mencken had deserved at least part of the credit, if not part of the blame.[16] Sterling Brown would later insist, after the decade was over, that rarely in fact did the age escape distorted portraiture, even among black writers, but the very word itself—"portraiture"—indicates that "realism" was recognized as the necessary narrative mode.[17] To be sure, Alain Locke would hold out for a more "poetic" realism over and against Mencken's advocacy of Dreiser as a model, but Walter White perhaps best expresses an attitude that by 1926 most black writers took for granted. Consider, for instance, his remark to Rudolph Fisher in 1925, a published novelist writing to an unpublished one: "Those black writers," said White, "who are writing about Negro life as it really exists are exploring a field which is as yet practically untouched. I remember a letter from Mr. Mencken shortly after I had been asked by a publisher to eliminate considerable portions of my own novel because of fear that it would offend the South. Mr. Mencken wrote me, 'the pussyfooting Southern novel is dead and the only hope in writing such fiction lies in complete honesty.' "[18]

Thus if we want to appreciate the impact that Mencken had on the members of the Harlem Renaissance we have to discuss his influence upon black literature before the Harlem Renaissance even existed. In 1920, Mencken's advice had the ring of novelty, because he was writing at a time when black caricature was the rule, not the exception; when black literature itself was synonymous with special pleading, not art; and when the idea of a Negro writing was akin to Dr. Johnson's remark about a woman preaching: It is not done very well, but one is surprised to see it done at all. In such a time, Mencken refused to speak down to the black writer; he spoke to him not as a trained dog but as a fellow artist, one who had obligations to craft, to honesty, to life as he knew it, as did all other artists. No wonder then that Walter White, J. A. Rogers, Theophilus Lewis, George Schuyler, Wallace Thurman, James Weldon Johnson, W. E. B. DuBois and others read him with enthusiasm in these early years before the Harlem Renaissance. Mencken not only seemed to share their perspectives upon "boobus Americanus" but he also shared their perspectives on black life in America. As with the young Richard Wright, what Mencken said about American culture did not so much surprise them; what surprised them was "how on earth anyone had the courage to say it."

II

To illustrate in greater detail the nature of Mencken's influence before the Harlem Renaissance began, I want to discuss his literary and personal relationship with one man, James Weldon Johnson, from their first meeting in 1916 through the publication of Johnson's anthology, *The Book of American Negro Poetry* in 1922. More specifically, I want to focus upon the impact on Johnson of two works by Mencken: "The Sahara of the Bozart" in *Prejudices: Second Series* (1920) and the first edition of *The American Language* (1919). Just as Walter White had admired Mencken's theory of the Negro novel, so Johnson admired his satiric achievement in "The Sahara of the Bozart." Moreover, Johnson saw that Mencken's relationship with words was not limited to his use of them. Mencken was also a student of the American language and Johnson realized that Mencken's defense of the American vernacular had a relevance to a theory of poetic diction that Johnson was developing for the Negro poet.

Like Mencken, the late Michel Foucault was a student of Friedrich Nietzsche, and a statement that Foucault has made about Nietzsche perhaps explains why James Weldon Johnson found so much to respond to in Mencken: "Rules are empty in themselves, violent and unfinalized; they are impersonal and can be bent to any purpose. The successes of history belong to those who are capable of seizing these rules . . . and redirecting them against those who had initially imposed them."[19] In these remarks, Foucault sees that Nietzsche's observations upon history can be used as a weapon by the colonized people of a culture. For Nietzsche perceived that the history of a culture imposed a kind of linguistic imperialism upon the people of that culture, and if the exceptional individual was to free himself from the burdens of the past, he had to reverse the meaning of the language that imprisoned him. Or as Ralph Ellison has put it in discussing the dilemma of the black writer, one must learn to "change the joke and slip the yoke."[20]

From the 1890s to the early years of the 1920s, the joke was definitely on black people in American culture, and from their point of view, it wasn't very funny. The history of America's racial attitudes during these years has been told many times, so I need not dwell upon the obvious: the crippling effect that the Jim Crow laws had upon the mind of the South, the revival of the Ku Klux Klan, the racial intolerance that led to the race riots of 1919, and the renewal of the stereotype of the black beast as evinced by the popularity of such novels as *The Leopard's Spots* (1902) and *The Clansman* (1905) by Thomas Dixon, and by the popularity of such pseudo-scientists as Madison Grant and Lothrop Stoddard.[21] In such a climate, it should not surprise us that D. W. Griffith's famous movie *The Birth of a Nation* (1915), based on *The Clansman*, should have had an opening run of seven months at Clune's Theater in Los Angeles. This was unprecedented even for a play, and people still conjecture that it may have been the most widely seen movie of all time.[22] Hence characters like Silas Lynch, Lydia Brown and Gus the renegade—villainous villains from the penny dreadfuls made more villainous because they were black—became firmly imprinted on the public's mind. And, as we know, the stereotype of the black beast was not the only one that shaped most Americans' conception of the Afro-American. The docile, watermelon-eating, lazy, crapshooting darkey was another favorite, as was the loyal, self-deprecating motherly Mammy. These stereotypes were kept alive well through the 1920s by such writers as Octavus Roy Cohen, E. K. Means, Irvin Cobb, Hugh Wiley, and Emma Speed Sampson.

We also have to remember that the years between 1905 and 1920 were not very good years for Afro-American letters. There were relatively few voices to counter the stereotypes and racial distortions. Charles Chesnutt had published his last novel in 1905; Paul Laurence Dunbar had stopped writing and Sutton Griggs went unread. True, W. E. B. DuBois had become the fiery editor of the *Crisis* in 1910 and author of the polemical novel *The Quest of the Silver Fleece* in 1911. And there were signs of life in Chicago with Fenton Johnson's poetry magazine, but by and large, 1905 to 1920 were not very good years for black literature. That James Weldon Johnson published his fine novel, *The Autobiography of An Ex-Colored Man*, anonymously in 1912 is perhaps symbolic of the uncertainties of the times.

It was in these uncertain times that James Weldon Johnson first made the friendship of H. L. Mencken, a man who, in 1914, had become co-editor of the *Smart Set* and was establishing himself as the foremost critic of American culture. Like Nietzsche, Mencken had his own quarrel with history, and it was not by accident that Mencken had written a book in 1908 explaining Nietzsche to Americans. For from 1908 to 1923, as a book reviewer for the *Smart Set*, Mencken did battle with "The Genteel Tradition" and American puritanism, two lingering diseases from the past that had weakened the American artist. Stifling propriety and bogus moralism had robbed the artist of both his energy and his vision and had kept him from seeing an unknown, vital America waiting to be expressed in song and story.

Because Mencken had voiced his anger with such wit and force, Johnson was determined to meet him, for as he said later in his autobiography, "Mencken had made a sharper impression on my mind than any American then writing."[23] When the two men finally did meet in Mencken's *Smart Set* offices in 1916, Johnson was enthralled by Mencken's conversation: "I had never been so fascinated at hearing anyone talk. He talked about literature, about Negro literature, the Negro problem, and Negro music." After a long conversation, Johnson was impressed that "a man as busy as he could give so much time to a mere stranger," and he "felt buoyed up . . . as though I had taken a mental cocktail." Evidently the conversation had had the same effect on Mencken, for soon the two men began to correspond regularly about matters concerning Afro-American art and life, and Mencken began reading Johnson's column, "Views and Reviews," in the *New York Age*. Although Johnson first mentioned Mencken in his column on 27 April 1918, he waited until 20 July 1918 before he pulled out all the stops. The entire article is devoted to Mencken ("American Genius and Its Locale") and Johnson called him "the cleverest writer in America today." But it wasn't just Mencken's cleverness that impressed Johnson—those who respond to him on that level alone, he said, "are missing the best part of him; the best part of Mencken is truth." And he tells the truth, continued Johnson, because he is absolutely fearless.

Two years later (21 February 1920), Johnson related Mencken's passion for truth to his way of depicting it: "Mr. Mencken's favorite method of showing people the truth," said Johnson, "is to attack falsehood with ridicule." There is a lesson to be learned here, insisted Johnson: "What could be more disconcerting and overwhelming to a man posing as everybody's superior than to find that everybody was laughing at his pretensions? Protest would only swell up his self importance." In other words, laughter cuts the enemy down to size; whereas protest merely inflates his ego. Reverse the sense of superiority, urged Johnson, and we have begun to slip the yoke.

Ironically, as Johnson was beginning to discuss the theme of liberation through satire with his black audience, Mencken was experiencing the full force of America's wartime hysteria. For during the year that Americans entered the war (1917), Mencken discovered what it meant to be a Negro. He found to his dismay that the Great War had given a new weapon to the defenders of puritanism: patriotism. One of these defenders, Stuart Sherman, wrote several articles insisting that Mencken's attacks upon American "kultur" were connected to his German ancestry. Given the hostile atmosphere, Mencken could not retaliate. He soon found himself barred from all magazines and newspapers except the *Smart Set*, the *Seven Arts*, and the *New York Evening Mail*. But that was not the worst of it. The government thought him a spy and harrassed him. Friends he had counted on suddenly grew frightened and deserted him.[24] This experience left its impact. Even thirteen years after the armistice, he could speak of himself "as a member of a race lately in worse odor among 100% Americans than either Jews or Negroes."[25]

Thus, although Johnson did not meet Mencken until 1916, their relationship is given special poignancy because of Mencken's harassment during the Great War. We find, for example, Mencken instantly agreeing with Johnson's assessment of the terrible race riots of 1919, which Johnson had expressed to Mencken in a letter. The "low-caste white man," said Mencken to Johnson, "is a poltroon under his hide [who] delights in operations which allow him to kill without risk. . . . As you say, fighting back changes the scene. Once he is convinced that chasing Negroes is dangerous, he will stop it."[26] But it wasn't just in letters to Johnson that Mencken began to identify with the Negro. A history of Mencken's revision of "The Sahara of the Bozart" also bears this out. When Mencken published the original version of the essay on 13 November 1917 in the *New York Evening Mail,* he had not even mentioned the Negro—all his emphasis was upon Southern decadence. His thesis was that the South's old civilization had died during the Civil War, and the poor whites had replaced the ancient aristocracy as the controlling force in Southern life. This fact explained why, in Mencken's famous hyperbole, the South is as vacous intellectually as the vast "interstellar spaces."

In the final version—the version in *Prejudices, Second Series* (1920) that created such a furore in the South[27]—Johnson's influence is present. Johnson had been following Mencken's pre-1920 attacks on the South, and had in the main agreed with Mencken's wasteland theme. However, in response to one article by Mencken ("Mr. Cabell of Virginia"), he proceeded in the *New York Age* to give his own explanation for the decline of intellectual life in the South. It happened to be the same article ("American Genius and Its Locale") in which Johnson had praised Mencken so fulsomely:

> We do not think that the destruction of the Old Southern Civilization or any innate inferiority of the poor white trash is the reason; the real reason is that the white South of today is using up every bit of its mental energy in this terrible race struggle. . . . All of the mental power of the white South is being used up in holding the Negro back, and that is the reason why it does not produce either great literature or great statesmen or great wealth.

That Mencken read Johnson's piece is of course conjectural, but the changes that Mencken made in the final version of the "Sahara" essay seem to indicate that he did. Now the Negro has a prominent place in the essay, and Mencken adopted Johnson's psychological explanation as one cause of Southern decline. Said Mencken of the poor whites who dominate the political scene, "the emerging black [is] the cornerstone of all their public thinking."[28]

And in Mencken's hands, the psychological explanation became a new source of satire. Only the lowly Negroes, said Mencken, show any signs of life in the South:

> . . . the only visible aesthetic activity in the south is wholly in their hands. No southern composer has ever written music so good as that of half a dozen white-black composers who might be named. Even in politics, the negro reveals a curious superiority. Despite the fact that the race question has been the main political concern of the southern whites for two generations, to the practical exclusion of everything else, they have contributed nothing to its discussion that has impressed the rest of the world so deeply and so favorably as three or four books by southern negroes.

And if this were not insulting enough, Mencken added that the only Southern prose writer in recent history to do anything of value (besides James Branch Cabell) was Joel Chandler Harris, and he turned out to be "little more than an amanuensis for the local blacks." His works, continued Mencken, "were really the products not of white Georgia, but of black Georgia. Writing afterward *as* a white man, he swiftly subsided into the fifth rank." But the best ironic touch in the new version of the "Sahara" essay was the implied Nietzschean perspective on the New South. The real aristocracy that has emerged since the Civil War is not white but black; it consists of the mulatto sons and daughters of the old aristocracy, for "the men of the upper classes sought their mistresses among the blacks." As for the poor whites, alas, they "went unfertilized from above."[29]

Near the end of "The Sahara of the Bozart," Mencken pays tribute to Johnson as a man who has transcended the limitations of his environment through his satire. Mencken refers to an article in a "stray negro newspaper" that had poked fun at an ordinance recently passed in Douglas, Georgia. It seems the good people of Douglas prohibited, on the penalty of a $500 fine, "any trouserspresser" from pressing the trousers of both white and black. The writer of this article, said Mencken, having more wit than the entire community of Douglas, noted that nearly all the clothing in the town was handled by black people and that it sometimes stayed in black homes "for as long as a week at a time."[30] As we might expect, the "stray negro newspaper" Mencken was referring to was the *New York Age*, and it was Johnson himself who had written the article on 27 March 1920.[31] Mencken's allusion to Johnson's article appears to be Mencken's way of saying that the arrangement between master and slave in the South should have been reversed.

Seen from the point of view of the black intellectuals, "The Sahara of the Bozart" did have that thrust. For what Mencken had done in this essay was to skewer the South in terms worthy of the comic genius of an Aristophanes or a Swift. The South is Aristophanes's Cloud-Cuckoo Land or it is Swift's Houyhnhnm-Land without the Houyhnhnms.[32] Or it might even be the empty world ruled by the mad Academy of Lagado in Book Three of *Gulliver's Travels*. Said Mencken of the South, it is a land so large that "nearly the whole of Europe could be lost in that stupendous region of . . . paralyzed cerebrums: one could throw in France, Germany, and Italy, and still have room for the British Isles."[33] In this intellectually vacuous world, populated primarily by Caucasian Yahoos, only James Branch Cabell, Mencken's friend, and the emerging black race show any sign of sanity.

Thus it was that Mencken's satire of the South provided Johnson and others like him with an approach that would redirect the rules imposed against them. Mencken's reversal of Southern categories—the black beast now the civilized man, the civilized Southerner now the Yahoo—gave the black intellectuals of the 1920s a position of strength from which they might deal with a culture that had denied them their humanity.[34] Mencken's example showed that Olympian ridicule was possible for a group of black intellectuals who were accustomed not to laughing but to asking favors. And Johnson's own contributions to Mencken's attack on the South helped Mencken to sharpen his argument. For it was one thing to attack the South for thinking that the invention of Coca-Cola was a genuine cultural achievement; it became doubly effective when that bogus achievement was contrasted with real cultural contributions like Negro folk tales and spirituals.

Mencken's intellectual relationship with Johnson did not end with satire. In the early 1920s, Johnson believed that a yoke was strangling the voice of the black poet. A poet himself, in addition to being a songwriter, a journalist, and a novelist, Johnson thought that the black poet was trapped by two poetic styles—one formal, the other informal—and these two styles made it impossible for him to capture the real experience of black people the way that Afro-American folk songs and spirituals could. For Johnson, the black poet either buried black life under a barrage of "fine" diction, as Phyllis Wheatley did when she imitated the English masters of the eighteenth century, or he illuminated only a small corner of black life, as Paul Lawrence Dunbar did, by descending to "Negro dialect," an instrument, in Johnson's view, that had only "two full stops: humor and pathos."[35]

Here was a true dilemma—how to steer between a formal style that allowed no room for the voice of the common people and an informal one that often reduced common life to one voice, that of the lowly, lovable, laughable darky. "Negro dialect," Johnson hastened to add, was not intrinsically a limited vehicle for Negro expression. Indeed, Dunbar had used it successfully in some of his poetry "for the true interpretation of Negro character and psychology." The problem lies in the limitations placed upon this vehicle by white influences. They have so warped it as a poetic instrument that at present it can only express certain kinds of Negro experiences. Dunbar, said Johnson, longed to escape its meshes but felt that white people would not let him write any other kind of poetry. They liked his dialect verse because they felt comfortable with the kind of Negro it created. Later in the 1930s, Johnson nostalgically wondered what would have happened if early black poets could have been allowed to develop dialect poetry "in its virgin state." It might have become as rich a medium as Burns's Scottish dialect, but in this age "the possibility of doing that . . . no longer exists."[36] If black poets are going to be true to the richness and variety of black life, they will have to find a new language.

Johnson began working toward a solution to this problem as early as 1920 when he wrote "The Creation," a poetical sermon spoken in the language of the black preacher, and in 1922 when he wrote the famous preface to his anthology *The Book of American Negro Poetry*. "The Creation"— which became one of seven poetical sermons published as *God's Trombones* in 1927—represented his practical solution to the problem, whereas his preface was his theoretical solution. The distinguished critic Louis D. Rubin, Jr. has called Johnson's "discovery for the black poet fully as useful as that which the Chicago poets and, more importantly, T. S. Eliot and Ezra Pound were making for American poetry in general."[37] I would like to argue that in making this "discovery," Johnson had a little help from Mencken's recently published treatise *The American Language* (1919).

When Johnson came to write his preface to *The Book of American Negro Poetry*, he sent a first draft to Mencken for suggestions. The suggestions Mencken made have little to do with his real presence in Johnson's preface.[38] The Mencken that appears in Johnson's preface is the Mencken who had discussed the richness of the American language, more specifically, of the American vernacular. Just as Mencken's defense of the American vernacular was a continuation of his quarrel with "The Genteel Tradition," so Johnson created a theory of poetic style that exposed past poetic practice as a trap, one that encased black writers within the stereotypes of the dominant culture.

The first edition of *The American Language* is both scholarly and polemical—certainly much more polemical than the fourth edition (1936), the book that most of us are familiar with. Indeed, this book needs to be read in conjunction with Mencken's *Smart Set* reviews and his *A Book of Prefaces* (1917), for it represents a Mencken trying to forge a new American literature, and continuing to do battle with puritanism as a "force" in American life. Mencken's conception of American puritanism reflects an idea about culture that he probably got from Nietzsche. For Nietzsche, while admitting that Apollo and Dionysius needed to be held in balance, complained of his own German culture that it had moved too far in the Apollonian extreme. It worshipped the god of restraint, of playing it safe, of following the rules. In an Apollonian culture, moral categories are clearly defined and rigorously enforced. Hence the natural impulses of man, that in certain historical periods manifest themselves in great creative outbursts, are restrained. The only fervor that is allowed is a moral fervor in defense of the established order, and in such an Apollonian world, that order symbolizes a reign of the dull, the lifeless, and the "genteel."

In this 1919 edition of the *American Language*, then, Mencken took after American pedagogues for trying to sterilize an exciting, living language. He wanted to show that the American vulgate, though vulgar in the sense that it belonged to the common people, was not vulgar if you consider its potentiality for artistic expression. The precise image, the striking metaphor, the exuberant hyperbole—these attributes made America's language superior to England's English. America's English retained the vitality and adventuresomeness of the Elizabethan immigrants who migrated to these shores; whereas England's English had the life taken out of it by the grammarians of the Eighteenth Century. Unfortunately, America's schoolmarms and schoolmasters insist upon stuffing proper English down children's throats. Fortunately, this English is never spoken outside the schoolroom. The real, vital language thrives in a far healthier climate, the world at large.

Obviously Mencken's approach was meant to be audacious, shocking the American academy and giving ammunition to the young American intellectuals who were already beginning to rebel against the first signs of Harding's "normalcy." Carl Dolmetsch has pointed out that immediately following the Great War, the *Smart Set* "opened its offensive against the prevailing tendencies in post-war American life and letters."[39] The first edition of the *American Language*, I insist, was part of that offensive, and its satiric strategy was perfect. For who could fault a book so self-consciously American, so conspicuously patriotic? Yet in celebrating our native tongue, Mencken set out to debunk the kind of language that produced a nation of middle-class, Anglo-Saxon goosesteppers. He set out to celebrate a goatish, rebellious, highly diversified language, one that reflected a culture that was in actuality a tossed salad, not a melting pot. Although the language was identifiable as a single language, its energy came from many sources, and the culture represented by these sources was the antithesis of the canned, self-satisfied, colorless version proclaimed by the jingoists.

Thus Mencken had two enemies in mind in the 1919 edition of *The American Language*: the Anglophiles and their slavish devotion to refinement, and the native-born patriots and philistines and their mindless devotion to the fatuous cliché. Both groups denied the existence of the diversified culture that gave birth to the real American language, whereas Mencken believed that within this diversified culture lay America's only hope for a genuine literary renaissance. Indeed, one purpose behind his analysis of the vernacular was to show the American writer the source of his true strength.

Mencken's major point is that there is a real difference between a dead language and a living one, and feigned elegance may only be hiding a dead carcass. Proper language is not the language that people speak, but it has become the language that people speak in books. For Mencken, real elegance is connected to the potentiality within the vernacular of realizing itself, and he was convinced that this potentiality had yet to be tapped in America. True, Mark Twain, Walt Whitman and Ring Lardner had scratched the surface, but where is the artist to exploit to the full the American's "bold experimenting in words, which was so Elizabethan" or his "extraordinary capacity for metaphor" or his "extravagant and often grotesque humor" or his "gypsy phrases," or his disquieting "terseness"? What the American vernacular needs, continued Mencken, "to make even pedagogues acutely aware of it, is a poet of genius to venture into it, as Chaucer ventured into the despised English of his day. . . . " And he added, "given the poet, there may suddenly come a day when our *theirns* and *would'a hads* will take on the barbaric stateliness of the peasant locutions of old Maurya in *Riders to the Sea*. They seem grotesque and absurd today because the folks who use them seem grotesque and absurd. But that is a too facile logic and under it is a false assumption. In all human beings, if only understanding be brought to the business, dignity will be found, and that dignity cannot fail to reveal itself. . . . "[40]

Mencken singled out the Irish playwright John Synge as a model to be followed, Synge who in his preface to *The Playboy of the Western World* told of how he acquired his "gypsy phrases" by overhearing the language of servant girls as they gossiped in the kitchen. But it wasn't just the individual words that created his distinct style; the style was created by throwing off the "artificial restraints" of the official language, and recreating "the less self-conscious grammar and syntax of a simple and untutored folk."[41]

This was a point that Mencken made over and over again in *The American Language*. The distinctiveness of the American language was not just a "difference in vocabulary" from England's English; its distinctiveness lay "in the whole fashion of using words"—in tone, in syntax, "in conjugation and declension, in metaphor and idiom." The reason an English novelist usually fails to capture the inner spirit of the language in his American characters is that he inevitably sticks to the surface of the language, to individual words. Said Mencken, "the thing lies deeper than vocabulary and even than pronunciation and intonation; the divergences [between English and American] show themselves in habits of speech that are fundamental and almost indefinable." But just read, he added, a "page from one of Ring W. Lardner's baseball stories" and "the thoroughly American color of it cannot fail to escape anyone who actually listens to the tongue spoken around him."[42]

This was just the kind of discussion that Johnson needed to formulate his own theory of language for the Negro poet, and when in the preface to *The Book of American Negro Poetry* Johnson alluded to Synge, he was paying Mencken the same kind of compliment Mencken had paid him in "The Sahara of the Bozart":

> What the colored poet in the United States needs to do is something like what Synge did for the Irish; he needs to find a form that will express the racial spirit by symbols from within rather than symbols from without, such as the mere mutilation of English spelling and pronunciation.

He needs a form that is freer and larger than dialect, but will still hold the racial flavor; a form expressing the imagery, the idioms, the peculiar turns of thought, and the distinctive humor and pathos, too, of the Negro, but which will also be capable of voicing the deepest and highest emotions and aspirations, and allow of the widest range of subjects and the widest scope of treatment.[43]

In other words, the "form" that Johnson was looking for should reflect the rich oral tradition of the folk that has many voices and that continues to be a living, vital tradition. Dialect, on the other hand, has only one voice, and that voice is fixed in an imaginary, pastoral past. When Johnson came to write the preface to *God's Trombones*, he claimed to have found that "form" in the rich language of the Negro preacher which, in its tremendous range of notes, was like the multi-voiced trombone.[44] Johnson's conception of the preacher's many voices within a single voice is quite similar to Mikhail Bakhtin's notion of "polyglossia." For Bakhtin, a literary form like the epic reflects a culture's connection to the past, to a world already completed and fulfilled. Other voices in the culture, however, reflect present, immediate, everyday concerns, and tend to challenge the reality implied by the single voice fixed upon the past. They incorporate the single voice and in so doing free reality "from the power of language in which it had been entangled as if in a net."[45] For Johnson, dialect was the net entangling the Negro poet, just as for Mencken "genteel" language was the net entangling the American artist. Both nets tied the artist to a sterile past, preventing him from expressing the multi-layered world around him.

Johnson believed that the Negro preacher's language might include dialect but that it was subsumed within a much larger context because the preacher's voice was a rich polyglot: "the sublime phraseology of the Hebrew prophets" coupled with the idioms of the King James Bible, and fused with the idioms, metaphors and imagery of Negro life. And added Johnson: in this heap of languages, "there may have been, after all, some kinship with the innate grandiloquence of [the] old African tongues."[46] The language, in short, could move up and down the music scale with ease, descending to the colloquial and rising to the sublime.

In *God's Trombones*, then, Johnson tried to fulfill Mencken's prophecy of the American poet who would express the inner life of his people by using to the full the vast flexibility and resources of the living American language. It is not surprising, that Mencken published one of Johnson's poetical sermons, "Go Down, Death!," in the *American Mercury* (April 1927), and called it in print "one of the most remarkable and moving poems of its type ever written in America."[47] Indeed, Johnson became a model for him of what could be done with the Negro idiom in poetry. When Carl Van Vechten sent Mencken some early poems by Langston Hughes, written in dialect, for possible publication in the *Mercury*, Mencken rejected them, telling Van Vechten that the young man in question ought to read Johnson's strictures on Negro language.[48] And as we know, Hughes must have gotten the hint that dialect poetry was not his medium, for he never wrote it again. After 1925, he began to develop his own unique vernacular style from his observations of real black life in the Harlem streets.

Thus, despite his neglect by critics of the Harlem Renaissance, Mencken is an inescapable presence in the history of this literary movement. Even its negative side, what Sterling Brown has called its penchant for "exotic primitives," might to some extent be laid at Mencken's door. Certainly the unjustly maligned Van Vechten should not bear the brunt of Brown's criticism, for the Dionysian world view of *Nigger Heaven* was already stale Pilsner by the time Van Vechten developed it. Still, I believe that Mencken's influence upon Harlem's intellectuals was mostly positive in its effects, especially when that influence is seen in a specific context such as the Johnson-Mencken collaborations of the late teens, early 1920s. Mencken gave Johnson and other black artists a perspective by which they could attempt, like Joyce's Stephen Dedalus, to "forge in the smithy of [their] soul[s] the uncreated conscience of [their] race." If the results did not quite match the glorious expectations, there were many other reasons for the Renaissance's failures besides Mencken's presence. Certainly what can be said of the pre-Renaissance collaborations of Johnson and Mencken is that they anticipated many of the major themes of the literary movement. Satire of the master race, the search for an authentic poetical language, a connection between the Harlem Renaissance and the Irish Renaissance, the conflict between pagan and puritan, youth and age, past and present—all these things Mencken and Johnson had touched on, and their legacy had a profound effect on the exciting, creative period to come.

Notes

1. Richard Wright, *Black Boy* (New York: Harper and Brothers, 1945), 217–18.

2. Floyd Calvin, "Interview with Countee Cullen," *Pittsburgh Courier*, 18 June 1927.

3. George Schuyler, "Views and Reviews," *Pittsburgh Courier*, 30 July 1927.

4. W. E. B. DuBois, "Mencken," *Crisis* 34 (October 1927):276.

5. Kelly Miller, "Mencken Mentions the Negro," *Baltimore Afro-American*, 8 October 1927.

6. George Schuyler, *Black and Conservative* (New Rochelle: Arlington House, 1966),142.

7. W. E. B. DuBois, "The Negro in Art: A Symposium," *Crisis* 31 (March 1926):220.

8. HLM to George Schuyler, 25 August 1927, in Carl Bode, ed., *The New Mencken Letters* (New York: Dial Press, 1977),213–14—hereafter cited as *New Letters*.

9. See Fenwick Anderson, "Black Perspectives in Mencken's *Mercury*," *Menckeniana* 70 (Summer 1979):5. Anderson also notes that between 1924–33, Mencken published 54 articles in the *Mercury* both by and about blacks, an extraordinary number in a magazine concerned with American culture in general.

10. Walter Lippman, "H. L. Mencken," *Saturday Review of Literature* 3 (11 December 1926):413.

11. See Carl Dolmetsch, "A History of the *Smart Set* Magazine, 1914–1923," Ph.D. diss., University of Chicago, 1957, 140. Also, see Guy Jean Forgue, *H. L. Mencken: l'Homme, l'Oeuvre, l'Influence* (Paris: Minard, 1967), 342–43.

12. Carl Van Vechten, *Nigger Heaven* (New York: Knopf, 1926), 223.

13. HLM, "Gropings in Literary Darkness," *Smart Set* 63 (October 1920):140.

14. Walter White, *A Man Called White* (New York: Viking Press, 1948), 65.

15. I trace the interesting history of this novel's publication in my book, *The Sage in Harlem: H. L. Mencken and the Black Writers of the 1920s* (Baltimore: Johns Hopkins University Press, 1984), 118–21. For an alternative view to mine, see Edward Waldron, *Walter White and the Harlem Renaissance* (Port Washington, N. Y.: Kennikat Press, 1978), 47–61.

16. In *Nigger Heaven*, Van Vechten directs some gentle satire Mencken's way. Durwood praises white novelist Roy McKain (probably Jim Tully, whom Mencken admired) for writing a "capital yarn" about a Negro pimp: "I don't suppose he even saw the fellow . . . but his imagination was based on a background of observation." Van Vechten proceeds to depict McKain as a man who can observe detail but who completely misperceives its moral implications. Since Van Vechten's narrative propensities lay toward comedy of manners, he may be gently attacking the limitations of a literal-minded realism, one that Mencken was sometimes (but not always) guilty of espousing. It is significant, I believe, that Van Vechten did not admire Dreiser; whereas for Mencken, he was a novelist of the "first rank." See Carl Van Vechten, *Fragments from an Unwritten Autobiography* (New Haven: Yale University Press, 1955), 2:6–7.

17. Sterling Brown, "A Century of Negro Portraiture in American Literature," *Massachusetts Review* 7 (Winter 1966): 73–96. Reprinted in *Black Voices*, ed. Abraham Chapman (New York: New American Library, 1968), 564–89.

18. Walter White to Rudolf Fisher, 12 March 1925, NAACP Executive Correspondence Files, Manuscripts Division, Library of Congress.

19. Michel Foucault, "Nietzsche, Genealogy, History," in *Language, Counter-Memory, Practice*, trans. Donald F. Bouchard and Sherry Simon (Ithaca: Cornell University Press, 1977), 151.

20. The title of a chapter in *Shadow and Act* (New York: Random House, 1964).

21. C. Vann Woodward has written the classic study of the South's capitulation to racism in the 1880s—see *The Strange Career of Jim Crow* (New York: Oxford University Press, 1955). Also, see Joel Williamson, *The Crucible of Race: Black-White Relations in the American South since Emancipation* (New York: Oxford University Press, 1984).

22. See Robert M. Henderson, *D. W. Griffith: His Life and Work* (New York: Oxford University Press, 1972), 156–59.

23. James Weldon Johnson, *Along This Way* (1933; rept. New York: Viking Press, 1968), 305–6.

24. The story of Mencken's difficulties during World War I has been told many times. See Isaac Goldberg, *The Man Mencken* (New York: Simon and Schuster, 1925), 208; Carl Bode, *Mencken* (Carbondale: Southern Illinois Press, 1969), 106–16; William Manchester, *Disturber of the Peace: The Life of H. L. Mencken* (New York: Harper, 1951), 98–111. On Mencken's warfare with Stuart Sherman and the "New Humanists," see Richard Ruland, *The Rediscovery of American Literature: Premises of Critical Taste, 1900–1940* (Cambridge: Harvard University Press, 1967), 11–165.

25. HLM, "The Curse of Prejudice," *American Mercury* 23 (May 1931):125.

26. HLM to James Weldon Johnson, 8 August 1919, in Bode, *New Letters*, 111.

27. In *Serpent in Eden: H. L. Mencken and the South* (Chapel Hill: University of North Carolina Press, 1974), Fred C. Hobson has convincingly shown that the reaction to "The Sahara of the Bozart" helped create what we now know as the Southern renaissance.

28. HLM, *Prejudices, Second Series* (New York: Knopf, 1920), 144.

29. Ibid., 142, 148–49, 150.

30. Ibid., 153.

31. The title of Johnson's article had a Menckenian ring: "Segregation of 'Pants' in Georgia."

32. Hobson, 16, makes a connection between "The Sahara of the Bozart" and Book Four of *Gulliver's Travels.*

33. HLM, *Prejudices, Second Series*, 136.

34. For instance, the theme of Southern (or white) insanity appears with some regularity in satires written by Afro-Americans during the 1920s, and Mencken's presence is usually acknowledged, either tacitly or explicitly. For three examples, see E. Franklin Frazier, "The Pathology of Race Prejudice," *Forum* 77 (June 1927):856–62; George Schuyler, "Traveling Jim Crow," *American Mercury* 20 (August, 1930):423–31; Walter White, *Rope and Faggot: The Biography of Judge Lynch* (1928; rpt. New York: Arno Press and the *New York Times*, 1969), 9, 11, 58.

35. James Weldon Johnson, ed., *The Book of American Negro Poetry* (1922; rept. New York: Harcourt, Brace and World, 1959), 41.

36. James Weldon Johnson, *St. Peter Relates an Incident: Selected Poems* (New York: Viking, 1935), 70.

37. Louis D. Rubin, Jr., "The Search for a Language, 1746–1923," in *Black Poetry in America* (Baton Rouge: Louisiana State University Press, 1974), 25.

38. Mencken urged Johnson to put more emphasis on contemporary poets, and he wanted Johnson to expand the section of the preface dealing with Negro music into an article or book: "Why not go into the history of ragtime at length, establishing names and dates accurately? It ought to be done. . . . Then you might do similar essays on negro poets and negro painters and sculptors, and so have a second book on the negro as artist. . . . I think a preface to poetry should stick to poetry pretty closely. . . . " HLM to James Weldon Johnson, undated letter (circa 1922), H. L. Mencken Papers, Rare Books and Manuscripts Division, The New York Public Library, Astor, Lenox and Tilden Foundations, hereafter cited as NYP.

39. Dolmetsch, 30.

40. HLM, *The American Language* (New York: Knopf, 1919), 58, 140, 162, 320–21.

41. Ibid., 320.

42. Ibid., 34, 139–40.

43. James Weldon Johnson, ed., *The Book of American Negro Poetry*, 41–42.

44. James Weldon Johnson, *God's Trombones: Seven Negro Sermons in Verse* (1927; rept. New York: Viking Press, 1969), 6–7.

45. M. M. Bakhtin, *The Dialogic Imagination*, trans. Caryl Emerson and Michael Holquist (Austin: University of Texas Press, 1981), 60.

46. *God's Trombones*, 49.

47. Mencken's praise appears on the book jacket of the first edition of *God's Trombones* (New York; Viking Press, 1927). There is a copy of Johnson's book, including book jacket, in the James Weldon Johnson Collection at Yale University (Beinecke Library). That Mencken allowed his statement to be published in just this way shows his high regard for Johnson's work, for he generally despised advertising puffery that passed itself off as a critical evaluation. He also included Johnson's poem in a collection that represented the best work published by the *American Mercury* in 1927. See *From the American Mercury* (New York: Knopf, 1928), 3–6. In 1942, Johnson's widow thanked Mencken for his generous "estimate of 'Go Down Death' on publication," and then added a comment about Mencken's personal relationship with her late husband that could stand as a general statement for Mencken's involvement with the black writers of his generation. Said Grace Johnson about Mencken's let-

ters to Johnson, "They are an interesting and valuable part of your range of thought *when most people were inarticulate who held the power of influence that you represented*" (italics mine). Grace Johnson to HLM, 25 August 1942, NYP.

48. HLM to Carl Van Vechten, 19 December 1925, James Weldon Johnson Memorial Collection of Negro Arts and Letters, Beinecke Rare Book and Manuscript Library, Yale University. Mencken complained that "the author . . . constantly mixes up 'the' and 'de.' Tell him to read James W. Johnson's remarks on the subject in the introduction to 'A Book of Negro Spirituals.' "

INDEX